BEACON OF HOPE:
THE PROMISE OF
EARLY HEAD START FOR
AMERICA'S YOUNGEST CHILDREN

BEACON OF HOPE:
THE PROMISE OF
EARLY HEAD START FOR
AMERICA'S YOUNGEST CHILDREN

Edited by Joan Lombardi and Mary M. Bogle

ZERO TO THREE®
PRESS
WASHINGTON, DC

Published by

ZERO TO THREE
2000 M St., NW, Suite 200
Washington, DC 20036-3307
(202) 638-1144; Toll-free orders (800) 899-4301; Fax: (202) 638-0851
Web: http://www.zerotothree.org

The mission of the ZERO TO THREE Press is to publish authoritative research, practical resources, and new ideas for those who work with and care about infants, toddlers, and their families. Books are selected for publication by an independent Editorial Board. The views contained in this book are those of the authors and do not necessarily reflect those of ZERO TO THREE: National Center for Infants, Toddlers and Families, Inc.

Cover design: Naylor Design, Inc.
Text design and composition: Design Consultants

Library of Congress Cataloging-In-Publication Data

Beacon of hope: the promise of Early Head Start for America s youngest children / [edited by] Joan Lombardi, Mary M. Bogle. -- 1st ed.
      p. cm.
   Includes biographical references.
   ISBN 0-943657-65-2
1. Early Head Start (Program) 2. Children with social disabilities--Services for--United States. 3. Poor children--Services for--United States. 4. Toddlers--Services for--United States. 5. Infants--Services for--United States. 6. Maternal and infant welfare--United States. 7. Child development--United States. I. Lombardi, Joan. II. Bogle, Mary M.
   HV741.B37 2004
   372.21--dc22

2004014675

First Edition First Printing October 2004

ISBN 0-943657-65-2

Printed in the United States of America

Suggested citations:

Book citation: Lombardi, J., & Bogle, M. M. (2004). *Beacon of hope: The promise of Early Head Start for America's youngest children*. Washington, DC: ZERO TO THREE Press.

Chapter citation: Solchany, J. E., & Barnard, K. E. (2004). First relationships: Infant mental health in Early Head Start. In J. Lombardi & M. M. Bogle, *Beacon of hope: The promise of Early Head Start for America's youngest children* (pp. 127 147). W ashington, DC: ZERO TO THREE Press.

DEDICATION

In memory of Helen H. Taylor,
whose leadership, dedication and wisdom
helped create a strong foundation for
Early Head Start; and whose
warmth and friendship remains
forever in our hearts.

TABLE OF CONTENTS

LIST OF TABLES AND FIGURES

PREFACE

Joan Lombardi

The first time it ever occurred to me that Head Start should serve children younger than age 3 was in 1972. At that time I was a graduate student in early childhood education and had just started teaching a group of 3-year-olds at a Head Start program in Boston. In early fall of that year, just after being hired, I visited the children in their homes to meet them before their first day of "preschool." I was touched by their affection and by their parents' personal interest and involvement. But from those very first moments with the children and families, I wondered why we had waited so long to reach them. Distressing signs already were emerging—asthma that had persisted for years, ear infections that had been left unattended, limited exposure to the array of words they would need to become successful readers.

Little did I know at the time, as a young convert to the emerging children's movement, that the wise founders of Head Start had recognized this same point some 7 years earlier, at the very dawn of the Head Start program. In January 1965, at the first exploratory meeting, Reginald Lourie (who 12 years later became the founding chairman of the National Center for Clinical Infant Programs, now ZERO TO THREE) pointed out that for many children, starting even at age 3 could be too late (1979, p. 98). In 1966, Joseph McVicker Hunt, professor of psychology and author of *Intelligence and Experience* (1961), chaired a task force that explored a range of issues related to Head Start. One year later, following the task force's recommendations, 33 Parent and Child Centers were established to serve children under age 3 and their families.

In 1969, when President Richard Nixon established the federal Office of Child Development, he observed, "Preliminary evaluations . . . indicate that Head Start must begin earlier in life and last longer to achieve lasting benefits" (Zigler & Muenchow, 1992, p. 74). That same year, Migrant Head Start programs began, eventually serving children from birth to age 5 as their parents worked in the fields across the United States. In 1970, three Parent and Child Development Centers were added as part of an intensive research and demonstration effort to test different models of parent–infant interventions.

During the 1970s and 1980s, additional efforts were made within Head Start and the Office of Child Development to plan for and address the needs of infants and toddlers. In the early 1970s, Child and Family Resource Programs began offering comprehensive services for children birth to age 8. In 1980, a task force on the future of Head Start—convened by President Jimmy Carter—recommended that the Head Start program itself be expanded to serve children under age 3. In 1983, a version of the Child Development Associate credential, designed specifically to test the competencies needed to care for infants and toddlers, was ready for field testing. And in the late 1980s—building on the promise of community-based initiatives in places such as Chicago, Illinois; Pittsburgh, Pennsylvania; and Brattleboro, Vermont—Comprehensive Child Development Programs were launched in multiple sites to provide intensive services to families with children under age 5. Many leaders of these programs broke new ground in serving very high-risk families with young children. Judith Jerald, for example, designed and directed the Comprehensive Child Development Program in Brattleboro before becoming coordinator of the national Early Head Start program.

Overall, however, Head Start was not meeting the needs of infants, toddlers, and their families during this period. Although Parent and Child Centers and programs serving the infants and toddlers of migrant parents continued to operate, their budgets did not even keep up with inflation. Technical assistance was limited. While serving on the education staff of the Head Start Bureau in the late 1970s, I listened to the directors of Parent and Child Centers and Migrant Head Start programs advocating tirelessly for resources to expand and improve services for children under the age of 3.

Twice during the 1980s—while working as a government employee and while at home caring for my young children—I was asked to work on the performance standards for Head Start programs serving infants and toddlers. Each time, many dedicated people inside and outside the government contributed to the work. Yet the standards we developed were never adopted. Head Start programs serving infants and toddlers never received the attention and support they needed to ensure quality. Although the National Head Start Association recommended in 1990 that Head Start programs be allowed to serve children from birth to age 5, depending on community needs, Congress did not include the recommendation in that year's Head Start reauthorization legislation. By the early 1990s, more than 25 years after the birth of Head Start, the 106 Parent and Child Centers and the network of migrant programs served fewer than 19,000 infants and toddlers (U.S. Department of Health and Human Services, 1993).

But suddenly in the early 1990s, something began to change. It was a pivotal time for infants and toddlers in the United States. Finally, people recognized that early intervention services could improve the developmental trajectory for very young children threatened by poverty. At the economic summit convened by then-President-elect Bill Clinton, Lisbeth Schorr, author of *Within Our Reach: Breaking the Cycle of Disadvantage* (1988) urged an expansion of Head Start downward to prebirth in order to support families for the whole first 5 years of their children's development. A few months later, in January 1993, the Carnegie Corporation's Task Force on Young Children heard the presentation of two papers calling for the improvement in existing Head Start services to very young children and the further expansion of the program to serve additional infants and toddlers.

It was against this backdrop that the idea of serving very young children in Head Start began to receive serious attention. Responding to the calls for improvement and expansion in the overall program, Secretary of Health and Human Services Donna Shalala convened an advisory committee to review the Head Start program and to make recommendations for the future. Mary Jo Bane, then assistant secretary, chaired the committee and led efforts to establish several subcommittees. Having served as the staff director to the committee, I can still recall long discussions and serious debates in the subcommittee on the appropriate role for serving infants and toddlers. The subcommittee discussed three main issues: (1) the improvements needed in programs already serving infants and toddlers, (2) how Head Start could take a leadership role and serve as a national laboratory for services to younger children, and (3) the best strategies for expansion to children under age 3.

After exchanging many drafts of the infant and toddler recommendations, the final report of the committee stated

> The overwhelming majority of Advisory Committee members recommend the development of a new initiative focused on serving families with children under age 3. This initiative should build on the accepted principles which are the foundation of Head Start's success, including the provision of comprehensive services, with a special focus on supporting the parent–child relationship. The initiative should be informed by previous and current efforts to serve younger children, including those of the Parent and Child Centers, Migrant Head Start, and the Comprehensive Child Development Programs. (U. S. Department of Health and Human Services, 1993, p. 52)

The advisory committee did not reach consensus on the scope of the initiative or the exact amount of funds needed. It recommended that the U.S. Department of Health and Human Services convene a high-level committee—similar to that which had planned the original Head Start program—charged with developing program guidelines that would allow Head Start to serve children under age 3.

Very shortly after the advisory committee released its report in December 1993, the administration began working with a bipartisan group of members from both houses of Congress to draft legislation to reauthorize Head Start. With the growing increase in public awareness about early child development, it became clear that the timing was right to use the reauthorization process to develop a new program for infants and toddlers.

Although the provisions calling for the improvement and expansion of services to infants and toddlers had broad bipartisan support, the issue was not without debate. Some members of Congress agreed philosophically with the need to serve children earlier but had some reservations about creating a new program; others thought it needed more study. Some constituents wanted to see the program opened up to new grantees; others wanted to target existing Head Start programs, providing the flexibility to serve children under age 3. Some felt that the administration had surpassed the recommendations of the advisory committee by establishing a specific new program in their proposed legislation, rather than establishing a high-level group to determine the approach; others felt that it was important for Congress to establish the program while interest in very young children was receiving popular attention.

Several factors helped ensure that the final bill would include a focus on younger children. First, the Carnegie Corporation's publication of the landmark report, *Starting Points: Meeting the Needs of Our Youngest Children* (1994), led to a new level of public awareness among parents, the media, professionals, and policymakers about the early years and the importance of early brain development. At the same time, more and more families with younger and younger children were entering the workforce, welfare reform was in full swing, and the need for quality infant and toddler care began to soar.

The 1994 legislation was successfully crafted through cooperation between the administration and a bipartisan group of members in the House and the Senate. The final legislation called for a set-aside of Head Start funds to provide family-centered services for low-income families with very young children and for pregnant women. The services would be designed to promote the development of the children and to enable their parents to fulfill their roles as parents and to move to self-sufficiency. The legislation also required the development of a set of program performance standards, targeted money for training and technical assistance, and a comprehensive evaluation of the program.

From the moment that the Head Start reauthorization bill was signed on May 18, 1994, significant care and attention was paid to how the new program would be implemented. Under the direction of Commissioner of the Administration for Children and

Families Olivia Golden, the Advisory Committee on Services for Families With Infants and Toddlers was established, bringing together a distinguished panel of academicians and practitioners (see Appendix A). Helen Taylor, then associate commissioner for the Head Start Bureau, provided outstanding leadership and wisdom to the advisory committee and throughout the implementation process.

The advisory committee convened three times during the summer of 1994 and held more than 30 focus groups with a range of stakeholders. There was strong consensus that the program should be an integral part of the Head Start family, build on Head Start's record of comprehensive services, ensure professional development, and support and address the growing needs of working families. As I recall, there was some debate about what name to give the program. Some people wanted to call it "Head Start for Infants and Toddlers," and others wanted to call it "Early Start." I believe that Julius Richmond, who had served as the founding director of Head Start in 1965 and later served on the advisory committee, came up with "Early Head Start." This name conveyed that the program was an integral part of Head Start while recognizing the distinction and special needs of serving younger children.

The committee recommended that the program be designed to produce outcomes in the following four domains:

1. **Child development**, including health and social, cognitive, and language development;

2. **Family development**, including parents' relationships with children, the home environment and family functioning, family health, parent involvement, and economic self-sufficiency;

3. **Staff development**, including professional development and relationships with parents; and

4. **Community development**, including enhanced child-care quality, community collaboration, and integration of services to support families with young children.

The Early Head Start program was announced on November 15, 1994. On that day Secretary Donna Shalala, while accepting the advisory committee report, called for a "new era of support to families with infants and toddlers." She pledged to use the guidelines in the report to establish "Early Head Start, a new program that would provide high-quality, comprehensive, and individualized support and services to families with very young children" ("Shalala Calls for a New Era," 1994, p. 1). Also marking the occasion, Commissioner Olivia Golden said, "We have designed an Early Head

Start program that will be suited to last well into the next century—always reshaping itself to America's youngest children and their families" ("Shalala Calls for a New Era," p. 1).

Once the advisory committee completed its work, the administration approached the early implementation with the enthusiasm that a new program with such potential deserved. Deborah Stark, the staff director for the advisory committee and early planning team, recalls that several principles guided the overall approach to implementation.

First, the process was to be inclusive. This meant that there was a commitment to hearing from as many people as possible—parents, Head Start providers, other leaders in early care, family advocates, mental health professionals, and researchers—and to understanding their hopes and desires for the new program. Second, the new program was to build on the lessons already learned in serving pregnant women and families with infants and toddlers through the Parent and Child Development Centers, Comprehensive Child Development Programs, and Migrant Head Start programs. Third, the new program was to involve partnerships at all levels across the federal government to secure commitment to the new program and identify opportunities for collaboration and enhancement. Among others, these partners included the Child Care Bureau, the Maternal and Child Health Bureau, the Center for Mental Health, and the Office of Special Education Programs. Fourth, participants were to focus on building the capacity of the program by addressing its training and technical assistance needs, developing clear performance standards, and including a comprehensive evaluation that would capture the multiple pathways to early child development. The first 68 Early Head Start programs were launched in fall 1995 with an appropriation of $106 million, and a firm foundation laid by the advisory committee.

I was very fortunate to serve as a member of the advisory committee and, along with my co-editor Mary Bogle, as a member of the overall implementation team. Mary, who had served as a project officer for the Comprehensive Child Development Centers, provided invaluable experience to the overall team and contributed greatly to its success. In those early days, neither of us could have imagined that we would later be given an opportunity to share a picture of Early Head Start's first decade.

The idea for this book emerged in 2000 as a way to honor Helen Taylor and all the people who contributed to the success of Early Head Start, particularly those people who worked in communities throughout the country. We continued our work as the promising results of the Early Head Start National Research and Evaluation Project were released in 2001 and 2002 and as the technical assistance team at the Early Head

Start National Resource Center at ZERO TO THREE worked to ensure continuous improvement. The cohort of Early Head Start programs announced on January 9, 2003, brought the total number of programs to 708. When making this announcement, Secretary of Health and Human Services Tommy Thompson said, "These Early Head Start grants will ensure that thousands more young children get needed support to promote early education, giving them a better chance for success when they eventually start school" ("HHS Awards $72 Million," 2003).

The purpose of putting together this volume is to celebrate Early Head Start and to provide a glimpse of the program's success. A wide variety of people, including researchers and program experts, wrote the 11 chapters. Chapters 1–3 of the book focus on the program's potential, providing a description of Early Head Start today and reporting on the findings of the evaluation. Chapters 4–9 describe the inner workings of the program, highlighting strategies for providing services to infants, toddlers, and pregnant women; reaching out to fathers and teen parents; meeting the mental health needs of children and families; and effectively including children with special needs. Finally, Chapters 10–11 address the emerging policy issues, including the need for increased federal and state investments to expand the program and ensure continuous improvement.

Early Head Start has earned its reputation as a beacon of hope for the nation's most vulnerable children. Mary and I hope that this book gives you a sense of the promise that Early Head Start provides, helps you appreciate Early Head Start's contributions to children and families across the United States, and, above all, leaves you with a renewed commitment to join in this effort as we work to improve the lives of babies, toddlers, and their families living in poverty.

Joan Lombardi
Washington, DC

REFERENCES

Carnegie Corporation of New York. *Starting points: Meeting the needs of our youngest children.* (1994). New York: Author.

HHS awards $72 million in Early Head Start grants nationwide. (2003, January 9). *HHS News.*

Hunt, J. M. (1961). *Intelligence and experience.* Hoboken, NJ: John Wiley and Sons.

Schorr, L. (1988). _Within our reach: Breaking the cycle of disadvantage._ New York: Doubleday.

Shalala calls for a new era of support to families with infants and toddlers. (1994, November 15). _HHS News._

U.S. Department of Health and Human Services. (1994). _The statement of the Advisory Committee on Services for Families With Infants and Toddlers._ Washington, DC: Author.

U.S. Department of Health and Human Services. (1993, December). _Creating a 21st century Head Start._ Final report of the Advisory Committee on Head Start Quality and Expansion. Washington, DC: Author.

Zigler, E., & Muenchow, S. (1992). _Head Start: The inside story of America's most successful educational experiment._ New York: Basic Books.

Zigler, E. & Valentine, J. (1979). Head Start, a retrospective view: The founders. In E. Zigler & J. Valentine (Eds.), _Project Head Start: A legacy of the war on poverty_ (p. 98). New York: The Free Press.

ACKNOWLEDGMENTS

Many people across the country contributed to this book and to making Early Head Start a success. We are particularly indebted to: all the chapter authors and the numerous reviewers; the entire staff of the Early Head Start National Resource Center at ZERO TO THREE, particularly Tammy Mann, Lillian Sugarman, Adrienne Sparger, and others working across the regions; to the staff of ZERO TO THREE including Matthew Melmed, Beatrice Dermer, Emily Fenichel, Nancy Guadagno, Bill McCall, Jennifer Moon, Rebecca Parlakian, Erica Lurie-Hurvitz, and Rachel Abbey; and to all the state officials and advocates and local Early Head Start program staff who took the time to provide input along the way.

We are very grateful for the work of the National Head Start Research and Evaluation Project research team, the insights and vision gained from The Advisory Committee on Services for Families with Infants and Toddlers (Appendix A), and the dedication of Judith Jerald in her work from Brattleboro to Washington, D.C. We remember the pioneering efforts of those who came before us including the staff of the Parent Child Centers, the Comprehensive Child Development Programs, and the Migrant Head Start programs; as well as the ongoing champions who believed in the power of starting early throughout the history of Head Start.

Finally, we are grateful to all the funders who invested in this work including: The Atlantic Philanthropies, The Heinz Endowments, the Conrad N. Hilton Foundation, the A.L. Mailman Family Foundation, Inc., and to the children and families across the country who make it all worthwhile.

EARLY HEAD START: AN OVERVIEW

Tammy L. Mann, Mary M. Bogle, and Rebecca Parlakian

E arly Head Start (EHS) offers what babies, toddlers, families, and communities need to thrive. It is the latest and boldest initiative of the Head Start program, which has been a national laboratory for child development and family support for almost 40 years. Head Start has continued to evolve during the past 4 decades, setting new standards for quality early childhood education and family support; inspiring innovative models for local, state, and federal collaboration; and propelling changes in how poor families are included in the design and implementation of family service programs. As national evaluation results demonstrate, EHS is producing real benefits for infants and toddlers in low-income families.

This chapter summarizes the design and scope of EHS; highlights families' experiences in EHS; profiles three distinctive EHS programs; and examines the infrastructure that supports, monitors, and ensures the continuous improvement of EHS services.

GETTING STARTED: ESTABLISHING EARLY HEAD START

In 1994, Congress passed legislation reauthorizing Head Start and establishing a program that would provide comprehensive support to children under age 3 in low-income families.[1] The first 68 EHS programs were funded in late 1995. By 2003, EHS had expanded to more than 700 programs, serving more than 62,000 children under age 3 (see Figure 1.1). Yet 2.1 million children under age 3 in the United States live in poverty (Song & Lu, 2002). EHS is currently reaching only about 3% of the infants and toddlers who are eligible for its services.

FIGURE 1.1

Ages of Children in Early
Head Start Program,
Program Year 2002

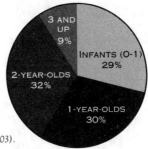

Reprinted with permission from Irish, Schumacher, & Lombardi (2003).

EHS programs operate in every state as well as in the District of Columbia and Puerto Rico (Administration for Children and Families, 2002). At the local level, they are administered by various public and private agencies, including schools, health care providers, tribal authorities, and community action agencies. Each EHS program serves between 60 and 200 children and their families, and many of these programs have long waiting lists (Judie Jerald, personal communication to Mary Bogle, September 2001).

The Head Start Bureau, which is part of the Administration for Children and Families, an agency of the U.S. Department of Health and Human Services, oversees the EHS program. The bureau selects EHS grantees that are capable of fulfilling the program's mission and oversees and supports programs after they have been funded. The national office also develops new policy guidance as EHS continues to evolve. Ten regional offices and centrally located offices for the migrant and seasonal programs and for the American Indian and Alaskan Native programs assist in these efforts.

HOW EARLY HEAD START MEETS BABIES' NEEDS

Even though each EHS program provides the same scope of services, the approach to providing these services varies based on the needs of a particular child and family, the community in which they live, and the design of the EHS program in that locale. Each local EHS program conducts regular community assessments to determine the best mix of services for low-income families with infants and toddlers. Programs modify their services as community demographics and needs change.

Because every family, regardless of income, must find its own way to nurture an individual child's growth while meeting the whole family's basic financial, social, and emotional needs, EHS programs work with families and children in several ways.

- **Home-based services** bring EHS staff into family homes every week to support child development and the parent–child relationship. Twice a month, all parents and children in the program have an opportunity to come together as a group for learning, discussion, and social activity.

- **Center-based services** offer children part- or full-time enrollment in an early care and education setting. In addition, staff members visit family homes at least twice a year.

- **Combination services**, as the term suggests, combine home visits and center-based services.

In the center-based and combination models of service, the child may be in a licensed family child-care home, a child development center run by the EHS program, or a community-based child development center that works in partnership with the EHS program. In 2002, approximately 46% of EHS programs were center based, 43% were home based, and others were combination models or locally designed options (see Figure 1.2).

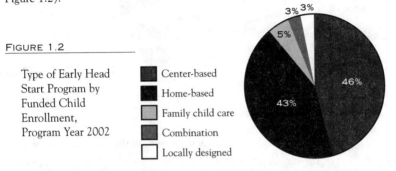

FIGURE 1.2

Type of Early Head
Start Program by
Funded Child
Enrollment,
Program Year 2002

■ Center-based
■ Home-based
▨ Family child care
▨ Combination
☐ Locally designed

Reprinted with permission from Irish, Schumacher, & Lombardi (2003).

EHS programs try to offer children and families the services in the format that best meets their needs at a particular time. A program may offer more than one service option to a family during the course of that family's enrollment. For example, a family with a newborn may begin in a home-based program, transition to a center-based child-care setting when a parent enters job training or becomes employed, then return to home-based services or a combination of home- and center-based services when the family's school or work situation changes.

Supporting parents in their efforts to improve their lives and the lives of their children is a mandate of EHS. For example, parents may access many social services through EHS, such as housing referrals, literacy programs, adult education, and job training. These outreach efforts are designed to promote adult self-sufficiency, and access to mental health services helps ensure that parents are able to offer a healthy, stable home to their children (see Figure 1.3). Responding nimbly to families' changing situations and shifting needs requires fiscal, programmatic, and administrative flexibility from EHS programs.

CARING AND RESPONSIVE RELATIONSHIPS

Head Start and EHS are designed to be "child focused" and "family centered." These terms emphasize the importance of responsive relationships for promoting each child's social, emotional, cognitive, and physical growth. The Advisory Committee on

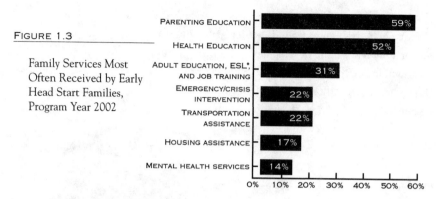

FIGURE 1.3

Family Services Most
Often Received by Early
Head Start Families,
Program Year 2002

*Note: ESL = English as a Second Language

Reprinted with permission from Irish, Schumacher, & Lombardi (2003).

Services for Families With Infants and Toddlers recognized the crucial role that relationships play in the delivery of quality services when it stated, "[T]he success of each program will rest on [that program's] ability to support and enhance strong, caring, continuous relationships which nurture the child, parents, family, and caregiving staff" (U.S. Department of Health and Human Services, 1994, p. 11).

Given the primacy of the parent–child relationship, families are critical partners with EHS staff in determining the intensity and types of services that they receive. A strong commitment to collaborate with parents on children's learning experiences and on decisions about program management is a hallmark of the Head Start approach.

Using health, child, and family assessments, EHS families and staff work together to establish a strong working relationship that supports parents as they progress through the family partnership agreement process—a discussion of their goals for their children and for themselves as well as their families. In many cases, this discussion culminates in a written plan, as staff and parents articulate goals for their children's development and learning as well as the experiences, activities, and materials needed to achieve these goals. EHS programs also maintain health records on each enrolled child and coordinate with parents and health care providers to ensure follow-up care (see Figure 1.4). For children with disabilities, health and development plans are integrated with their Individualized Family Service Plan (IFSP), a federally mandated tool for supporting the development of infants and toddlers with special needs. An IFSP includes a written description of services to be provided to the child and family.

Partnership with families is so fundamental to effective home-based work that EHS home visitors plan the content of each visit (for example, how to support children's development and meet their needs) jointly with parents. In addition to supporting the

FIGURE 1.4

MEDICAL SCREENINGS, TREATMENT, AND SERVICES FOR EARLY HEAD
START CHILDREN, PROGRAM YEAR 2002

Percentage of Early Head Start children receiving medical screening	81% (49,404)
Percent diagnosed as needing treatment, of those screened	23% (11,370)
Early Head Start children receiving follow-up services, of those needing treatment	93% (10,543)
Conditions for which services were provided*:	
Asthma	33%
Anemia	15%
Hearing Difficulties	12%
Overweight	9%
Vision problems	7%

*Note: The PIR survey only captures the services listed in this chart. There is also an "Other" category that accounts for 24% of the children receiving services, but there is no indication of what services are included in this category.

Reprinted with permission from Irish, Schumacher, & Lombardi (2003).

quality of their work with careful plans, equipment, and curricular materials, home visitors remain open to the opportunities that each visit will present. For instance, EHS home visitors always seek to model to parents successful ways of relating to their very young children. In addition, they build on "teachable moments" to coach parents about how they might better respond to a child's cues or match their own behavior to a child's interests and developmental needs. Home visitors also use their close relationships with families to introduce, provide, or arrange for all other EHS supports, including medical, dental, and social services.

In addition, home-based programs offer families group socialization activities at a central location, usually the main offices or meeting space of the EHS program. Group socializations are much more than playgroups; rather, they focus on the relationship between very young children and their parents. During socializations, parents interact with their children directly through planned and spontaneous activities such as finger plays, simple art projects, singing, and rolling balls. Parents also develop friendships with other EHS parents for emotional and practical support. Sometimes expectant parents are invited to attend socializations so that they can draw support and excitement from their peers who have already become new parents. Home visitors participate in the socializations and often use them to enhance the skills on which they are working with parents in their homes.

In center-based settings and family day care homes, EHS regulations, training, and guidance materials work together to enforce and promote the creation of close, nurturing bonds between caregivers and children. Appropriate staffing patterns and "best practices" classroom organization help to create an intimate, home-like setting in EHS programs. For example, infants and toddlers benefit from EHS's small classrooms and low child-to-teacher ratios. These features help to ensure high-quality one-on-one interactions between child and teacher.

In addition, each child is assigned a primary caregiver—a person who is primarily responsible for his or her care—thus allowing families and teachers to get to know one another well. As a shared history develops, teachers can better individualize their approaches based on their knowledge of a particular child and thus can better meet that child's needs. Such skills are integral to meeting EHS's goal of providing responsive and relationship-based care to every enrolled child. EHS caregivers also build responsive relationships with families. These partnerships are forged mostly through daily communication between parent and caregiver about the infant's activities, achievements, and feelings.

EXAMPLES OF EARLY HEAD START PROGRAM MODELS

How are EHS services and practices implemented at the local level? The short answer is, the approach at every site is different. EHS serves communities from Alaska to Maine and from Hawaii to Puerto Rico. The diversity of approaches used to provide comprehensive services to very young children and their parents is matched only by the diversity of the families that participate in EHS. The three profiles of EHS programs that follow cannot begin to represent the full range of experiences within EHS, but they do offer a glimpse into several distinctive programs and the parents, children, staff, and community partners who are building these programs together.

Puget Sound Educational Services District

The Puget Sound Educational Services District Early Head Start (Puget Sound EHS) is an excellent example of how EHS programs often bend and blend to meet a particular community's needs. Puget Sound EHS operates seven sites that are scattered throughout Tacoma–Pierce County, Washington.

Three sites are home based; 7 staff members visit a combined total of 45 families per week (Wendy Jans & John Naegele, personal communications to Mary Bogle, February and May 2002; Puget Sound Educational Services District, 2001). Three center-based sites serve teen parents and their very young children at the Challenger, Oakland, and Henderson Bay alternative high schools. Weekly home visits ensure that teens enjoy continuity of services even when school is not in session. The Henderson Bay and Oakland sites also operate small home-based programs for teens who have graduated, are pregnant, or are temporarily out of school. When and if home-based teens return to school, they transition to the center-based programs.

Comprehensive services to the teens and their children at the alternative high schools are planned by staff members, such as a child development coordinator and a health/ nutrition coordinator. Each site also has at least one family educator who provides social service support to families. To leverage cost-effective infant–toddler care services that achieve EHS quality levels, the Puget Sound EHS has developed close partnerships with local child-care providers. The child-care programs use state subsidies to pay for care that meets licensing requirements for the 60 infants and toddlers served across the sites. The Puget Sound EHS enhances this care by paying for additional teachers, an extra hour of planning time for each teacher's day, and supplemental educational supplies and materials. In addition, the program provides 60 hours per year of training in child development for child-care staff and reimburses the career development costs of caregivers who are seeking Child Development Associate (CDA) certificates and early childhood degrees.

As its seventh site, Puget Sound EHS has set up a residential parenting program in the Washington Corrections Center for Women (WCCW) through a partnership with the Washington State Department of Corrections. Women who have been convicted of nonviolent offenses and whose sentences will expire in fewer than 3 years may enroll in the program. Pregnant women at WCCW attend parenting and childbirth classes. They receive prenatal and delivery care at facilities outside the prison, and they and their children continue to receive health services that meet the Head Start Program Performance Standards (2002). Family educators visit pregnant women and mothers of newborns in the prison for 90 minutes at least once a week.

Similar to women on public assistance throughout Washington state, women at WCCW are required to return to work after their babies are 6 weeks old. The WCCW–Puget Sound EHS partnership offers various educational and vocational training programs, in addition to prison and community job opportunities. Other services include mental heath counseling, intensive parenting and life skills classes, support groups on anger management, and, as is often needed, substance abuse intervention.

The heart of the Puget Sound EHS program at WCCW is an on-site child development center that is supervised by qualified child development specialists. When not at work, mothers assume full responsibility for their children and live with them in their rooms, which have been decorated with colorful airplanes, jungle animals, and mobiles by inmates, volunteers, and EHS staff. Inmate caregivers, specially selected and trained by EHS Staff, are on call to support mothers by caring for children as needed in the evening and on holidays and weekends.

Mid-Iowa Community Action Agency

Similar to the Puget Sound program, the EHS program of the Mid-Iowa Community Action Agency, which serves 69 children across five rural counties, is constantly evolving to keep pace with the community's profile. Currently, agriculture provides the community's economic base; other employment opportunities are available in the heating and cooling, retail sales, and meat packaging industries. Although jobs are available in this community, families that participate in Mid-Iowa EHS emphasize that, without more education, they cannot compete for the (better-paying) positions that require technical skills (Administration on Children, Youth, and Families, 1999a).

The Mid-Iowa EHS program began in 1996 as a home-based model. An infant–toddler specialist visits homes each week to assist parents in building loving and supportive relationships with their young children. A family development specialist, who focuses on the broader needs of the whole family, visits each month (Administration on Children, Youth, and Families, 1999a).

During the past few years, the Mid-Iowa EHS program has opened two infant–toddler development centers to provide high-quality care to approximately 24 children while their parents meet the increased training and work obligations brought on by welfare reform. The Mid-Iowa EHS program also has established a partnership contract with an independent child-care provider to meet the full-day needs of additional children with working parents. These families will continue to receive the full complement of home-based services until the Mid-Iowa EHS program and its new child-care partner agree that all Head Start Program Performance Standards for center-based care of very young children can be fully and consistently met (Kathie Readout, personal communication to Mary Bogle, July 2002).

Red Cliff Band of Lake Superior Chippewa

The EHS program of the Red Cliff Band of Lake Superior Chippewa uses a center-based model to meet the needs of its community, which is located along the southern shores of Lake Superior. Because births to teen mothers account for more than one quarter of all births in this American Indian community, the Red Cliff EHS program targets adolescent and single mothers.

Red Cliff teachers and parent educators promote learning for not only infants but also their adolescent parents, who are approaching the age of majority in a community in which 43% of the adult population does not have a high school degree or equivalent certificate. As teen parents attend classes during the day, EHS cares for their infants and toddlers in a center that reflects the Red Cliff Band's traditional culture. Teachers sing, read, and speak to the children in Ojibwe and English (the primary language of the community). In addition to reclaiming their native language with the children, parents and other members of the community take part in weekly events at which children participate in traditional dances and fathers accompany the singing and dancing with ceremonial drums.

A partnership with T. Berry Brazelton's Touchpoints project provides an opportunity for parents to enhance their understanding of early development and their parenting skills. Red Cliff program designers have adapted the Touchpoints program to emphasize relationships between fathers and children (Early Head Start National Resource Center, 2001, pp. 13–15; Rob Goslin, personal communication to Mary Bogle, August 2002).

FOUR CORNERSTONES FOR
EARLY HEAD START PROGRAM DESIGN

What makes EHS work for children and families? One of the most unique and powerful attributes of EHS is its infrastructure, which is designed to support, monitor, and ensure the continuous improvement of local programs nationwide. In its 1994 statement, the Advisory Committee on Services for Families With Infants and Toddlers identified the four cornerstones that would lay this critical foundation for EHS: child development, family development, community building, and staff development.

- The **child development** cornerstone is foremost and focuses attention on the development of the whole child, encompassing social–emotional, physical, and intellectual domains. EHS considers the parent–infant bond as primary and preeminent and directs programs to provide activities that promote loving and consistent parent–child interaction.

- The **family development** and **community building** cornerstones acknowledge that no child can be raised in isolation. Children need parents who have committed themselves to the task of child rearing; parents need community support as they undertake this responsibility. EHS programs offer a "two-generational" model of care that serves expectant parents, parents, and children. Community building in EHS begins with needs assessments that help programs offer appropriate services, engage in collaborative agreements with local service providers, and ensure culturally sensitive planning.

- The **staff development** cornerstone grew out of the advisory committee's observation that "programs are only as good as the individuals who staff them" (U.S. Department of Health and Human Services, 1994). It recognizes that EHS cannot achieve the goals outlined in the first three cornerstones without properly selecting, training, and supporting the people who actually bring the programs to life.

BUILDING ON THE CORNERSTONES: HEAD START PROGRAM PERFORMANCE STANDARDS

A solid grounding in research evidence and sound guiding principles are necessary but not sufficient for program effectiveness. A key element of EHS's success, identified by the Early Head Start National Research and Evaluation Project, is the Head Start Program Performance Standards. Revised in 1996 to address both prenatal and birth-through-5 development, the performance standards emphasize high quality, accountability, and flexibility in the design and delivery of services. They build on the cornerstones of EHS, with sections on early childhood development and health services, family and community partnerships, and program design and management (including staff development). The evaluation found that in the group of EHS programs it studied, those that fully implemented the performance standards achieved the strongest patterns of impacts for the children and families they serve (Administration for Children and Families, 2002).

The Head Start Program Performance Standards emphasize accountability and flexibility in the design and delivery of services. The standards are grounded in science and are designed to ensure that children and families receive high-quality, appropriate, and relevant care. As the advisory committee had hoped, the standards comprise a detailed framework for high-quality infant–toddler services—a framework that is built on the wisdom and knowledge base of early childhood research and practice. For example, regulations within the Early Childhood Development and Health Services section of the performance standards speak to the importance of the infant forming close relationships over time with a limited number of staff members. Because this concept is so fundamental to healthy infant–toddler development, the entire section begins with a focus on relationships and builds from that point to other aspects of development.

The rigor of the revised regulations comes through in requirements that are more stringent than those found in most state child-care regulations. These requirements address issues such as the following:

- Teacher qualifications, which require that teachers in EHS centers have, at minimum, a CDA credential or its equivalent at the time of hire or within 1 year of hire.

- Small child-to-teacher ratios, set by regulation at no more than 4 infants and toddlers per fully qualified caregiver. Parents and other volunteers, who are usually present, do not count toward the ratio.

- Primary caregiver assignments, which give each child one caregiver who is primarily, but not exclusively, responsible for his or her care.

- Small groups, which are limited to no more than 8 children so that the environment promotes close relationships and focused learning.

- Continuity of care, which aims to keep each child with his primary caregiver throughout his tenure in the EHS daily care setting.

The performance standards ensure that each enrolled child and family receives access to the same comprehensive scope of services through EHS. Delivery of these services varies from site to site. Fortunately, the performance standards offer individual programs broad latitude to respond to the unique needs of the children, families, and communities they serve. For example, under the Family and Community Partnerships section of the performance standards, grantees must seek volunteers from the community to participate in EHS and Head Start programs. Grantees may use various strategies to implement this rule, such as encouraging program parents to communicate volunteer opportunities to friends and relatives by word of mouth. And indeed, EHS programs respond in several ways to the outreach requirement, using outlets such as paid volunteer coordinators—including parents—or agreements with civic organizations that serve as volunteer pipelines. Ultimately, every method reflects the unique composition of families served and the community resources at hand; the standards to do not attempt to interfere with local innovation.

PROGRAM SUPPORTS FOR EHS

Like its parent program (Head Start), EHS is a federal-to-local program. Federal officials support the delivery of high-quality comprehensive services in communities across the country through activities associated with four critical program supports: program monitoring, training, partnership building, and research and evaluation

(U.S. Department of Health and Human Services, 1994). Today, these elements have become the load-bearing walls that create a sturdy, stable structure for EHS (Fenichel & Mann, 2001).

Program Monitoring

To monitor EHS programs' progress toward full implementation of the performance standards, teams of federal representatives and consultant specialists spend 5 days on site at a program, reviewing all aspects of its operations. They gather data from direct observation and interviews with the program management team, staff, participating families, child-care partners, and others. Because the review is conducted in partnership with the grantee, the process includes regular opportunities to receive feedback from the review team, to provide information, and to respond to reviewers' concerns. Program reviews are designed in this way to help program staff members continuously improve their efforts to meet the unique needs of their communities, agencies, children, families, and personnel. Programs are monitored every 3 years.

Training and Technical Assistance

To work effectively with families, EHS program staff must represent a wide range of skills, knowledge, and cultures. They also must have the personal strength necessary to partner with families during intensely stressful periods and through challenges that may include mental illness, substance abuse, domestic violence, and child custody disputes. Depending on the needs of the families and the communities they serve, staff members may bring or develop special expertise in serving specific populations, such as homeless families, teen parents, or new immigrants.

Because staff must arrive endowed with impressive backgrounds, skills, and personal characteristics, EHS program directors pay close attention to the process of recruitment and selection. Finding the right staff people frequently reminds managers of the disparity between the demand for and supply of qualified workers. For example, with regard to child development staff, few colleges offer degrees in infant–toddler development; more often than not, a 4-year early childhood curricula may offer only one or two courses in infant development. Many more people earn the CDA credential for work with preschool children than for work with infants and toddlers. As a result, EHS programs must shoulder significant responsibility for ensuring the professional development of their staff members. The methods that EHS programs use to support all new and veteran staff members include written materials about the program and its mission; verbal and written policies and procedures; opportunities for novice staff members to "shadow" experienced staff members; role-playing to prepare for challenging situations; development of case studies; observation of videotapes of classroom and home visit experiences; staff mentors; interdisciplinary group staff meetings; and workshops, seminar series, and conferences (Early Head Start National Resource Center, 1999).

Staff retention is a second challenge for EHS. Continuity of staff is essential for developing and maintaining strong relationships with young children and their parents. However, turnover rates in the early childhood field in general, and among child-care providers specifically, are among the highest of any profession, hovering at 30% per year. By comparison, only 6.6% of public school teachers leave their jobs each year (Bureau of Labor Statistics, 1998). In 2002, teacher turnover rates in EHS were 18%, compared with only 11% in Head Start. Furthermore, 19% of the teacher vacancies in EHS remained unfilled for 3 months or longer (Irish, Schumacher, & Lombardi, 2003).

For these reasons, technical assistance and staff development activities represent a significant portion of the federal effort on behalf of EHS children and families. At the national level, the Head Start Bureau contracts with ZERO TO THREE: National Center for Infants, Toddlers, and Families and its partner organization—WestEd, an early childhood academic and research facility—to manage the Early Head Start National Resource Center (EHS NRC). The center develops materials to support program planning and implementation, hosts large-group training conferences and workshops, and provides guidance on innovative approaches such as using satellite television to train staff members who work in remote areas. In addition, the EHS NRC formerly employed a network of experienced senior early childhood associates who consulted with federal staff members on EHS-related matters in the 10 regional EHS offices across the country and in the Washington, D.C.–based offices that oversee the migrant and seasonal programs as well as the American Indian and Alaskan Native Head Start programs.

WestEd offers the Program for Infant and Toddler Caregivers—an intensive train-the-trainer program in infant–toddler development and caregiving practice to all EHS programs. During the first 7 years of EHS's existence, the EHS NRC partnered with 28 regionally based Quality Improvement Centers that employed infant and toddler specialists to provide technical assistance directly to EHS programs. Recently, the Head Start Bureau has redesigned the regional component of its technical assistance system.

Creative partnerships at the national and local level provide EHS programs with access to ongoing training and staff development. The Hilton/EHS Training Program, jointly funded by the Head Start Bureau and the Conrad Hilton Foundation, provides training to EHS parent and staff teams from across the country on including infants and toddlers with significant disabilities in EHS programs. At the local level, EHS programs have established several training partnerships with community colleges and universities. For example, several programs "purchase" infant–toddler development courses from their local colleges. The program pays a flat fee to the college, chooses the instructor, and designs the curriculum to reflect and support Head Start Program Performance Standards as well as to meet trainees' educational needs. Classes are held at times and places that are convenient for EHS staff, and many programs offer meals and child care to maximize staff members' ability to attend. Because EHS programs may make courses available to staff members of community child-care partners, the entire community benefits through such arrangements (Judie Jerald, personal communication to Mary Bogle, September 2001).

Within Early Head Start, supervision is the glue that brings experience, training, and personal insight together. Home visitors, child caregivers, and social-service planners receive a range of guidance, including "reflective supervision" sessions, which are regularly scheduled opportunities to meet and discuss the progress of work with children and families, to problem solve, and to develop new approaches for meeting the needs of participating families.

Partnership Building

EHS programs cannot provide or pay for all of the services that participating families need, nor are they expected to do so. These programs are encouraged to establish collaborative relationships with providers of health and child development services, schools and civic groups, and the faith community. Key EHS partners include agency officials and community providers that carry out the infant–toddler requirements of the Individuals with Disabilities Education Act; community mental health centers; federal, state, and local offices that oversee Welfare-to-Work initiatives; and the federal Child Care Bureau and state Child Care Development Block Grant offices.

Partnerships between EHS and child-care providers have become increasingly important as programs grapple with the mandate to ensure that enrolled infants and toddlers who have parents at work or in training receive child care that meets the Head Start Program Performance Standards. Although some EHS programs fulfill this requirement by offering center-based care themselves, others form partnerships with licensed family child-care homes and child-care centers in their communities. Collaborating child-care providers must meet Head Start Program Performance Standards. Partnership agreements include provisions for training and technical assistance, regular visits to homes and centers by EHS staff, and general quality control for child-care services to EHS children (Judie Jerald, personal communication to Mary Bogle, September 2001).

Many EHS programs blend their own resources with state subsidies for child care. A former partnership between the Head Start Bureau and the Child Care Bureau helped facilitate this "braiding" of EHS and subsidy dollars. The Quality in Linking Together (QUILT) Project, a training and technical assistance effort, was designed to support partnerships among child care, EHS and Head Start, prekindergarten, and other early education programs. The QUILT Project used its knowledge of promising practices emerging across the country to help EHS programs ensure that the child care received by enrolled children met Head Start Program Performance Standards wherever it was provided.

Evaluation, Research, and Continuous Improvement

As the flagship for infant–toddler efforts across the country, EHS relies on solid data to drive its claims of success and plans for the future. Three main approaches are used to evaluate the effect and implications of EHS services and to identify opportunities for enhancing services: evaluation, research, and continuous improvement.

Continuing Head Start's tradition as a national laboratory on how to support the healthy development of young children, EHS uses rigorous, independent evaluation to assess its methods and document outcomes for children and families. In 1996 and 1997, the Administration on Children, Youth, and Families selected 17 of the original 68 EHS programs to participate in an intensive study of child and family outcomes, progress in implementing the Head Start Program Performance Standards, and programs' effect on the availability and quality of child care in the communities they serve (Administration on Children, Youth, and Families, 1999b). Because the 17 chosen programs broadly resembled the entire pool of EHS programs—they represented a balance of program background, race or ethnicity, region, and urban or rural setting—lessons learned could be applied to the whole. Roughly 3,000 families participated in this rigorous, independent evaluation effort, reflecting the socioeconomic and political context of low-income families throughout the United States (Raikes, Kisker, Paulsell, & Love, 2000). Chapters 2 and 3 contain detailed discussions of the most recent findings from the evaluation, including a summary of EHS's positive effect on children's cognitive, language, and social–emotional development.

The EHS program also is an important source of research on issues affecting infants, toddlers, and their families. Sixteen of the evaluation sites have conducted special research projects with help from university partners (John Love, personal communication to Mary Bogle, September 2002). For example, researchers in Logan, Utah, completed an infant attachment study; researchers in Yakima Valley, Washington, studied children's language and social development, particularly the role of Mexican American culture in influencing service effectiveness and child development; and researchers in Jackson, Michigan, focused on family health, particularly family mental health (Administration on Children, Youth, and Families, 1999a). EHS evaluators also have conducted program-wide studies on fatherhood, children with disabilities, and the effect of welfare reform on enrolled families.

Finally, EHS programs are challenged to use data to demonstrate concrete results for children and families and to guide continuous improvement of their services. Continuous improvement refers to ongoing activities designed to measure—and improve—program performance across a range of categories, including program management, child health, cognitive development, and parent involvement. To assist with these efforts, tools, techniques, and data from the national evaluation are regularly shared with EHS programs, child-care providers, and migrant and seasonal Head Start grantees at an annual Birth-to-Three Institute. Attendees are given advice and assistance on translating the implications of the data into more effective program practices at home.

Other continuous improvement efforts are developed and administered locally. For example, at the Panhandle Early Head Start program in Tallahassee, Florida, home visitors document the frequency of their visits and the topics that they discuss with each parent. They enter this information into a database; the data is then used for supervision purposes, for evaluation of service quality, and for tracking of program outcomes. Supervisors also use the data to provide home visitors with objective feedback about their performance compared with that of others in the same role. In addition, analyzing home visitors' data allows program managers to determine whether specific approaches or services have a measurable effect on families. For example, Panhandle EHS staff members have discovered that more frequent discussion of breast-feeding with pregnant women and new mothers promotes longer duration of breast-feeding for program participants (Graham et al., 1997).

CONCLUSION

Today, EHS is a national laboratory and a national model for best practices in promoting healthy child development, supporting the families of infants and toddlers, and building strong communities—not only for poor families but for all families. Building on 40 years of evidence from research and practice, EHS is enriching the world's knowledge base of very young children through its national and local research and evaluation projects. It has advanced the field of infant–toddler care through thoughtfully designed and delivered services, and its federal infrastructure of support, accountability, and results-based improvement.

Since EHS began serving children in 1995, the numbers of children served and the resources available to serve them have increased steadily. This is an extraordinary testament to the nation's demand for high-quality infant–toddler services and to policymakers' confidence in the program. Even with such rapid growth, EHS has maintained its high standards. It has continued to evolve programmatically, adapting its services and structure to meet the needs of a diverse set of communities and families across the United States during a time of rapid social change. Most important, research shows that EHS works: It produces important benefits for participating families. EHS designers and managers are fostering innovations and partnerships that are changing federal, state, and local systems. EHS staff and parents are changing lives.

DISCLAIMER

The views expressed in this chapter reflect those of the authors and not those of the Administration for Children and Families, Administration on Children, Youth, and Families, Head Start Bureau.

NOTE

1. The Head Start Act is Title VI, Subtitle A, Chapter 8, Subchapter B of the Omnibus Budget Reconciliation Act of 1981, Pub. L. No. 97–35 (August 13, 1981). Minor amendments to this act were made by the Technology-Related Assistance for Individuals With Disabilities Amendments of 1993, Pub. L. No. 103–218 (March 9, 1994). This act was most recently reauthorized, through fiscal year 2003, by the Coats Human Services Amendments of 1998, Pub. L. No. 105–285 (October 27, 1998).

REFERENCES

Administration on Children, Youth, and Families. (1999a). *Leading the way: Characteristics and early experiences of selected Early Head Start programs. Vol. 2: Program profiles.* Washington, DC: U.S. Department of Health and Human Services.

Administration on Children, Youth, and Families. (1999b). *Leading the way: Characteristics and early experiences of selected Early Head Start programs. Executive summary, vols. 1, 2, and 3.* Washington, DC: U.S. Department of Health and Human Services.

Bureau of Labor Statistics. (1998). *Occupational projections and training data.* Washington, DC: U.S. Department of Labor.

Early Head Start National Resource Center. (1999). *Early Head Start program strategies: Staff development.* Washington, DC: U.S. Department of Health and Human Services and ZERO TO THREE.

Early Head Start National Resource Center. (2001). *Linguistic diversity and early literacy: Serving culturally diverse families in Early Head Start.* Technical assistance paper no. 5. Washington, DC: U.S. Department of Health and Human Services and ZERO TO THREE.

Fenichel, E., & Mann, T. L. (2001). Early Head Start for low-income families with infants and toddlers. *The Future of Children,* 11(1), 135–141.

Graham, M., Stabile, I., Powell, A., Pruett, R., Hakes, A. Z., & Butler, B. (1997, October/November). Serving pregnant women within Early Head Start: Lessons from the Panhandle Healthy Start and Early Head Start. *Zero to Three,* 22(1), 31–36.

Head Start program performance standards and other regulations. 45 C.F.R. §§ 1301, 1302, 1303, 1304 and guidance, 1305, 1306, and 1308 and guidance. (Government Printing Office 2002).

Irish, K., Schumacher, R., & Lombardi, J. (2003). *Serving America's youngest: A snapshot of Early Head Start children, families, teachers, and programs in 2002.* Washington, DC: Center for Law and Social Policy.

Puget Sound Educational Services District. (2001). *Fact sheets and correspondence on EHS program design and structure.* Burien, WA: Author.

Raikes, H., Kisker, E., Paulsell, D., & Love, J. (2000, October). Early Head Start National Research and Evaluation Project: Meeting the child care needs of families. *Head Start Bulletin,* 69, 7.

Song, Y., & Lu, H. (2002, March). *Early childhood poverty: A statistical profile*. New York: National Center for Children in Poverty.

U. S. Department of Health and Human Services. (1994). *The statement of the Advisory Committee on Services for Families With Infants and Toddlers*. Washington, DC: Author.

U.S. Department of Health and Human Services, Administration for Children and Families. (1995, March 17). *Early Head Start Program grant availability* (Program Announcement No. ACYF-HS-93 600.952). 60(52): 14547–14579.

Administration for Children and Families. (2002). *Making a difference in the lives of infants and toddlers and their families: The impacts of Early Head Start*. Washington, DC: U.S. Department of Health and Human Services.

ABOUT THE AUTHORS

Tammy L. Mann is director of the Early Head Start National Resource Center at ZERO TO THREE. Prior to her work at ZERO TO THREE she served as James Marshall Public Policy Fellow at the American Psychological Association where her work focused on child and family policy issues.

Mary M. Bogle is the former executive director of Grantmakers for Children, Youth, and Families. Prior to serving in that position, she was a program specialist for the Head Start Bureau. She served on the Early Head Start design team and is a staff co-author of *The Statement of the Advisory Committee on Services for Families With Infants and Toddlers* (U.S. Department of Health and Human Services, 1994) and the initial *Federal Register* announcement that launched Early Head Start. Currently, she is a private consultant on early childhood, youth development, and nonprofit management.

Rebecca Parlakian is a staff writer at ZERO TO THREE. She has developed and written two series of publications for infant–family program leaders—one on best practices in infant–toddler program management and the other on supporting children's social–emotional development in the first 3 years of life.

CHAPTER 2

WHAT WORKS: IMPROVING THE ODDS
FOR INFANTS AND TODDLERS IN
LOW-INCOME FAMILIES

Helen H. Raikes, John M. Love, Ellen Eliason Kisker,
Rachel Chazan-Cohen, and Jeanne Brooks-Gunn

C hildren who participated in Early Head Start (EHS) had better child development outcomes at age 3, and their parents fared better across a broad range of parenting and self-sufficiency measures than control group counterparts. This pattern of impacts was found in a rigorous experimental design evaluation of 17 programs from the first two cohorts of programs funded, across multiple program approaches, a widely heterogeneous population, and diverse communities[1] (Administration for Children and Families, 2002). Table 2.1 provides data on the key characteristics of families entering the EHS research programs.

The wide range of impacts—augmented by larger impacts in some subgroups—suggests that the new EHS program is making a difference in areas associated with children's school success and parents' ability to support children's development. Findings from the evaluation also point to ways the program can build on the initial promising findings to produce even stronger impacts in the future.

The study was conducted under contract with Mathematica Policy Research and Columbia University's National Center for Children and Families at Teachers College, in conjunction with researchers in 15 universities who collected data and were partners in decision making about the research process and analysis.[2] The Early Head Start National Research and Evaluation Project recruited 3,001 children and their families when the mothers were pregnant or when children were less than 1 year old. Half of the families were randomly assigned to enroll in the program and half were assigned to a control group that could participate in any services available in the community but could not enroll in EHS. The 17 EHS research programs resembled all first-wave EHS programs in terms of the demographic characteristics of the families they enrolled and program features. Thus, the findings are believed to apply to EHS programs more generally.[3]

A BROAD PATTERN OF IMPACTS

EHS produced favorable impacts across a wide range of child, parenting, and self-sufficiency outcomes. The findings show that, compared with their control group

TABLE 2.1

Key Characteristics of Families Entering
the Early Head Start Research Programs

	Percentage of families	Number of families or program sites			Percentage of families	Number of families or program sites
Child and family characteristics						
Age of focus child			**Primary caregiver received welfare benefits?**[1]			
In utero	25	761	Yes		35	842
0+	75	2,240	No		65	1554
Primary caregiver's race/ethnicity			**Living arrangement of primary caregiver**			
African American	35	1,014	With spouse		25	752
Hispanic	24	693	With other adults		39	1,157
White	37	1,091	Alone		36	1,080
Other	5	135	**Gender of primary caregiver**			
Mother's age at birth of first child			Male		51	1,510
Younger than 20	39	1,142	Female		49	1,448
20 or older	61	1,771	**Enrolled child is firstborn in family?**			
Mother's education			Yes		63	1,858
Less than 12th grade	48	1,375	No		37	1,112
Grade 12 or attained a GED	29	822	**Maternal Risk Index**[2]			
			0 to 2		42	1,333
Greater than 12th grade	24	682	3		31	835
Primary caregiver's occupational status			4 to 5		26	706
Employed	24	677	**Mother at risk for depression?**[3]			
In school or training	22	630	Yes			
Neither	55	1,590	(CES-D at least 16)		48	617
Primary caregiver's primary language			No			
English	71	2,265	(CES-D less than 16)		52	658
Other	29	615				
Program characteristics						
Program approach			**Overall implementation among mixed-approach programs**			
Center based	20	4				
Home based	46	7	Early		54	3
Mixed approach	34	6	Late or incomplete		46	3
Overall implementation						
Early	35	6				
Late	35	6				
Incomplete	30	5				

Note: Totals may not add to 100% due to rounding.

1. Data pertain to families with focus children who were born at baseline.

2. This index was constructed by adding the number of the following risk factors that the mother faced: being a teenage mother, having no high school credential, receiving public assistance, not being employed or in school or training, and being a single mother.

3. The Center for Epidemiological Studies–Depression Scale (CES-D) was administered at baseline to sample members at eight sites in connection with local research data collection at those sites.

counterparts, children who were enrolled in EHS experienced significantly better social–emotional, cognitive, and language outcomes at age 3 and demonstrated some health-related advantages, as well. Their parents were observed to be more supportive in interactions with their children and to provide home environments that were more supportive of child development. EHS parents were also found to read more to, to play more with, and to be less physically punitive toward their children. These parents participated more frequently in training and education programs and were more likely to be employed than control group parents. In most cases, impacts were sustained or broadened from 2-year-old assessments reported in an interim impacts report (Administration on Children, Youth, and Families, 2001a, 2001b). Although most effect sizes[4] were in the range of 10–20%, the pattern of significant differences across many types of outcomes for children and parents, across widely heterogeneous groups, and across multiple program approaches leads us to conclude that the program has been effective. We next examine the findings in greater detail. Differences reported below are statistically significant[5], and all are in the expected direction.

The programs had favorable impacts on multiple aspects of social–emotional development at age 3, and impacts were stronger than at age 2. Compared with children in the control group, children who participated in EHS engaged their parents more, were less negative toward their parents, and were more attentive to objects during play. They were rated lower in aggressive behavior by their parents.

EHS had positive impacts on various features of 3-year-old children's cognitive development, sustaining the pattern found when children were 2 years old. Children who participated in EHS scored higher on the Bayley Scales of Infant Development Mental Development Index (MDI; mean of 91.4% vs. 89.9% for the control group; Bayley, 1993). In addition, a smaller percentage of EHS children than control group children scored in the at-risk range of developmental functioning—that is, below 85 on the MDI (27.3% vs. 32.0%, respectively). Although children who participated in EHS still scored below national norms, they scored better than children in the control group[6].

At age 3, EHS children scored higher on the Peabody Picture Vocabulary Test (PPVT-III; 83.3% vs. 81.1% for the control group; Dunn & Dunn, 1997), a measure of receptive vocabulary. Significantly fewer children in EHS than in the control group (51.1% vs. 57.1%, respectively) scored in the at-risk range of developmental functioning (below 85).

Children who participated in EHS at age 3 were more likely to have received immunizations, although children in both the program and control groups had high rates of immunization (99% for the program group vs. 98% for the control group, a significant difference). Children who participated in EHS were less likely to be hospitalized for accidents and injuries during their third year than control group children, although such hospitalizations were relatively uncommon occurrences for both groups.

Children who participated in EHS were more likely to be identified as eligible for early intervention services and were more likely to receive these services than control children. Although EHS prevented delays in cognitive and language development, special education services were more likely to have been offered for children who had identified disabilities. Early provision of these services is believed to be important for optimizing the potential of children with disabilities.

EHS is a two-generation program with services provided for parents as well as children. Accordingly, many program impacts on aspects of parenting were observed.

Parents of 3-year-olds who participated in EHS were observed to be more emotionally supportive, less detached, and less negative toward their children than control group parents, continuing the pattern seen when children were 2 years old.

EHS parents of 3-year-olds continued to provide more stimulating home environments than did control group parents, as measured by the Home Observation for Measurement of the Environment (HOME; Caldwell & Bradley, 1984). Stimulation included providing more language and cognitive stimulation as measured by a factor score on HOME. A higher percentage of EHS parents than control group parents (56.8% vs. 52.0%, respectively) reported reading daily to their children. A smaller percentage of EHS parents of 3-year-olds reported spanking their children during the previous week than control parents (46.7% vs. 52.0%, respectively), and EHS parents suggested fewer punitive discipline strategies in response to hypothetical situations.

Although the program had no overall impact on parent-reported symptoms of depression, parents in programs that fully implemented the performance standards early tended to report fewer symptoms of depression when children were 3 years old compared with their control group counterparts. In eight programs in which depression was measured at baseline, there was also a trend showing a reduction in mother's depressive symptoms when children were 3 years old for those who reported depressive symptoms at the time of program enrollment. The overall impact on reducing parenting stress seen at age 2 was not sustained at age 3, although it was found in several subgroups when children were 3 years old. This is one of the few areas in which impacts were not sustained from age 2 to age 3.

Analyses from a subset of 12 sites focused specifically on fathers, and in seven sites, father–child play was observed. Compared with fathers and father figures in the control group, the EHS fathers were less likely to report spanking their children during the previous week (25.4% vs. 35.6%, respectively) and were observed to be less intrusive when interacting with their children; their children were more able to engage their fathers and attend to objects during father–child play.

EHS parents were more likely to participate in education or job training activities than control group parents (60.0% vs. 51.4%, respectively) during the 26 months after enrollment, continuing a pattern observed at 15 months after enrollment. Rates of employment increased in both groups during the evaluation period, but 26 months after enrollment EHS parents were more likely than control group parents to have ever been employed (86.8% vs. 83.4%, respectively). This trend was not observed during the earlier assessment period, suggesting that effects on employment may have emerged late in families' program involvement.

Impacts were broad in another respect: Significant impacts were found in most subgroups[7] defined by family and program characteristics. Across 35 major subgroups of families studied, significant favorable impacts on child development were found in 31 subgroups and on parenting outcomes in 32 subgroups. This pattern of findings demonstrates the potential of the program across a breadth of subgroups and across a wide array of outcomes.

Significant impacts were found within all program approaches, whether center-based, home-based, or a combination thereof. However, the impacts were broadest and largest in the mixed-approach programs (see "Depth of Impacts," p. 29 of this chapter).

Programs that fully implemented the Head Start Program Performance Standards (*Head Start program performance standards and other regulations*, 2002) had a broader pattern of impacts when children were 3 years old than programs that did not fully implement these standards. This finding, although not as strong as when children were 2 years old, illustrates the importance of implementing the program as it was designed—to maximize attaining the breadth of outcomes.

In summary, the EHS program showed impacts across a broad range of outcomes, providing a base for the future development of the relatively young EHS program.

PROGRAM IMPLEMENTATION AND SERVICE USE

For any program evaluation, it is important to ascertain which services and other features of the program children and families actually used. The EHS evaluation collected extensive, in-depth data about program implementation, unique features of the three program approaches, and the program services that children and families received. The implementation findings are reported in depth in the EHS implementation study reports (Administration on Children, Youth, and Families, 1999a, 1999b, 2000a, 2000b; Administration for Children and Families, 2003). A description of program services and comparisons of the services received by program and control group families during the 26 months after random assignment appear in the interim and final impact reports (Administration on Children, Youth, and Families, 2001a, 2001b; Administration for Children and Families, 2002).

Programs selected home-based, center-based, or mixed approaches. The early childhood literature suggests that EHS programs could have different outcomes according to the program models selected. On the basis of family and community needs assessments, EHS programs determine whether to provide home-based, center-based, or a mixture of these services to families.[8] When the research programs were funded, about one third of the programs offered center-based services to children and families (which included center-based child development services, parenting education, and at least two home visits per year), about one third offered home-based services (which included weekly home visits, group parent–child socializations, and verification that any child care used was high quality), and about one third of the programs initially were classified as "mixed approach" because they offered home- and center-based services, according to families' needs. Over time, the mixed-approach program model came to predominate; at the time of the third site visit in fall 1999, two thirds of the research sites were mixed-approach programs, one fourth were center-based programs, and only about one tenth were home-based programs.

As a part of the EHS evaluation, programs were asked to report on their theories of change—to identify their intended outcomes and the mechanism(s) by which these outcomes would be achieved (see discussions of EHS program theories of change in *Leading the Way, Vol. 1* [Administration on Children, Youth, and Families, 1999a, chapter II] and *Pathways to Quality and Full Implementation in Early Head Start Programs* [Administration for Children and Families, 2003, chapter III]). Home-based programs more frequently identified parenting outcomes as their priority outcomes and changes in parenting as the mechanism by which they aimed to influence child development outcomes. Center-based programs more frequently targeted the child directly, and mixed-approach programs tended to target the parent and child, although they targeted the parent–child interaction more frequently than other aspects of parenting and targeted social–emotional development more frequently than other aspects of child development.

Although all programs needed to adhere to the service requirements prescribed by the performance standards, there were some differences according to program approaches.

For example, center-based programs provided more services to children directly and aimed to affect children's development. Home-based programs provided home visits to parents and children, but many aimed to affect children's development through their parents. Mixed-approach programs provided services directly to children in centers and directly to parents through frequent home visits; these programs targeted child and parent outcomes, often emphasizing parent–child relationships. Mixed-approach programs emphasized fitting services to family needs and had more flexibility to do so with both home- and center-based options. Some of the mixed-approach programs offered both center-based and at least monthly home-based services to the same families, and others offered center-based services to certain families and home-based services to others within their program population.

Programs varied in attainment of implementation of the performance standards. The EHS implementation study included a systematic assessment of implementation of the Head Start Program Performance Standards (Administration on Children, Youth, and Families, 1999a, 1999b, 2000a, 2000b; Administration for Children and Families, 2003; Head Start *program performance standards and other regulations*, 2002). Using extensive data collected during site visits to each of the programs over the course of the study, a panel of experts met twice (following visits in fall 1997 and fall 1999) to develop consensus-based ratings of each program's degree of implementation of key elements of the performance standards (using 24 elements in 1997 and 25 in 1999). From these individual ratings, the expert panel developed overall ratings of program implementation. These ratings, developed before the impact analyses were conducted, facilitated descriptions of the implementation process and enabled the evaluation team to explore variations in impacts according to degree of implementation.

About one third of the 17 research programs were early implementers (i.e., they were judged to be fully implemented about 1 year after beginning to serve families), about one third were later implementers (i.e., fully implemented within 3 years after beginning to serve families), and about one third were incomplete implementers (i.e., they did not fully implement the comprehensive standards within the first 3 years of service to families). Early-implementing programs included two center-based programs, one home-based program, and three mixed-approach programs. Most programs had served infants and toddlers in some capacity before becoming EHS programs.[9]

The later-implemented programs tended to be home-based programs that required program monitoring and time to incorporate requirements for rigorous child development services and child-care quality into their designs. Incompletely implemented programs included some family support programs that had not incorporated rigorous child development services into the model and a few programs that were unable to meet the management demands that the EHS program requires. Former Comprehensive Child Development Programs, Head Start programs, and community programs were about equally distributed among the programs implemented early, late, and incompletely.

Many families received intensive services. In interviews with families at regular intervals after random assignment, the evaluation measured services that program and control families received (Administration for Children and Families, 2002). Program families generally received significantly more services than the control group did. Specifically, program parents (93%) were significantly more likely than control group parents to receive core child development services such as home visits, center-based care, and group parenting activities that EHS programs delivered, although 58% of the control group received some of these types of services in their communities. EHS parents were nearly twice as likely as control families (71% vs. 37%, respectively) to participate in group parenting–focused activities such as parenting classes or events and parent–child or parent support group activities.

EHS parents were much more likely than control parents to participate in intensive home visiting services. The majority of EHS parents (58%) across all program approaches participated in EHS home visits monthly for at least 15 months, and about one third (35%) did so weekly during that length of time. In contrast, very few control parents received monthly (5%) or weekly (2%) home visits during a comparable period of time.

Based on data from 12 EHS programs that participated in the father studies, nearly one half of the EHS fathers participated in at least one of the seven EHS activities about which they were asked. In addition, comparisons of fathers' participation in activities indicate that 34% of EHS fathers reported that they had participated in a home visit (vs. 5% of control group fathers); 45% dropped off or picked up their child at an EHS or other child-care center (vs. 41% of control group fathers); 25% participated in a parenting education program (vs. 11% of control group fathers), and 20% participated in a parent–child program (vs. 8% of control group fathers). EHS fathers were also much more likely than control group fathers to report participating in these activities frequently.

We turn now to describing the services that the EHS families received across program approaches and level of implementation. Here, rather than emphasizing differences between the program and control groups, we focus on within-program descriptions to show the levels of services that may have produced the outcomes. At the same time, it is important to note that in nearly every case for which both program and control group data were available, data of the program group were significantly higher than those of the control group (Administration for Children and Families, 2002).

In home-based programs, about 61% of parents participated in monthly home visits and 43% in weekly home visits for at least 15 months. In mixed-approach programs, 53% of the families participated in monthly home visits and 31% participated in weekly home visits for at least 15 months. As expected, rates of regular home visit completion were low in center-based programs (2% of parents received monthly home visits, and no parents reported weekly home visits over at least 15 months).

In center-based programs, when children were 14 months of age, 59% of children received center-based care for 30 hours a week; by the time the children were 3 years of age, the proportion had increased to 68%. When all forms of child care (including care during evenings and weekends) were cumulated, 66% of children in center-based programs received 30 hours a week or more at 14 months old, increasing to 74% by age 3. As expected, the percentage of children receiving full-time center-based care was lower in mixed-approach programs (23% at 14 months, 54% at 3 years) and home-based programs (14% and 40%, respectively) than in center-based programs. Similarly, the percentage of children receiving 30 hours or more of all forms of care was lower for mixed-approach programs (50% at 14 months, 67% at 3 years) and home-based programs (37% and 51%, respectively). Interestingly, child-care use varied considerably over the assessment period, contributing to a lower average of total hours of child-care use than might be expected. For example, despite high point-in-time usage in center-based programs, total child care across the entire assessment period averaged 21 hours a week, and use of center-based care averaged 14 hours a week (Administration for Children and Families, 2004).

Implementation affected service use. Early-implemented programs were more likely than other program groups to have families reporting monthly and weekly home visits. Additionally, children in early-implemented programs were in center-based care about 1.6 times the number of hours of those in programs that were implemented later or incompletely.

EHS staff rated the involvement of parents in the program: 37% of program parents were rated as highly engaged, 32% as variably engaged, 18% as consistently engaged at a low level, and 13% as not engaged. Staff in early-implemented programs rated more families as highly engaged in the program. Center-based programs had the most parents rated as highly engaged (47%), relative to home-based (39%) and mixed-approach (38%) programs. Staff at one site in which engagement was studied in depth noted that many of the parents who were unengaged or who had low levels of engagement had greater needs that made it difficult for them to follow through on commitments and to participate in the program (Pan & Bratton, 2000).

Families participated in the program for an average of 21 months. The duration was slightly longer for families in early-implemented programs (23 months) than for programs that were implemented later or incompletely (22 months). Duration did not vary appreciably according to program approach.

Depth of Impacts

Variability in program and demographic features led to different impacts; several subgroups demonstrated larger impacts, illustrating the potential of the program for depth and breadth of effects. Variability in program features as well as variability in family demographic features would be expected to influence outcomes in a sample as heterogeneous as that of the EHS study. For example, we expected to find the largest impacts in early-implemented programs, in program models incorporating the features of home- and center-based programs, among families who received services during the longest period, and among families who did not have extreme barriers to engagement and service use. In fact, several subgroups did show large impacts. Larger favorable impacts were observed among families in mixed-approach programs, especially those that were fully implemented, families in which the mother enrolled during pregnancy, families with a moderate number of demographic risk factors (3), and African American families. Some of the sample subgroups (such as African American families or teenage mothers) approximated the homogeneity of samples used in earlier infant–toddler intervention studies (Olds, Henderson, Tatelbaum, & Chamberlin, 1986; Ramey & Campbell, 1991).

Larger impacts were found among mixed-approach programs. Mixed-approach programs produced a strong pattern of larger and broader impacts than was true for programs overall. In mixed-approach programs, favorable program impacts with effect sizes greater than 20% were found for child language and social–emotional development; observed parent–child interaction (supportiveness, quality of assistance in a teaching task, and detachment); daily reading to children; spankings during the previous week and use of mild and not severe discipline; and parent education or training and employment.[10] Although home-based and center-based programs both produced significant, favorable impacts, the larger impacts found in the mixed-approach programs are likely to be due to the ability of mixed-approach programs to target parenting and child outcomes fairly equally, their flexibility in creating a good fit between program services and family needs, and a tendency to focus on the parent–child relationship more than other programs. As noted, the mixed-approach model became the most predominant approach among EHS research programs.

The largest impacts were found in early-implemented mixed-approach programs. Among the six mixed-approach programs, three were able to fully implement the performance standards early in the evaluation period. These programs demonstrated even larger impacts than the other mixed-approach programs while maintaining the broad pattern of impacts seen in the sample at large. These mixed-approach programs were carrying out the program as it was designed to be implemented among all EHS sites; this group of mixed-approach programs was able to do so soon after the evaluation began. Thus, families in the study sample experienced the program as fully implemented from enrollment or very soon after. Early-implemented mixed-approach programs achieved

- Impacts with effect sizes greater than 50% on parental daily reading to child and in use of mild and not severe discipline strategies;

- Impacts with effect sizes in the range of 40–50% on observed child social–emotional development (engagement of parent during play and sustained attention) and observed parent supportiveness in a teaching task;

- Favorable impacts with effect sizes in the range of 30–40% on child language development (prevention of delays), observed parent detachment, and parent participation in training and education; and

- Favorable impacts with effect sizes in the range of 20–30% on child cognitive development (Bayley MDI scores and prevention of delays), observed child negativity, observed parent–child interaction outcomes (quality of assistance in a teaching task, detachment, and intrusiveness), reported parent–child activities, parent's completion of a General Educational Development (GED) diploma, and parent's employment.

Together, these findings indicate that a pattern of large and broad favorable impacts is possible when programs implement the performance standards as they were intended and take a mixed approach to program services.

Families enrolled during pregnancy demonstrated larger impacts. About one quarter of EHS families in the research sample enrolled during pregnancy, and the remaining families enrolled during the first year of the child's life. Although those who enrolled later also demonstrated the general pattern of broad impacts across a range of outcomes, the effects among those who enrolled during pregnancy were notably larger:

- Effect sizes on child social–emotional development (engagement of parent during play, sustained attention) and on observed parent–child interaction (supportiveness during play) were 40–60%;

- An impact with an effect size of 30–40% was observed on an additional child social–emotional development outcome (engagement of parent during a teaching task); and

- Favorable impacts with effect sizes in the range of 20–30% were observed on child cognitive development, additional child social–emotional development outcomes (persistence, negativity toward parent during play), additional parent–child interaction outcomes (supportiveness during a teaching task, detachment), spanking during the previous week, whether parents were employed or in training during the evaluation period, and welfare receipt in one of the latter quarters of the evaluation.

Families with a moderate number of risk factors had larger impacts. Among the sample of families studied, about 45% of the families had two or fewer demographic risks, about 30% had three demographic risk factors, and about 25% had extreme numbers of (four or five) demographic risks. Previous studies have demonstrated the negative effects of cumulative risks on children and families, especially at the highest cumulate levels (Sameroff & Fiese, 2000). The demographic risks observed in the current study included being a teenage mother, being neither in school nor employed, being a single parent, lacking a high school diploma or GED credential, and receiving public assistance. Families enrolled in the EHS program demonstrated notably larger impacts, while maintaining the broad pattern of impacts seen in the sample at large, among a group of families who had three demographic risks. Favorable impacts, though smaller in magnitude, were observed among families with up to two demographic risks, and in one of the few exceptions to the broad pattern of favorable impacts, the program did not have favorable impacts on children and families with extreme numbers of demographic risk factors, except for reducing subsequent births. The strong pattern of favorable impacts seen among families with three demographic risks was found across a broad range of outcomes:

- Among families with three demographic risks, impacts in the range of 30–40% were observed for parent–child interaction (supportiveness during play, supportiveness during a teaching task, detachment), parent–child play, daily reading, and bedtime reading to children; and

- Among this group at moderate level of risk, favorable impacts with effect sizes in the range of 20–30% were observed on child cognitive development, child social–emotional development (engagement of parent during play), observed parent–child interaction (quality of assistance during the teaching task), parenting stress, hours in education and training, Temporary Assistance for Needy Families (TANF) receipt toward the end of program enrollment, and food stamp use (increased).

African American families demonstrated larger impacts. Three racial or cultural groups of roughly comparable size were included in the study: African American, Hispanic, and White. Although the EHS program demonstrated favorable impacts on Hispanic families and children (including promising findings regarding children's language development)[11] and some favorable impacts for White children and families, impacts for African American families were larger as well as broader:

- Impacts for African American children and parents with effect sizes of 40–50% were found on child social–emotional development (engagement of parent in play and during a teaching task, sustained attention) and observed parent–child interaction (supportiveness during play);

- Favorable impacts in the range of 30–40% for effect size were observed in additional areas of child social–emotional development (negativity and aggressive behaviors) and whether the parent was ever employed or in training; and

- Favorable impacts with effect sizes in the range of 20–30% were observed for child language development, child social–emotional development (persistence), home environment, parental warmth, adherence to a regular bedtime, at-home support for language and learning, observed parent–child interaction outcomes (quality of assistance, support during a teaching task, intrusiveness during play and a teaching task, negative regard), reported parent–child dysfunctional interaction, parenting stress, hours in education or training, employment, TANF benefits, and total welfare benefits of all kinds.

METHODOLOGICAL EMPHASES

Findings were developed using state-of-the-art evaluation techniques. Evaluators used a number of procedures and techniques to pursue questions that are sometimes challenges for evaluations. Some procedures had been used previously in other disciplines but not in early childhood programs. Several techniques were selected for their relevance to program practices and program improvement efforts. Six methodological features of the study are highlighted in the following list.

1. **Successful implementation of random assignment and good comparability between the program and control groups at each assessment.** Families were systematically and randomly assigned by Mathematica Policy Research with no exemptions granted. Random assignment resulted in program and control groups with very few differences in baseline characteristics at the outset and at all follow-up points. The presence of local research teams at each site working in close cooperation with Mathematica facilitated the success of random assignment. To control for any possible differences that may have existed between the groups, 20 categories of variables were entered as controls in the regression-adjusted impact analyses.

2. **Analyzing implementation within the experimental design.** The evaluation collected extensive implementation data, created an implementation variable to use in the impact analyses, and completed analyses of the effects of implementation within the experimental design.

3. **Studying impacts on services.** The study systemically collected data on a wide range of services received by both program and control groups; with this information, researchers could establish that even though control families received many services, EHS program families received more intensive services as a result of their program participation.

4. **Analyzing impacts on the basis of participation as well as intent to treat.** Using techniques employed in econometric studies (Bloom, 1984) and an operational definition of participation as 1 home visit or 2 weeks of center care, it was possible to analyze impacts in a way that was credible to programs that were unable to provide initial services to a few families, without undermining the integrity of the experimental design. Sensitivity analyses showed that results were nearly identical using the two methods of analysis (Administration for Children and Families, 2002).

5. **Interpretation of patterns of impacts.** Given the large number of variables analyzed, this evaluation drew conclusions based on patterns of impacts rather than emphasizing isolated or single-variable impacts. Although the majority of impacts were statistically significant at the 0.05 and 0.01 levels, impacts at the 0.10 level were also considered when associated with a pattern of significant impacts.

6. **Continuous program improvement.** The evaluation sought to follow the recommendation of the Advisory Committee on Services for Families With Infants and Toddlers (U.S. Department of Health and Human Services, 1994) to provide findings that programs could use for continuous program improvement. Targeted subgroup analyses provided one mechanism by which the study was able to be responsive to that recommendation and to the recommendation of another committee of experts, the Head Start "Blueprint" Committee, to investigate for whom and under what conditions the program was effective (U.S. Department of Health and Human Services, 1990). To address the potential of subgroup confounding, multiple regression sensitivity analyses were conducted that validated, to a general extent, the separate analyses of nonoverlapping groups (Administration for Children and Families, 2002a).

SUMMARY AND LESSONS FOR THE FUTURE

The findings from the study should be useful to the relatively young EHS program, given its commitment to data-driven continuous program improvement (U.S. Department of Health and Human Services, 1994). The main findings from the study and their implications for the future of the program follow.

1. **EHS showed a pattern of broad impacts with implications for ways to build in the future to enhance specific outcomes.** The pattern of impacts across a wide range of child and parenting outcomes over many population groups and program approaches is encouraging. EHS programs produced impacts in all areas of child development and in most areas of parenting, parent well-being, and self-sufficiency as well as on fathers, across a heterogeneous population and multiple program approaches. This broad pattern of findings underscores the benefits of the comprehensive nature of EHS services.

Specific child and parenting outcomes suggest focused implications. Relatively strong findings in the area of social–emotional development suggest potential for future effects. In general, the program can build on cognitive and language development findings that were significant and promising but modest overall, and on findings relating to home environments and the stimulation of children's language and literacy skills by emphasizing these areas of development in their program activities and through more intensive and innovative curricula. Relatively strong impacts on mother–child relationships and promising outcomes for maternal discipline practices and self-sufficiency, as well as for some parenting practices of fathers, can be built upon and extended through enhanced focus in each area. Relatively weak impacts—with some promising findings in several subgroups—in the area of mental health can be strengthened by emphasizing the features of support and relationships that promote mental health, through the targeted use of specialized mental health interventions, and by building infant mental health service capacity in communities.[12]

2. **Impacts were broader when programs were fully implemented, underscoring the importance of adherence to the performance standards.** The fact that impacts are broader when programs are fully implemented underscores the importance of the Head Start Program Performance Standards—quick implementation of the standards after funding and continued adherence to the standards in all program approaches appear to bring about the best results.

3. **EHS programs produced larger impacts in mixed-approach programs, which balanced center-based with home-based services, and impacts were larger still when mixed-approach programs were fully implemented; these findings underscore the importance of both child-focused and parent-focused services and of tailoring services to fit family needs, as well as adhering to the performance standards.** Findings showing impacts with relatively large effect sizes in mixed-approach early-implemented programs demonstrate the potential of the program for the future. Early Head Start can build on these findings by further balancing child development services (through quality center-based services and focused child development efforts in home-based services) with parenting emphases (through intense home-based services and parenting education) and fine-tuning the fit between service options and parent needs to optimize outcomes.

4. **EHS programs produced larger impacts among families in which the mother enrolled during pregnancy, pointing to the advisability of enrolling families early.** Findings for families enrolled during pregnancy further demonstrate the potential for the program to have larger impacts while maintaining the breadth of impacts seen more generally. The evaluation results indicate that families and children benefit from longer and/or timely exposure to EHS services and underscore the importance of beginning services early in the child's life or, preferably, prebirth.

5. **Early Head Start programs produced larger impacts among families that had a moderate number of demographic risks but not among families at highest risk.** The findings suggest that current program strategies are appropriate for most families but also highlight the need to develop new strategies for families at extreme levels of risk. Larger impacts observed among families at moderate levels of demographic risk demonstrate the effectiveness of current strategies for these families; the lack of positive impacts for families with extreme levels of risk (i.e., families having four or five risks) signals challenge for the future. This pattern of impacts is not unique to EHS. Negative outcomes for families at extreme levels of demographic risk have been observed in other studies (Jones, Forehand, Brody, & Armistead, 2002; Liaw & Brooks-Gunn, 1994; Rutter, 1979). These results suggest that comprehensive programs need to create different patterns of services, stronger community partnerships with service providers, or services with greater intensity to serve these families effectively. Often called the "hard to serve," families with extreme numbers of demographic risks are also more likely to suffer from other chronic conditions such as mental and physical health problems. Some enhanced intervention strategies for families who have specific risk factors such as mental health problems are being developed in the Early Promotion and Intervention Research Consortium (Administration on Children, Youth, and Families, 2002).

Taken together, the findings of Early Head Start National Research and Evaluation Project send three key messages:

1. Significant, positive impacts were observed across a broad range of child, parent–child, parenting, and parent self-sufficiency outcomes when children were 3 years old; these findings illustrate the promise of the new EHS program.

2. The findings showing larger impacts viewed against a backdrop of a

broad range of outcomes in subgroups demonstrate the potential of the program—when fully implemented, with services fine-tuned to differential family needs—to achieve depth as well as breadth of impacts.

3. By applying lessons from the evaluation, the program has the potential to have even greater impact for the nation's largely underserved low-income families with infants and toddlers.

ACKNOWLEDGMENTS

The findings reported in this chapter are based on research conducted as part of the national Early Head Start National Research and Evaluation Project funded by the Administration on Children, Youth and Families (ACYF), U.S. Department of Health and Human Services, under contract 105-95-1936 to Mathematica Policy Research in Princeton, New Jersey, and the Center for Children and Families at Columbia University's Teachers College in New York, in conjunction with the Early Head Start Research Consortium. The consortium consists of representatives from the 17 programs that participated in the evaluation, 15 local research teams, the evaluation contractors, and ACYF. Research institutions in the consortium (and principal researchers) include Administration for Children and Families (Rachel Chazan-Cohen, Judith Jerald, Esther Kresh, Helen H. Raikes, and Louisa Tarullo); Catholic University of America (Michaela Farber, Harriet Liebow, Lynn Milgram Mayer, Christine Sabatino, Nancy Taylor, Elizabeth Timberlake, and Shavaun Wall); Columbia University (Lisa Berlin, Christy Brady-Smith, Jeanne Brooks-Gunn, and Alison Sidle Fuligni); Harvard University (Barbara Alexander Pan, Catherine Ayoub, and Catherine Snow); Iowa State University (Dee Draper, Gayle Luze, Susan McBride, and Carla Peterson); Mathematica Policy Research (Kimberly Boller, Jill Constantine, Ellen Eliason Kisker, John M. Love, Diane Paulsell, Christine Ross, Peter Schochet, Cheri Vogel, and Welmoet van Kammen); Medical University of South Carolina (Richard Faldowski, Gui-Young Hong, and Susan Pickrel); Michigan State University (Hiram Fitzgerald, Tom Reischl, and Rachel Schiffman); New York University (Mark Spellmann and Catherine Tamis-LeMonda); University of Arkansas (Robert Bradley, Mark Swanson, and Leanne Whiteside-Mansell); University of California, Los Angeles (Claire Hamilton and Carollee Howes); University of Colorado Health Sciences Center (Robert Emde, Jon Korfmacher, JoAnn Robinson, Paul Spicer, and Norman Watt); University of Kansas (Jane Atwater, Judith Carta; and Jean Ann Summers); University of Missouri–Columbia (Mark Fine, Jean Ispa, and Kathy Thornburg); University of Pittsburgh (Beth Green,

Carol McAllister, and Robert McCall); University of Washington School of Education (Eduardo Armijo and Joseph Stowitschek); University of Washington School of Nursing (Kathryn E. Barnard and Susan Spieker); and Utah State University (Lisa Boyce and Lori Roggman).

The authors thank the consortium reviewers who commented on early drafts of this chapter under the guidelines of the Early Head Start Research Consortium publication policies. The authors express appreciation for the involvement of the children, families, and staff and the Early Head Start program directors from the research sites for their dedication to the national study.

DISCLAIMER

The content of this chapter does not necessarily reflect the views or policies of the U.S. Department of Health and Human Services, nor does the mention of trade names, commercial products, or organizations imply endorsement by the U.S. government. Correspondence concerning this chapter should be addressed to Helen Raikes (hraikes@neb.rr.com).

NOTES

1. In addition to the rigorous experimental design, the evaluation results reported in this chapter are based on well-established analytic approaches that take into account data collection nonresponse and levels of program participation. Methodological analyses showed that random assignment was implemented successfully, biases in the impact estimates due to differential data collection nonresponse were minimal, estimates of impacts per participant and impacts per eligible applicant were very similar, and estimated subgroup impacts were similar when other characteristics were controlled. A full explanation of the research design, analytic methods, and sensitivity analyses can be found in volumes I and II of *Making a Difference in the Lives of Infants and Toddlers and Their Families: The Impacts of Early Head Start* (Administration for Children and Families, 2002).

2. The contractor, government project officers, and local researchers comprised the Early Head Start Research Consortium, which met twice annually and more frequently in working groups to plan implementation of the research design and the analyses and to interpret findings.

3. Fifteen research sites were purposely selected using several criteria: (a) programs had to be able to recruit twice as many families as they could serve; (b) programs had to

have a viable research partner; and (c) in aggregate, the programs had to provide a national geographic distribution that represented the major programmatic approaches and settings and that reflected diverse family characteristics thought to be typical of EHS families nationally. Applying these criteria resulted in fewer center-based programs than desired, so in 1996 one additional center-based program from Wave I was selected and in 1997 another center-based program from Wave II was selected.

4. The *effect size* provides a way of comparing effects across different measures in terms of the size of the program control difference relative to the standard deviation of the measure. Typically expressed as a percentage or proportion of the standard deviation, it is calculated by dividing the estimated impact per participant on the outcome measure by the standard deviation of the measure among the control group. Thus, for example, if a measure has a standard deviation of 12 points, and the program control difference (i.e., the impact) is 6 points, then the effect size would be 0.50 or 50%. If the program's impact were 10 points on a measure that had a standard deviation of 20, we would conclude that the magnitude of these two impacts was the same.

5. Although most impacts were significant at the 0.05 and 0.01 levels of probability, differences at the 0.10 level are also reported when part of a pattern of significant differences or when the differences could indicate notable trends emerging late in the evaluation period.

6. It is important to note that, because of EHS enrollment policies, the EHS study sample (both program and control groups) included a higher percentage of children with identified disabilities than that of the population at large.

7. The program's impacts were examined for 35 subgroups: 29 based on family characteristics (defined at the time of random assignment) and 6 based on program characteristics. The family characteristics included whether the mother was a teenage or older parent at the time of the child's birth (2 subgroups), race or ethnicity (3 subgroups), main language spoken at home (2 subgroups), mother's highest grade completed (3 subgroups), mother's primary occupation (3 subgroups), family's living arrangements (3 subgroups), whether the child was firstborn (2 subgroups), whether the family was receiving cash assistance at enrollment (2 subgroups), mother's pregnancy status at enrollment (2 subgroups), child's gender (2 subgroups), number of demographic risks (3 subgroups), and risk for depression in 8 sites at which depression was measured at baseline (2 subgroups). In addition, program-related characteristics included the program's pattern of implementation (3 subgroups) and program approach (3 subgroups). The subgroups that were defined based on one characteristic at a time naturally overlap. In sensitivity analyses, the patterns of differential impacts remained largely the same after potential confounding characteristics were controlled.

8. For research purposes, the combination of home- and center-based services is referred to as the "mixed-approach" program model, although this term does not reflect an official Head Start option.

9. Although early-implementing programs were able to meet most of the performance standards assessed, anecdotally, most contended that in 1999 they were still improving their services.

10. We use the term "favorable impacts" to describe both increases among EHS participants relative to the control group on positive outcomes (e.g., significantly higher levels of parent supportiveness) and reductions in negative outcomes (e.g., significantly lower levels of spanking or detachment).

11. Effect size of the impact for English-speaking Hispanic children on the *Peabody Picture Vocabulary Test* was 30–40%, and the effect size for Spanish-speaking children on the *Test de Vocabulario Imagenes Peabody* (Dunn, Padilla, Lugo, & Dunn, 1986) was 20–30%. Although the effect sizes are interesting, because the sample was relatively small, the impacts were not significant.

12. Nationally, EHS is already addressing program needs for greater resources in this area through an infant mental health initiative. Additionally, five new research grants comprising the Early Promotion and Intervention Research Consortium will extend the knowledge base by developing and measuring the effects of enhanced intervention strategies (Administration on Children, Youth, and Families, 2002).

REFERENCES

Administration on Children, Youth, and Families. (1999a). *Leading the way: Characteristics and early experiences of selected Early Head Start programs. Volume 1: Cross-site perspectives*. Washington, DC: U.S. Department of Health and Human Services.

Administration on Children, Youth, and Families. (1999b). *Leading the way: Characteristics and early experiences of selected Early Head Start programs. Volume 2: Program profiles*. Washington, DC: U.S. Department of Health and Human Services.

Administration on Children, Youth, and Families. (2000a). *Leading the way: Characteristics and early experiences of selected first-wave Early Head Start programs. Volume 3: Program implementation*. Washington, DC: U.S. Department of Health and Human Services.

Administration on Children, Youth, and Families. (2000b). *Leading the way:*

Characteristics and early experiences of selected first-wave Early Head Start programs. Executive summary, vols. 1, 2, and 3. Washington, DC: U.S. Department of Health and Human Services.

Administration on Children, Youth, and Families. (2001a). *Building their futures: How Early Head Start programs are enhancing the lives of infants and toddlers in low-income families.* Summary report. Washington, DC: U.S. Department of Health and Human Services.

Administration on Children, Youth, and Families. (2001b). *Building their futures: How Early Head Start programs are enhancing the lives of infants and toddlers in low-income families. Vol. 1: Technical report and Vol. 2: Technical report appendices.* Washington, DC: U.S. Department of Health and Human Services.

Administration for Children and Families. (2002). *Making a difference in the lives of infants and toddlers and their families: The impacts of Early Head Start.* Washington, DC: U.S. Department of Health and Human Services.

Administration for Children and Families. (2003). *Pathways to quality and full implementation in Early Head Start programs.* Washington, DC: U.S. Department of Health and Human Services.

Administration for Children and Families. (2004). *The role of Early Head Start programs in addressing the child care needs of low-income families with infants and toddlers: Influences on child care use and quality.* Washington, DC: U.S. Department of Health and Human Services.

Administration on Children, Youth, and Families. (2002, March 4). FY02 Head Start discretionary research funding announcement. *Federal Register, 67(42):* 9745–9756.

Bayley, N. (1993). *Bayley scales of infant development* (2nd ed.). Manual. New York: The Psychological Corporation, Harcourt Brace & Company.

Bloom, H. (1984). Accounting for no-shows in experimental evaluation designs. *Evaluation Review, 8,* 225–246.

Caldwell, B. M., & Bradley, R. H. (1984). *Home observation for measurement of the environment: Administration manual* (Rev. ed.). Unpublished manuscript. Little Rock: University of Arkansas at Little Rock.

Dunn, L. M., & Dunn, L. M. (1997). *Peabody Picture Vocabulary Test* (3rd ed.). Circle Pines, MN: American Guidance Services.

Dunn, L. M., Padilla, E. R., Lugo, E. R., & Dunn, L. M. (1986). *Examiner's manual for the Test de Vocabulario en Imagenes Peabody (Peabody Picture Vocabulary Test), adaptación hispánoamericana (Hispanic-American adaptation)*. Circle Pines, MN: American Guidance Service.

Head Start program performance standards and other regulations. 45 C.F.R. §§ 1301, 1302, 1303, 1304 and guidance, 1305, 1306, and 1308 and guidance. (Government Printing Office 2002).

Jones, D. J., Forehand, R., Brody, G., & Armistead, L. (2002). Psychological adjustment of African American children in single mother families: A test of three risk models. *Journal of Marriage and the Family*, 64, 105–115.

Liaw, F., & Brooks-Gunn, J. (1994). Cumulative family risks and low birthweight: Children's cognitive and behavioral development. *Journal of Clinical Child Psychology*, 23, 360–372.

Olds, D. L, Henderson, C., Tatelbaum, R., & Chamberlin, R. (1986). Prevention of child abuse and neglect: A randomized trial of nurse home visitation. *Pediatrics*, 78, 65–78.

Pan, B., & Bratton, L. (2000, June 28–July 1). *Parenting stress and maternal communication with toddlers*. Presentation at Head Start Fifth National Research Conference, Washington, DC.

Ramey, C. T., & Campbell, F. (1991). Poverty, early childhood education, and academic competence: The abecedarian experiment. In A. Huston (Ed.), *Children in poverty: Child development and public policy* (pp. 190–221). New York: Cambridge University Press.

Rutter, M. (1979). Protective factors in children's responses to stress and disadvantage. In W. M. Kent & J. E. Rolf (Eds.), *Primary prevention of psychopathology: Social competence in children*, Vol. 3 (pp. 49–74). Hanover, NH: University Press of New England.

Sameroff, A., & Fiese, B. (2000). Models of development and developmental risk. In C. Zeanah (Ed.), *Handbook of infant mental health* (2nd ed.) (pp. 3–19). New York: Guilford Press.

U.S. Department of Health and Human Services. (1990, September). *Head Start research and evaluation: A blueprint for the future. Recommendations of the Advisory Panel for the Head Start Evaluation Design Project*. Washington, DC: Author.

U.S. Department of Health and Human Services. (1994). *The statement of the Advisory Committee on Services for Families With Infants and Toddlers*. Washington, DC: Author.

ABOUT THE AUTHORS

Helen H. Raikes is affiliated with the Gallup Organization and the University of Nebraska. This manuscript was prepared when she was a Society for Research in Child Development fellow and visiting scholar at the Administration on Children and Families.

John M. Love is a senior fellow at Mathematica Policy Research in Princeton, New Jersey.

Ellen Eliason Kisker was a senior researcher at Mathematica Policy Research in Princeton, New Jersey, at the time this chapter was written.

Rachel Chazan-Cohen is a senior social science research analyst at the Administration for Children and Families, U.S. Department of Health and Human Services.

Jeanne Brooks-Gunn is Virginia and Leonard Marx Professor in Child Development and Education at Teachers College, Columbia University.

CHAPTER 3

EARLY HEAD START'S ROLE IN PROMOTING GOOD-QUALITY CHILD CARE FOR LOW-INCOME FAMILIES

John M. Love, Helen H. Raikes, Diane Paulsell, and Ellen Eliason Kisker

In 1994, the year before Early Head Start (EHS) began, 40 policymakers, program specialists, and researchers concluded a series of meetings convened by the secretary of the Department of Health and Human Services with a set of recommendations that were to have far-ranging consequences. These recommendations, embodied in The Statement of the Advisory Committee on Services for Families with Infants and Toddlers, called for sweeping changes in Head Start services by establishing the framework for the new EHS program (U.S. Department of Health and Human Services, 1994). Along with discussion of all of the other EHS dimensions (described in other chapters in this book) was a single paragraph that, as welfare reform took hold around the country, stated the intention to create a new foundation for assisting working parents. The committee declared that:

> As programs provide child development services, they must ensure that infants and toddlers who need child care receive high-quality part- and full-day services. Such child care can be provided directly or in collaboration with other community providers as long as the Early Head Start program assumes responsibility for ensuring that all settings meet the Early Head Start Performance Standards (U.S. Department of Health and Human Services, 1994, p. 16).

Two years later, the revised Head Start Program Performance Standards were published for comment in the *Federal Register*, formalizing specific requirements for the quality of EHS services (Administration for Children and Families, 1996); the standards became effective in January 1998. Through the standards on early childhood development services, the Head Start Bureau also established a clear set of expectations for the quality of center-based child development services, including child care provided in community child-care settings. Among other things, the standards require child-to-staff ratios of 4:1 and a maximum group size of 8 infants and toddlers in center-based child-care settings. They also require child-care staff to have a Child Development Associate (CDA) credential (or higher degree) within 1 year of being hired as an infant–toddler teacher (Administration for Children and Families, 1996).[1]

In keeping with the advisory committee's recommendation, the Head Start Bureau expects programs to help all families who need child care find child-care arrangements. Moreover, programs must make significant efforts to ensure that these child-care arrangements—whether provided through a program-operated child-care center or a community child-care provider—adhere to the Head Start Program Performance Standards. Grantees are charged with developing systems to support and monitor this effort.

This chapter summarizes findings from the national EHS evaluation; these findings highlight the levels of child-care quality that EHS programs have achieved. This information is presented in the context of the programs' strategies for working toward meeting the Head Start Bureau's child care mandate and highlights the successes and challenges that programs have faced in working to ensure good-quality child care for all families who need it. The chapter concludes with a set of recommendations for programs.

METHODS

As part of the Early Head Start National Research and Evaluation Project, Mathematica Policy Research obtained extensive data at several points in time on child-care quality and programs' efforts to meet the Head Start Bureau's child-care mandate. Site visits conducted in fall 1997 and fall 1999 as part of the implementation study enabled researchers to learn about the programs' strategies for meeting families' child-care needs while addressing the child-care quality requirements of the performance standards (for details on the implementation study, see Administration for Children and Families, 2003; Administration on Children, Youth, and Families, 1999a, 1999b, 2000a, 2000b). Observations of program children's child-care arrangements, conducted when they were approximately 14 and 24 months old, supplemented the onsite interviews conducted for the implementation study and enabled researchers to assess the quality of child-care arrangements that program families used.[2]

Observations include data collected using a slightly shortened version of the Infant/Toddler Environment Rating Scale (ITERS; Harms, Cryer, & Clifford, 1990) and the Family Day Care Rating Scale (FDCRS; Harms & Clifford, 1989), as well as observed child-to-teacher ratios and group sizes.[3] These widely used scales consist of 35 items that assess the quality of care.[4] The scales produce scores on each item ranging from 1 to 7, in which 3 is described as minimal care, 5 as good care, and 7 as excellent care.

CHILD CARE FOR INFANTS AND TODDLERS IN THE UNITED STATES TODAY

Previous research indicates that many parents of infants and toddlers from low-income households have difficulty finding child care. Licensed or regulated child care is less available for infants and toddlers than for older children (Fuller & Liang, 1996; Fuller, Choong, Coonerty, & Kipnis, 1997). Chronic shortages also exist for children with special needs and for sick children (Collins, Layzer, Kreader, Werner, & Glantz, 2000). Substantial proportions of low-income mothers work during nonstandard hours, when licensed and regulated care is especially difficult to find (Ross & Paulsell, 1998). Information about child-care options and subsidies to pay for them is often difficult for parents to obtain (Gong et al., 1999).

Families are challenged to find quality child care. Extensive research has shown that variations in quality are associated with child outcomes across a wide age spectrum (Love, Schochet, & Meckstroth, 1996), particularly for infant–toddler care (Love, Raikes, Paulsell, & Kisker, 2000). Researchers and policymakers consider good-quality child care to be care in a safe, healthy environment that meets professional standards and promotes healthy child development (Love et al., 1996).

By most definitions, a large proportion of child care for infants and toddlers is not of good quality (Fenichel, Griffin, & Lurie-Hurvitz, 1999). For example, the Profile of Child Care Settings Study (Kisker, Hofferth, Phillips, & Farquhar, 1991) found an average group size of 10 for classrooms of 1-year-olds (compared with the Head Start Program Performance Standards specification of 8) and an average child-to-staff ratio of between 6:1 and 7:1 (whereas the National Association for the Education of Young Children [NAEYC] recommends 5:1 in a group size of 10 and 4:1 in a group size of 12, and Head Start standards specify 4:1 for that age group). Of the centers in that national survey, more than one third of those serving 2-year-olds exceeded the maximum group size recommended.

Process quality, typically measured by ITERS (Harms et al., 1990) and the Early Childhood Environment Rating Scale–Revised (ECERS–R; Harms, Clifford, & Cryer, 1998) for center care and FDCRS (Harms & Clifford, 1989) for family settings, has also been low. The National Child Care Staffing Study found average quality scores of 3.2 and 3.6 in centers serving infants and toddlers, respectively (Whitebook, Howes, & Phillips, 1989). Only 12% of the study classrooms exceeded the score of 5 typically associated with "good" classroom practices. Similarly, a more recent study (Cost, Quality, and Child Outcomes Study Team, 1995) found the average infant–toddler quality score to be 3.4; 40% of infant–toddler classrooms scored below 3.0, and only 8% achieved quality ratings better than 5.0.

Evidence also suggests that the child care used by poverty-level families may be of lower quality than the care more affluent families obtain. Kontos, Howes, Shinn, and Galinsky (1995) found a direct relationship between family income and quality of the family child-care settings used (with mean FDCRS scores of 2.6, 3.1, and 3.8 for low-, middle-, and high-income families, respectively). The Cost, Quality, and Child Outcomes Study Team (1995) found that more highly educated parents placed their children in higher quality settings, and a Canadian study (Schliecker, White, & Jacobs, 1991) found a positive correlation between ECERS classroom quality scores and family socioeconomic status.

CHILD CARE USE BY EARLY HEAD START FAMILIES

EHS families made extensive use of child care, and usage increased as children grew older (see Chapter 1 of this book and the special child-care policy report [Administration for Children and Families, 2004] for more details). Across the entire sample of EHS families, two thirds of all children were in a regular child-care arrangement for at least 10 hours a week when they were 14 months old: 25% of all families used a relative as their primary child-care arrangement, 10% used a nonrelative provider, and 30% used center-based care. By age 3, 84% of all children were receiving at least 10 hours of child care per week, 23% of the children were in primary child care provided by a relative, 12% were in child care provided by a nonrelative, and 48% were in center-based care for 10 hours a week or more.

As might be expected, the use of center-based child care differed by program approach. When children were 3 years old, 68% of children in center-based programs were in center-based care as their primary arrangement, 50% of children in mixed-approach programs were in center-based care as their primary arrangement, and 36% of children in home-based programs were in center-based care as their primary arrangement.

QUALITY OF CHILD CARE FOR EARLY HEAD START CHILDREN

The Early Head Start National Research and Evaluation Project investigated the quality of child care that EHS children received at the 17 research sites under the 3 settings that served EHS children:

- EHS center-based care (i.e., centers operated by the EHS center-based programs),

- Community child-care centers that EHS children attended, and

- Family child-care homes (regulated and unregulated) that EHS children attended in their communities.

Nine of the 17 programs that participated in the national evaluation (referred to here as "the research programs") offered child care in EHS centers in 1997, and 12 did so in 1999. In addition, many EHS children received care in other community child-care centers or family child-care homes. In this chapter, we report on observations conducted between October 1997 and September 1999 in EHS centers at 9 research sites, community child-care centers at 16 sites, and family child-care homes at 14 sites.[5]

Quality in Early Head Start Center-Based Care

Our analysis indicates that the quality of care provided by EHS centers during their first 2 years of serving families was good.[6] All nine programs that operated centers had average center scores above 4 (the middle of the "minimal care" range) on the ITERS; the average program-level score was 5.3 (in the "good care" range). Moreover, in 1997–98[7], five of the nine programs had average ITERS scores above 5.0; in 1998–99, six programs averaged above 5.0. The Cost, Quality, and Child Outcomes Study Team (1995) found that only 8% of classrooms had ITERS ratings above 5. When we examined the 31 EHS classrooms observed in 1997–98 and the 42 observed in 1998–99 (which were the basis for calculating the program-level quality averages reported here), we found that 45% of the classrooms in the earlier period and 60% in the later period had ITERS scores of 5 or higher. Observed child-to-teacher ratios in EHS centers also indicated good quality; they were low and well within the maximum allowed by the revised Head Start Program Performance Standards at both observation points (2.3 children per teacher in 1997–98 and 2.9 children per teacher in 1998–99), as were average group sizes (on average, 5.3 children per teacher in 1997–98 and 5.9 in 1998–99).

Quality in Community Child-Care Centers and Family Child-Care Homes

Our analysis suggests that the quality of care received by EHS children in community child-care centers varied widely but was minimal, on average. These observations included centers that EHS children attended in their communities, regardless of whether the program had recommended the center to the family. The average ITERS score in community child-care centers was 3.7 in 1997–98 and 4.4 in 1998–99, indicating that the quality of care in community child-care settings was considerably lower than the quality provided by EHS centers, but that it may have improved over time.[8, 9]

The quality of child care observed in family child-care homes for EHS children was consistently minimal. These homes included family child-care homes that EHS children attended, regardless of whether the program had helped select the child-care setting. In general, EHS programs formed partnerships more often with community center-based care providers than with family child-care providers; thus, the observed family child-care sites were less likely to be associated with partnerships. Average FDCRS scores were 3.3 in 1997–98 and 3.5 in 1998–99, following a pattern seen in community center–based child care in which average scores increased over the period of the study.[10] However, observed child-to-teacher ratios and group sizes were in most cases lower than those set by the revised Head Start Program Performance Standards. The average child-to-caregiver ratios in the family child-care settings that we observed were 3.3 children per caregiver in 1997–98 and 4.2 in 1998–99. The average group sizes in the family child-care settings that we observed were 4.2 children in the first year and 5.0 children in the second year.

Figure 3-1 summarizes the average quality across the two observation periods reported in the EHS implementation study plus a third period that is described in the EHS

FIGURE 3.1 _____

Quality of Child Care Used
by Early Head Start Families
Across Settings and Time

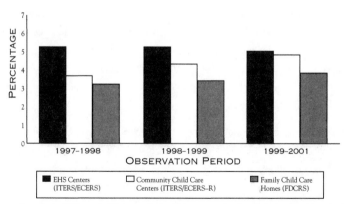

Sources: Average ITERS scores for EHS centers are based on 96 observations conducted between October 1997 and September 1998 and 130 observations conducted between October 1998 and September 1999. Average ECERS–R scores in EHS centers are based on 120 observations conducted between January 1999 and July 2001. Average ITERS scores for community child care centers are based on 45 observations conducted between October 1997 and September 1998, and 75 observations conducted between October 1998 and September 1999. Average ECERS–R scores for community child care centers are based on 196 observations conducted between January 1999 and July 2001. Average Family Day Care Rating Scale (FDCRS) scores are based on 65 observations conducted between October 1997 and September 1998, 65 observations conducted between October 1998 and September 1999, and 55 observations conducted between January 1999 and July 2001.

evaluation's child-care policy report (Administration for Children and Families, 2004). Over time, the quality of EHS centers remained at 5.0 or better (in the "good" range of the ITERS and ECERS–R) during this period while the quality of care received by EHS children in community child-care centers and family child-care homes improved somewhat but was somewhat lower than the quality of the centers operated by EHS programs.

PROGRAM STRATEGIES TO IMPROVE CHILD-CARE QUALITY

Following the guidance of the Advisory Committee on Services for Families With Infants and Toddlers, programs took many steps to improve program families' access to good-quality child care between fall 1997 and fall 1999. The programs took stock of families' child-care needs, program resources, and community resources and then implemented a range of strategies for addressing families' needs and improving the quality of child care they used.

In this section, we identify the main strategies used by programs, including EHS programs offering their own center-based child care and programs that helped families find other child-care arrangements in the community. The national evaluation report on program implementation describes these strategies in greater detail (Administration for Children and Families, 2002a).

Strategies to Improve Quality in Early Head Start Centers

By 1999, 60% of the classrooms in center-based programs had achieved scores in the "good" quality range (compared with 8% found by the Cost, Quality, and Child Outcomes Study Team [1995]). Research programs that provided center-based child care (including center-based programs and mixed-approach programs that provided child care to at least some families) took several direct steps to provide good-quality care in those centers. The most prevalent of the strategies they used to ensure quality included the following.

- **Achieving NAEYC accreditation.** By 1999, EHS centers at four programs had obtained accreditation from NAEYC. Program staff reported that the self-study process required for accreditation helped them to identify new ways to enhance the quality of care they provided.

- **Making important changes toward meeting the revised Head Start Program Performance Standards.** The programs that participated in the national evaluation worked on achieving compliance with the revised Head Start Program Performance Standards for center-based child development services. For example, some programs that needed to reduce group sizes to meet the standards did so. Others rearranged classroom staffing to meet requirements for assigning primary caregivers to children and to promote continuity of care by keeping children and teachers together for longer periods of time. Most EHS centers followed a curriculum, and many individualized the curriculum for each child. Programs also supported teachers in working to obtain CDA credentials and other training.

- **Increasing self-monitoring.** Most programs developed systematic ways to monitor their own centers for compliance with performance standards. Some observed center classrooms using the ITERS and used the results to provide feedback to teachers.

- **Adding more classrooms or centers, or increasing hours of operation.** To reduce group size or to provide child-care services to more families, some programs added classrooms, and several added centers. Although most of the new centers were small (serving 8 or fewer children), programs were able to provide child care to some children directly and to serve as a model of good-quality child care in their communities.

- **Increasing resources.** Several programs obtained additional funds from child-care subsidies, states, and other sources to help them expand the quantity and quality of the child care offered.

Strategies to Improve Quality in Community Child-Care Settings

Many programs that did not provide center-based care directly to all families who needed it developed strategies for improving the quality of care that program children received in community child-care settings. Some of the most prevalent strategies for improving quality that EHS children used in community settings included the following.

- **Forming partnerships with community child-care providers.** Several programs formed partnerships with child-care providers in their communities (child-care centers and family child-care homes) and referred families who needed child care to those providers. The main purpose of the partnerships was to support the providers in working toward compliance with the Head Start Program Performance Standards. Some programs formalized these partnerships through written agreements that established clear expectations for the EHS program as well as the child-care partner. Many programs assessed the quality of care provided by the partner using the ITERS, FDCRS, or other tools and provided ongoing feedback to the provider. The level of support offered to child-care providers through these partnerships varied from intensive to minimal across the research programs.

- **Providing resources to community partners and other providers.** Programs provided a range of resources to providers, including enhancement funds, toys and equipment, and training. Several programs and their community partners began offering free training and materials to child-care providers. One program also offered a stipend to caregivers for attending monthly training sessions.

- **Visiting children in community child-care settings.** To maintain relationships with children and to coordinate with child-care providers, EHS staff at some programs visited children regularly in their child-care settings, whether in centers or family child-care homes. During the visits, staff modeled developmentally appropriate care, conducted activities with the children, shared information with the providers about the children's developmental progress and family matters of relevance, and offered feedback to child-care teachers about the care they were providing.

- **Forming community collaborations.** Some programs attempted to improve child-care quality and work on meeting the performance standards in community child-care settings by collaborating more broadly with community organizations. For example, some programs offered broad-based training to community child-care providers and provided toys and equipment through lending libraries and other initiatives. Others participated in community coalitions and other collaborations with local organizations to work on raising community awareness about the importance of good-quality child care and to increase the supply and quality of infant–toddler care in the community.

- **Seeking additional funds.** Some EHS research programs sought outside funding to pay for efforts to improve the quality of care in the community—grants for expansion or quality improvement from the Head

Start Bureau, state funding for expanding EHS quality enhancement efforts to additional community providers, child-care subsidy funds, and other grants.

- **Helping families find child care.** Many of the research programs worked with enrolled families to provide education about the importance of good-quality child care for their children's development and indicators of quality they should look for when choosing a child-care arrangement. Some programs referred families to good-quality care in the community, and some collaborated with local resource and referral agencies to help families search for good quality care. In addition, staff at some research programs accompanied parents on visits to prospective child-care providers.

SUCCESSES, CHALLENGES, AND RECOMMENDATIONS: THE MULTIPLE SUCCESSES OF EARLY HEAD START

EHS programs that participated in the national evaluation have experienced notable success in providing consistently good-quality care in EHS centers. Moreover, these programs' use of the Head Start Program Performance Standards as a tool for improving quality in community child-care settings appears to be promising. Whether the programs provided child care directly or in collaboration with community providers, they implemented several strategies to help all families who needed child care find care that met the performance standards.

Although programs made progress in working toward this goal, they faced some significant challenges. By fall 1999, some programs had been able to surmount these challenges in innovative ways, and others were still tackling them.

Challenges in Early Head Start Centers

In EHS centers, the main challenges were staff retention, staff qualifications, and hours of operation. As in child-care centers everywhere, EHS centers struggled to retain staff. In the year preceding the 1999 site visits, 39% of direct care center staff left and were replaced across the 11 programs that offered all or some center-based care (Administration for Children and Families, 2003). Several programs reported losing teachers to school districts and other employers that offered higher wages for staff with similar skills. At the time of the 1999 site visits, many programs were addressing staff turnover by revising salary scales and enhancing training and educational opportunities.

In part because of the high rate of teacher turnover, several of the research programs that operated child-care centers struggled to meet the requirement that all child-care teachers obtain a CDA credential or higher degree within 1 year of hire. These programs supported staff in obtaining their CDAs by providing or paying for training and arranging substitutes so teachers could have release time to attend training. However, when teachers left and new ones were hired, the programs had to start over on CDA training with the new teachers. By 1999, 62% of child-care teachers in center-based programs had a CDA or higher degree, and another 19% were working on obtaining a CDA credential.

EHS centers did not meet the child-care needs of parents who worked nonstandard hours. Although most centers were open full-time during standard working hours, none offered care during evenings, nights, or weekends. Parents who worked non-standard hours had to "patch together" other child-care arrangements for their children before their EHS center opened or after it closed. Often, these parents relied on relatives and other informal providers during these hours. At the time of our 1999 site visits, the research programs had not yet focused on working with these secondary providers to improve the quality of other arrangements for EHS children.

Challenges in Community Child-Care Settings

In most communities, the supply of good-quality child care for infants and toddlers was insufficient, making it difficult for EHS programs to find community child-care partners that offered good-quality care. When a promising partnership was formed, it took time and resources to meet the performance standards, even under the best of circumstances. Time and resources are required for staff training, reducing ratios and group sizes, and renovating facilities when needed. It takes time to build the relationships with community child-care providers that serve as the foundation for solid partnerships. Another challenge was that EHS families often relied on several forms of community child care. Thus, even when programs formed one or several effective partnerships with child-care providers, program efforts to support quality were not always embraced by families or providers, and EHS children could still find themselves in low-quality child-care settings. In the initial years of the effort, EHS programs often had greater success in working with community centers than with community family child-care providers. Often it was administratively easier to work with the centralized program that a center offered than with the many home-based providers needed to obtain services for a comparable number of children.

Subsequent research has shown that these challenges are common to other EHS child-care partnerships as well (Paulsell et al., 2002). Despite these challenges, in a few short years, the 17 EHS research programs have shown leadership in their efforts to help families access good-quality child care for their infants and toddlers. Moreover, a promising trend has been observed in the research programs' efforts to use the Head Start Program Performance Standards as a tool for improving child-care quality in EHS centers and extending their reach into community child care. This research conducted with the new EHS program demonstrates that the vision of the Advisory Committee on Services for Families With Infants and Toddlers has made a difference for the quality of child-care services that low-income families can obtain.

Recommendations

Our findings suggest several steps that EHS programs could take in the future to enhance the good beginning in providing quality child care across multiple child-care settings.

Continue to rely on the performance standards as a benchmark for quality in all settings. All indications are that when programs follow the performance standards— whether in EHS centers, partnering community child-care centers, or in community family child care—the quality of child care is upheld.

Focus on strategies to retain front-line staff. Although child-care capacity in communities appears to be growing as staff trained by EHS increase in numbers and move into community positions (or stay with EHS), the implications of turnover for very young children remain a concern. Programs should continue to increase wages, enhance benefits, and provide positive workplace climates that encourage the retention of teaching staff.

Address family needs for child care during nonstandard hours. A portion of EHS parents appear to need child care during evenings, nights, and weekends, when many EHS centers are not open. Programs should ensure the quality of these settings and work with families to ensure the best possible continuity for the children.

Continue to build partnerships with community child-care centers and family child-care providers. Partnerships with community child-care providers offer tremendous promise for infant–toddler child care. Many challenges are inherent to this process because programs must necessarily play a dual role to monitor and empower in community partnerships. We recommend that the best practices in this complex new work be identified and that additional support and awareness be extended through training, technical assistance, and monitoring to enhance these new processes.

Communities, programs, trainers, and federal monitors may then learn about the most promising approaches as programs work with established child-care providers in their communities.

Provide support and build relationships with informal care providers who care for EHS children—the kith and kin providers who may not recognize themselves as part of the formal child-care system. These providers may be offered toys and materials, guidance and training, and relationship support from the EHS program.

Continue the procedures that have demonstrated promise for enhancing quality in EHS programs, communities, and states. Many new and creative initiatives have begun under the EHS mandate to ensure quality care. Quality of care for infants and toddlers in low-income households would be expected to continually improve as momentum and innovation build within these initiatives.

ACKNOWLEDGMENTS

The findings reported in this chapter are based on research conducted as part of the National Early Head Start Research and Evaluation Project funded by the Administration on Children, Youth, and Families (ACYF), U.S. Department of Health and Human Services, under contract 105-95-1936 to Mathematica Policy Research in Princeton, New Jersey, and the Center for Children and Families at Columbia University's Teachers College in New York, in conjunction with the Early Head Start Research Consortium. The consortium consists of representatives from the 17 programs that participated in the evaluation, 15 local research teams, the evaluation contractors, and ACYF. Research institutions in the consortium (and principal researchers) include ACYF (Rachel Chazan Cohen, Judith Jerald, Esther Kresh, Helen H. Raikes, and Louisa Tarullo); Catholic University of America (Michaela Farber, Harriet Liebow, Lynn Milgram Mayer, Christine Sabatino, Nancy Taylor, Elizabeth Timberlake, and Shavaun Wall); Columbia University (Lisa Berlin, Christy Brady-Smith, Jeanne Brooks-Gunn, and Alison Sidle Fuligni); Harvard University (Barbara Alexander Pan, Catherine Ayoub, and Catherine Snow); Iowa State University (Dee Draper, Gayle Luze, Susan McBride, and Carla Peterson); Mathematica Policy Research (Kimberly Boller, Jill Constantine, Ellen Eliason Kisker, John M. Love, Diane Paulsell, Christine Ross, Peter Schochet, Cheri Vogel, and Welmoet van Kammen); Medical University of South Carolina (Richard Faldowski, Gui-Young Hong, and Susan Pickrel); Michigan State University (Hiram Fitzgerald, Tom Reischl, and Rachel Schiffman); New York University (Mark Spellmann and Catherine Tamis LeMonda); University of Arkansas (Robert Bradley, Mark Swanson, and Leanne Whiteside-Mansell); University of

California, Los Angeles (Claire Hamilton and Carollee Howes); University of Colorado, Health Sciences Center (Robert Emde, Jon Korfmacher, JoAnn Robinson, Paul Spicer, and Norman Watt); University of Kansas (Jane Atwater, Judith Carta, and Jean Ann Summers); University of Missouri–Columbia (Mark Fine, Jean Ispa, and Kathy Thornburg); University of Pittsburgh (Beth Green, Carol McAllister, and Robert McCall); University of Washington, School of Education (Eduardo Armijo and Joseph Stowitschek); University of Washington, School of Nursing (Kathryn E. Barnard and Susan Spieker); and Utah State University (Lisa Boyce and Lori Roggman).

The authors thank the consortium reviewers who commented on early drafts of this chapter under the guidelines of the Early Head Start Research Consortium publication policies.

DISCLAIMER

The content of this chapter does not necessarily reflect the views or policies of the U.S. Department of Health and Human Services, nor does the mention of trade names, commercial products, or organizations imply endorsement by the U.S. government. Correspondence concerning this chapter should be addressed to John M. Love (jlove@mathematica-mpr.com).

NOTES

1. In August 2000, the U.S. Department of Health and Human Services issued draft performance standards for services provided through family child-care homes (U.S. Department of Health and Human Services, 2000). Under these standards, teachers in family child-care homes must have the same qualifications as center-based teachers. Ratio and group size requirements limit groups to 6 children per teacher when 2 or fewer children are under age 3. If more than two children are under age 3, the maximum group size is four children, with no more than two children under age 2.

2. In addition, observations of 36-month-old children's child-care arrangements were conducted after the implementation study was completed by using the Early Childhood Environment Rating Scale-Revised (ECERS–R; Harms, Clifford, & Cryer, 1998); those data are reported here as well. We also collected observation data on control group children at all three ages and on both program and control group children at 36 months of age. We present a more extensive analysis of child-care use and quality in a special policy report (Administration for Children and Families, 2004).

3. To compute average ITERS scores for EHS centers, we began by averaging the observations for each classroom. Classrooms were observed as often as once per quarter (or more often if staff or children had changed since the last observation), depending on when EHS children were in care. We then averaged the classroom scores for each center. If a program operated multiple centers, we averaged the center scores to generate an average program score. Thus, the average ITERS scores reported here do not reflect the average quality of care received by individual children. Rather, they represent the average quality of EHS centers, determined at the classroom level. To compute average ITERS scores for community child-care centers, we computed an average score for each center, and then averaged these center scores to compute an average site score. Similarly, to compute average Family Day Care Rating Scale (FDCRS) scores, we computed an average score for each family child-care home and then averaged these home scores to compute an average site score. The average ITERS and FDCRS scores reported here have not been weighted to reflect the number of program children participating in each classroom, center, or home. Observed child-to-teacher ratios and group sizes were calculated based on children and adults counted during the structured observations of child-care settings.

4. The shortened version of the ITERS that we used excludes 3 items from the adult needs category (opportunities for professional growth, adult meeting area, and provisions for parents).

5. See *Pathways to Quality* for a detailed description of our assessment of these data (Administration for Children and Families, 2003). In addition, a special policy report on child care in EHS presents a more extensive analysis of child-care use and quality (Administration for Children and Families, 2004).

6. These average ITERS scores are based on 96 observations conducted between October 1997 and September 1998 and 130 observations conducted between October 1998 and September 1999. During those years, observed children were either 14 or 24 months old.

7. We conducted additional child-care observations when children were 3 years old using the ECERS–R (Harms, Clifford, & Cryer, 1998). Although most of those observations were conducted after the implementation study was completed and analyses were done at the individual child (rather than program) level, the findings are consistent with the ITERS scores found in 1997–98 and 1998–99. The average ECERS–R score was 5.1, based on 120 3-year-old children observed in EHS centers between January 1999 and July 2001.

8. We are cautious in making this interpretation because response rates were low in some sites. With fewer than 5 observations at several sites, we may not have sufficient data to consider this to be a representative sample of EHS children's community child-care arrangements. These average ITERS scores for community child-care centers include 45 observations conducted from October 1997 through September 1998 and 75 observations conducted between October 1998 and September 1999.

9. The average ECERS–R score for EHS 3-year-old children in community child-care centers was 4.9 (N = 196 children), a level of quality quite close to that observed in EHS centers. These observations were completed when children turned 3 years of age between January 1999 and July 2001. Most of those observations were conducted after the implementation study was completed, and the analyses were done at the individual child (rather than the program) level.

10. These data are based on observations in 65 family child-care homes in 1997–98 and 1998–99. Most of those observations were conducted after the implementation study was completed, and the analyses were done at the individual child (rather than the program) level. The average FDCRS quality rating for 3-year-olds in community family child-care homes was 3.9 (N = 55). These observations were completed between January 1999 and July 2001.

REFERENCES

Administration for Children and Families. (1996, November 5). Head Start program: Final rule. *Federal Register*, 61(215), 57186–57227.

Administration for Children and Families. (2000, August 29). Head Start program: Proposed rule. *Federal Register*, 65(168), 52394–52400.

Administration for Children and Families. (2003). *Pathways to quality and full implementation in Early Head Start programs*. Washington, DC: Author.

Administration for Children and Families. (2004). *The role of Early Head Start programs in addressing the child care needs of low-income families with infants and toddlers: Influences on child care use and quality*. Washington, DC: Author.

Administration on Children, Youth, and Families. (1998, June). *Head Start program performance measures: Second progress report*. Washington, DC: Author.

Administration on Children, Youth, and Families. (1999a). *Leading the way: Characteristics and early experiences of selected first-wave Early Head Start programs. Volume 1: Cross-site perspectives*. Washington, DC: Author.

Administration on Children, Youth, and Families. (1999b). *Leading the way: Characteristics and early experiences of selected first-wave Early Head Start programs. Volume 2: Program profiles*. Washington, DC: Author.

Administration on Children, Youth, and Families. (2000a). *Leading the way: Characteristics and early experiences of selected first-wave Early Head Start programs. Volume 3: Program implementation*. Washington, DC: Author.

Administration on Children, Youth, and Families. (2000b). *Leading the way: Characteristics and early experiences of selected first-wave Early Head Start programs.* [Executive summary]. Washington, DC: Author.

Collins, A., Layzer, J. I., Kreader, J. L., Werner, A., & Glantz, F. B. (2000, November). *National study of child care for low-income families: State and community substudy report.* Cambridge, MA: Abt Associates.

Cost, Quality, and Child Outcomes Study Team. (1995, January). *Cost, quality, and child outcomes in childcare centers: Public report* (2nd ed.). Denver: University of Colorado at Denver, Economics Department.

Fenichel, E., Griffin, A., & Lurie-Hurvitz, E. (1999). *Quality care for infants and toddlers.* Washington, DC: U.S. Department of Health and Human Services, Child Care Bureau.

Fuller, B., & Liang, X. (1996). *Can poor families find child care? Persisting inequality nationwide and in Massachusetts.* Cambridge, MA: Harvard University.

Fuller, B., Choong, Y., Coonerty, C., & Kipnis, F. (1997). *An unfair Head Start: Unequal child care availability across California.* Berkeley, CA: Graduate School of Education—PACE.

Gong, J. A. C., Bussiere, A., Light, J., Scharf, R., Cohan, M., & Leiwant, S. (1999, January–February). Child care in the post-welfare reform era: Analysis and strategies for advocates. *Clearinghouse Review, 32*(9–10), 373.

Harms, T., & Clifford, R. (1989). *Family Day Care Rating Scale.* New York: Teachers College Press.

Harms, T., Clifford, R. M., & Cryer, D. (1998). *Early Childhood Environment Rating Scale* (rev. ed.). New York: Teachers College Press.

Harms, T., Cryer, D., & Clifford, R. (1990). *Infant/Toddler Environment Rating Scale.* New York: Teachers College Press.

Kisker, E. E., Hofferth, S. L., Phillips, D. A., & Farquhar, E. (1991). *A profile of child care settings: Early education and care in 1990.* Washington, DC: U.S. Department of Education.

Kontos, S., Howes, C., Shinn, M., & Galinsky, E. (1995). *Quality in family child care and relative care.* New York: Teachers College Press.

Love, J. M., Raikes, H., Paulsell, D., & Kisker, E. E. (2000). New directions for studying quality in programs for infants and toddlers. In D. Cryer & T. Harms (Eds.), *Infants and toddlers in out-of-home care.* Baltimore: Brookes.

Love, J. M., Schochet, P. Z., & Meckstroth, A. L. (1996). Are they in any real danger? What research does—and doesn't—tell us about child care quality and children's well-being. In *Child care research and policy papers: Lessons from child care research funded by the Rockefeller Foundation.* Princeton, NJ: Mathematica Policy Research, Inc.

Paulsell, D., Cohen, J., Stieglitz, A., Lurie-Hurvitz, E., Fenichel, E., & Kisker, E. (2002, March). *Partnerships for quality: Improving infant–toddler child care for low-income families.* Princeton, NJ: Mathematica Policy Research.

Ross, C., & Paulsell, D. (1998, December 31). *Sustaining employment among low-income parents: The problems of inflexible jobs, child care, and family support. A research review.* Princeton, NJ: Mathematica Policy Research, Inc.

Schliecker, E., White, D. R., & Jacobs, E. (1991). The role of day care quality in the prediction of children's vocabulary. *Canadian Journal of Behavioral Science, 23*(1), 12–24.

U.S. Department of Health and Human Services. (1993, December). *Creating a 21st century Head Start.* Final report of the Advisory Committee on Head Start Quality and Expansion. Washington, DC: Author.

U.S. Department of Health and Human Services. (1994). *The statement of the Advisory Committee on Services for Families With Infants and Toddlers.* Washington, DC: Author.

Whitebook, M., Howes, C., & Phillips, D. (1989). *Who cares? Child care teachers and the quality of care in America.* National Child Care Staffing Study, final report. Berkeley, CA: Child Care Employee Project.

About the Authors

John M. Love is a senior fellow at Mathematica Policy Research in Princeton, New Jersey.

Helen H. Raikes is affiliated with the Gallup Organization and the University of Nebraska. This manuscript was prepared when she was a Society for Research in Child Development fellow and visiting scholar at the Administration for Children and Families

Diane Paulsell is a senior researcher at Mathematica Policy Research in Princeton, New Jersey.

Ellen Eliason Kisker was a senior researcher at Mathematica Policy Research in Princeton, New Jersey, at the time this was written.

CHAPTER 4

THE WHOLE 9 MONTHS AND BEYOND: EARLY HEAD START SERVICES FOR PREGNANT WOMEN

Mireille B. Kanda and George L. Askew

Pregnancy is more than a physiological state. It is a process of becoming. Over 9 months, expectant parents prepare for parenthood. At the same time, the stages of prenatal development unfold. Both paths involve critical periods and important milestones. Both paths offer opportunities to be lost or gained.

For each family, the experience of pregnancy is unique and constantly changing. The mother's body provides the nourishment and hormones that govern her baby's growth and development. Her sensations and feelings may range from pleasure to discomfort, from satisfaction to anxiety. The father's experience of his changing role may cascade from anticipation to fear, from pride to uncertainty.

Although most pregnancies proceed smoothly, the costs of a troubled or unsupported pregnancy can be high. For the newborn infant, birth defects, low birth weight, and premature delivery are the potential consequences. Lifelong consequences for the child may include avoidable disabilities or other learning, social, and behavioral problems. For the parents, depression, marital stress, and poor bonding with the new baby may be the price of inadequate support, preparation, and celebration of the pregnancy and birth.

To be early enough to support good outcomes for families, the continuum of Early Head Start (EHS) services begins at pregnancy (see Figure 4-1). As a matter of program design and practical reality for thousands of enrolled families, EHS's attention to pregnancy is paying off. Results from the Early Head Start National Research and Evaluation Project show gains for children in language, cognitive, and social–emotional development that are greatest for youngsters whose mothers enrolled while pregnant with them (Administration for Children and Families, 2002; see also Chapter 2). This chapter discusses how the policies and practices of EHS align with today's best information on pregnancy and prenatal care.

FIGURE 4.1
PREGNANT WOMEN ENROLLED IN EARLY HEAD START, PROGRAM YEAR 2002

Enrollment of pregnant women in Early Head Start	7,669
Percent of pregnant women enrolled under the age of 18	23%
Pregnant women whose pregnancies were identified as medically "high risk"	24%
Health services received by pregnant women:	
Prenatal and postpartum health care	94%
Prenatal education on fetal development	92%
Information on benefits of breast-feeding	92%
Mental health interventions	28%

Reprinted with permission from Irish, Schumacher, & Lombardi (2003).

HIGH STANDARDS

The Head Start Program Performance Standards related to services for pregnant women are consistent with the 1989 recommendations of the Public Health Service Panel on the Content of Prenatal Care. According to the panel, the broad objective of prenatal care is to promote the health and well-being of the pregnant woman, the fetus, the infant, and the family. Care extends from preconception to 6 weeks beyond delivery and is a bridge to a medical home for the child and family. The panel's recommendations emphasize that prevention is preferable to treatment and that prenatal care has 3 basic components: (1) early and continuing risk assessment, (2) health promotion, and (3) medical and psychosocial interventions and follow-up. The panel's report is the standard against which prenatal care programs in the United States are measured (Expert Panel on the Content of Prenatal Care, 1989).

The Head Start Program Performance Standards acknowledge that pregnant women and families may not receive all, or even most, of their prenatal services directly from an EHS program (*Head Start program performance standards and other regulations*, 2002). Thus, programs are required to provide many pregnancy-related services directly, and when appropriate, programs are expected to rely on the resources of other agencies—particularly medical providers—for assistance in supporting healthy pregnancies.

THE CONTENT OF PRENATAL CARE IN EARLY HEAD START

Every pregnant woman is unique. And every pregnancy is different from previous or subsequent ones to the same woman. EHS programs tailor their prenatal services to each woman and family. Consistent with the recommendations of the Expert Panel on the Content of Prenatal Care, these services can be grouped into three categories:

(1) risk assessment, (2) health promotion, and (3) emotional support to pregnant women and their families.

Risk Assessment

EHS programs begin their support for each expectant mother with risk assessment, which continues throughout the pregnancy and after birth. Risks to a successful pregnancy include hazards such as exposure to toxins in the environment, inadequate nutritional resources, and domestic violence.

Income and maternal education are important demographic factors in the health of pregnant women as well as in the welfare and survival of their children. The infant mortality rate is almost double for infants of mothers with fewer than 12 years of education than for those whose mothers' educational level is 13 or more years (U.S. Department of Health and Human Services, 2000). Furthermore, pregnancy risks are disproportionately borne by low-income, minority women. Although the national infant mortality rate is declining, the infant death rate among African Americans is still more than double that of Whites. American Indians and Alaska Natives have an infant death rate almost double that of Whites. The maternal mortality rate among African Americans was 3.6 times that of Whites in 1997.

Behind these numbers lurks inadequate prenatal care. According to data collected in 1997, African American women and Hispanic women were twice as likely as White women to have delayed or no prenatal care (Department of Health and Human Services, 2000). More recent data confirm that, although early prenatal care utilization continues to increase, important racial and ethnic differences persist (National Center for Health Statistics, 2002). Barriers to access to prenatal care account for many of these disparities. Data from the Pregnancy Risk Assessment Monitoring System (PRAMS) suggest that the reasons women do not get prenatal care during the first 3 months of pregnancy include not knowing they are pregnant, lack of money or insurance, not being able to get an appointment, and lack of transportation (Centers for Disease Control and Prevention, 2000).

EHS mitigates these risks and barriers for its diverse population of families. One example is the Drake University EHS program, which serves the Des Moines area in Polk County, Iowa. Polk County has the fourth highest infant mortality rate among counties in the United States. In addition, smoking, methamphetamine addiction, low birth weight, and low rates of breast-feeding initiation and duration are prevalent. About 25% of uninsured Des Moines–area females fall within the child-bearing age range of 15 to 44.

The staff of the Drake University EHS has developed a comprehensive pregnancy risk and health assessment to evaluate how these and other factors affect the health of enrolled pregnant women. The tool assesses a woman's family resources; nutritional status; and expectations and knowledge about pregnancy, labor, and delivery. As is typical at all EHS programs, when Drake staff encounter a newly enrolled pregnant woman who has yet to receive services from a physician or midwife, they immediately arrange a medical home and prenatal care for her. Because the risks facing the women of Polk County are so great, the program also employs two perinatal support specialists to work with women throughout their pregnancies and 6 months postpartum, with follow-up visits at 9 and 12 months postpartum (Early Head Start National Resource Center, 2000; Kari Lebeda-Townsend, personal communication, November 2002).

In some instances, the risk-assessment capabilities of EHS staff exceed those of health care providers. For example, women with an unintended pregnancy, particularly if it is unwanted, are at higher risk of physical violence from their partners than women with intended pregnancies, regardless of other characteristics (Gazmararian et al., 1995). Most pregnant women, however, do not report that their prenatal care providers discuss physical abuse with them (Durant, Colley Gilbert, Saltzman, & Johnson, 2000), even though violence against pregnant women is reported to occur more frequently than other complications, such as gestational diabetes, toxemia, and preeclampsia (Gazmararian, Lazorick, Spitz, Ballard, Saltzman, & Marks, 1996). Failure to screen for domestic violence may be due, in part, to inadequate professional training for health care workers and the limited time that doctors have to develop rapport with pregnant women. EHS staff fill this void with training in empathic listening and finding the time to form trusting relationships in a safe, confidential environment.

Conflicts between the differing cultural value systems of providers and pregnant women are often a barrier to adequate prenatal care. In some cultures, people may see pregnancy as a natural process that does not require medical intervention, thus causing resistance against a Western medical model based on problem identification and treatment. In addition, the Western model, which is based on individualism and efficiency, may be perceived by the patient as cold, impersonal, and lacking in human warmth and genuine interest in the total person. Western medicine also requires the immediate sharing of very private information such as personal history. Providers may perceive the answers of patients who prefer to build the relationship gradually as vague. Ultimately, the provider may become more detached and the patient may fail to return for follow-up visits (Delgado, Metzer, & Falcon, 1995).

EHS's emphasis on cultural and linguistic competence for staff is an enormous benefit to expectant families. For example, the Des Moines area attracts many Sudanese refugees, and several Sudanese families are enrolled in the Drake University EHS. First-generation Sudanese generally find it offensive to ask a woman whether she is pregnant. Often, a Sudanese woman will not disclose that she is pregnant until the pregnancy is visible to others. This is a challenge for Drake EHS staff, because early entry into prenatal care by expectant women is a programmatic goal. Drake staff members address this dilemma at recruitment by offering Sudanese women general information about the program and specific information about the importance of early prenatal care. Sudanese women are not asked whether they are pregnant, and a translator often assists staff to communicate the information. In the experience of Drake staff, pregnant Sudanese women often choose to disclose their condition after receiving information about the program and early prenatal care.

EHS staff are trained to realize that pregnancy-associated cultural practices may offer certain health benefits and should not be discounted a *priori*. Says Kari Lebeda-Townsend, coordinator of the Drake University EHS, "Staff need to be aware that we don't always understand why things are done the way they are, but that there may be good, solid reasons why certain cultural practices began. Staff must appreciate that a practice may work well in a certain culture, country, or refugee camp but respectfully consider how the practice may work today in Des Moines, Iowa" (Mary Bogle, personal communication, 2002).

Often, Drake staff encounter cultural practices that are optimal for maternal and child health. For example, the Sudanese culture is very supportive of breast-feeding, so home visitors need to do little to initiate this practice among new Sudanese mothers. Here, American culture presents the challenge. Despite the known benefits of breast-feeding, women in the United States often are pressured by the media and peers to bottle-feed their babies. Drake staff provide Sudanese and other nursing mothers with positive reinforcement and tangible support, such as loaner breast pumps, to sustain breast-feeding for as long as mother and baby wish to continue.

The data on cultural protective factors in pregnancy support the Drake experience. For example, although Hispanic women tend to have a later entry into prenatal care, they also have a low prevalence of low-birth-weight infants (U.S. Department of Health and Human Services, 2000). Lower rates of smoking and substance abuse, and strong cultural values of family and community may have a protective effect for this population.

Health Promotion

Pregnancy plans in EHS delineate the prenatal health care, healthy behaviors, and education a woman needs to support a healthy pregnancy. Thus, they cover a broad spectrum of services. For example, just one expectant family may require support ranging from transportation to prenatal care to assistance with enrolling for public benefits such as the Special Supplemental Food Program for Women, Infants, and Children (WIC).

The needs of each family, available community resources, and the resourcefulness and ingenuity of the program staff shape the contents of each individual pregnancy plan. Problems such as limited English proficiency or a special medical condition or disability of the pregnant woman require flexible and creative resolutions. EHS staff members are trained to assess the individual needs and desires of the expectant family and to tailor solutions accordingly. For example, EHS staff members have learned that the parity of a woman (number of previous pregnancies she has experienced) and the extent of her support system may influence the level of intensity of the services that she will desire and accept.

As each pregnancy progresses, EHS programs educate expectant parents on what is happening now and what to expect next. The Clermont County EHS program in Cincinnati, Ohio, has developed a multimedia prenatal education program using a pregnancy curriculum tailored to the unique concerns of their largely White, low-income population of Appalachian families. Videos, monthly planning guides, flip charts, and audiovisual equipment are available for home loan. These materials support education on fetal development, nutrition, breast-feeding, maternal changes, hazards during pregnancy, and postpartum issues. Clermont home visitors assist parents in using the pregnancy curriculum, tracking their prenatal visits, pursuing healthy habits, and following up on recommendations from health care providers (Early Head Start National Resource Center, 2000).

Of the 20 pregnant women who used the Clermont pregnancy curriculum in the 1998–99 program year, 100% received prenatal care during the first trimester; 92% kept all prenatal appointments; 61% made a positive lifestyle change such as decreased caffeine intake, decreased or ceased smoking, and increased exercise; and 100% kept all postpartum follow-up and first-newborn doctor visits. These figures surpass even some of the objectives of *Healthy People 2010*, the Public Health Service blueprint for the health of the nation, which has set a target of increasing the proportion of pregnant women who receive early and adequate prenatal care from 74% in 1998 to 90% in 2010 (U.S. Department of Health and Human Services, 2000).

Many EHS programs provide home visits to expectant families. The home is an ideal place for services to expectant families, because women may suffer mobility challenges as their pregnancies progress, and families are often more receptive to guidance and education on their own turf. Using data from an internal study of home visits to pregnant women, the staff of the Panhandle Healthy Start/Early Head Start have demonstrated that the content of the home visit correlates with successful outcomes for mother and child. For example, more frequent discussion of smoking cessation by staff during home visits appears to increase the birth weights of children born to mothers who smoke (Florida State University Center for Prevention and Early Intervention Policy, 1999).

To ensure the quality of their home visits, Panhandle staff have developed a curriculum for working with pregnant women that researchers and program designers from the Florida State University EHS program have refined into the Partners for a Healthy Baby, Home Visiting Curriculum for Expectant Families. The curriculum enables the home visitor to use each contact with the mother to maximum advantage by providing a planned sequence of topics that promote a healthy pregnancy. For example, the curriculum guides the staff person through discussion of topics such as how the woman and her family feel about the pregnancy, changes that will occur for the mother and the baby during the first 3 months of pregnancy, the importance of eating nutritious foods and avoiding some foods altogether, and the dangers of using drugs and alcohol (Florida State University Center for Prevention and Early Intervention Policy, 1999).

The health promotion efforts of EHS staff often complement and extend those of physicians and midwives. Says Kathleen Shivaprasad, program manager of the EHS program of the Fresno County Economic Opportunities Commission in California, "We have a 19-year-old mom who went into preterm labor at 24 weeks. Fortunately, it was stopped, and her doctor prescribed bed rest. Probably because she is so young, she defined bed rest very loosely and was up and about all the time. Her family development specialist and the program's maternal/child health and disabilities coordinator were able to convince her to stay in bed by educating her on the serious consequences of her baby arriving too early. They also gave her activities she could do while in bed. The baby went to term" (Mary Bogle, personal communication, 2002).

In preparation for the baby's arrival, EHS staff educate expectant parents on topics such as physical care of the infant, understanding child development, age-appropriate discipline, and prevention of child abuse and neglect. In addition, EHS staff often help parents to arrange a prenatal visit to a pediatrician. Such visits can positively influence several health care outcomes, including breast-feeding initiation, number of emergency room visits, and the doctor–patient relationship (Serwint, Wilson,

Vogelhut, Repke, & Seidel, 1996). Many programs similar to the Drake University EHS offer expectant parents tangible resources for bonding with their newborns, such as baby slings and training in infant massage (Early Head Start National Resource Center, 2000).

The time frame for prenatal health promotion in EHS includes the postpartum period. Home visitors assist the pregnant woman to make the transition from a pregnancy to a postpregnancy physiological state as well as to adapt to the new responsibilities of parenting a newborn. To support breast-feeding, EHS programs offer everything from loaner breast pumps and home visits from lactation specialists to places at the EHS site where mothers can breast-feed comfortably. In addition, EHS programs arrange for a health care provider to visit the mother and newborn at home within 2 weeks of delivery.

Partnerships with other high-quality agencies are essential to the provision of services to pregnant women in EHS, especially health promotion and education services. Among the many Des Moines–area agencies that the Drake University EHS program calls on are

- Refugee Services, which provides translation services and cultural training for staff;

- Young Women's Resource Center, which provides support services for pregnant women and car seats for newborns;

- La Clinica de la Esperanza, which offers free health and perinatal care, consultation, translation, and assistance with government-benefits paperwork to a mostly Hispanic clientele;

- Creative Visions, which provides support and assistance for urban youth;

- House of Mercy, which provides health care, free lead screening, housing (for recovering, homeless, or adjudicated teens), and substance abuse treatment for addicted pregnant and parenting women; and

- Doulas in Des Moines, an organization that links expectant families to volunteer doulas (U.S. Department of Health and Human Services, 2000; Early Head Start National Resource Center, 2000).

Because free health care clinics are scarce in Des Moines, the Drake University EHS program has worked with community partners and business leaders to support the establishment, in 2000, of a clinic that is available to women and children throughout Polk County. This clinic, known as Heart and Hands: Women and Children's Health Center, is housed in the same church facility where the EHS program is based.

Box 4.1 Partner in a One-Stop Shop: The Nation's Capital Child and Family Development Early Head Start

The District of Columbia Developing Families Center is a partnership between the Nation's Capital Child and Family Development (NCCFD) agency, the D.C. Birth Center, and the Healthy Babies Project. Housed under one roof across from a shopping mall in northeast Washington, D.C., the three agencies collaborate under an umbrella organization—the D.C. Developing Families Center—to provide continuous, complementary services such as well-woman, prenatal, and pediatric health care; labor and delivery in on-site birth rooms or at a nearby hospital, as appropriate; health, childbirth, and parenting education; outreach, case management, and social support; mental health assessments and counseling; and early childhood development and education services to Early Head Start (EHS) and other families throughout the community.

A one-stop shop, that begins with pregnancy, supports in-depth relationships between providers and families. Says co-director Linda Randolph, "In most models, social service providers refer families to clinical settings in order to meet their medical needs. I find that too distant, because in a clinical setting a practitioner will often not see a pregnant woman or child long enough to set appropriate goals and provide good anticipatory guidance. In a child and family development setting like EHS, however, you see pregnant women, new families, and children consistently over long periods of time. When the clinical setting is colocated, this can make a big difference to maternal and child health."

She continues, "At the Developing Families Center—where a mother can receive prenatal care, deliver her baby, and receive parenting and child development services after the child is born—important health and development issues are tracked over time in the same location by staff people who know the whole family and respect their knowledge of their child's development. It's a warmer and more empowering experience for families. In addition, staff from across the agencies receive joint training and an opportunity to understand what is happening for each family together" (Linda Randolph & Travis Hardmon, personal communication to Mary Bogle, March 2002).

As its share of the partnership, the NCCFD manages a six-room infant/toddler center for 64 children within the Developing Families Center. The EHS program uses 14 of the center slots, mostly for infants of mothers who have received care from the Healthy Babies Project and who have delivered at the D.C. Birth Center. In addition, EHS families receive the full gamut of program services, including a family service worker who visits homes four times per year and education and employment services such as a General Educational Development (GED) program and a child care worker training program, which NCCFD offers at its headquarters just across the street from the Developing Families Center.

Source: Linda Randolph & Travis Hardmon, personal communication to Mary Bogle, March 2002.

Lebeda-Townsend sees program visibility and access for families—in both directions—as the greatest benefit of the colocation arrangement: "On the one hand, Early Head Start families already knew Early Head Start and were comfortable in the building. Now there is a health clinic, too. On the other hand, families who use the clinic also discover Early Head Start as a result. We have had several women come to our door to learn more about participating in Early Head Start. While we receive referrals from many community agencies and other providers, it's a great start when a family initiates an interest themselves; it promotes investment in the program from the beginning" (Mary Bogle, personal communication, 2002).

SOCIAL AND EMOTIONAL SUPPORT FOR THE PREGNANT WOMAN AND FAMILY

The birth of a child is a positive event in most cultures and families. Pregnancy and birth validate the parents' ability to procreate and perpetuate family and community traditions, values, and mores. However, pregnancy can also be a time of stress, causing mother, child, and family to be more vulnerable to poor health consequences. Expectant parents may experience poor self-esteem or anxiety about specific concerns such as whether family finances will be adequate to meet the needs of their new child.

Some researchers have tried with limited success to attribute pregnancy complications to specific stressors in the lives of pregnant women (Perkin, Bland, Peacock, & Anderson, 1993), whereas others have shown that babies of particularly stressed moms are more likely to have low birth weight or to be born premature (Wadwa, Sandman, Porto, Dunkel-Schetter, & Garite, 1993). These variations speak to the complexities of life and to the uniqueness of each family. On their journey to new or expanded families, parents need peer support, self-help resources, and services such as home visits, financial counseling, and coaching to prepare for childbirth.

Most pregnant women receive advice and support for childbearing, delivery, and infant care from several formal and informal sources. In addition to professionals, family and friends help to shape a family's preferences on decisions such as hospital delivery versus home delivery, whether to circumcise a male infant, and whether and how long to breast-feed. Extended family members often provide tangible assistance to the pregnant woman and her family, including child care, relief from domestic tasks, entertainment, housing, and transportation. For example, Lebeda-Townsend says that the "lying in" practices of Des Moines–area Asian immigrant families benefit mothers and newborns considerably. After the birth of a baby, the new mother's own mother, grandmother, or aunt attends to all household chores for several weeks. The mother is encouraged to stay in bed with her infant so that she can focus on bonding, breast-feeding, and recovering from delivery.

Often, other EHS families and the staff members themselves become sources of emotional and social support. Says Shivaprasad of the Fresno EHS, "We've had a run on twins lately. Just recently, we connected a mother of premature newborn twins with other mothers in the program who have been where she is now" (Mary Bogle, personal communication, 2002). At the Drake University EHS program, pregnant and post-partum women attend a monthly support group.

EHS programs also pay close attention to the emotional support needs of expectant fathers. Building on previous research, Diemer (1997) has shown that the attendance of expectant fathers at prenatal classes designed for men can expand social support and coping skills. At the Drake University EHS program, fathers are offered a men's group and support from a male involvement coordinator.

Says Lebeda-Townsend, "Staff recognize that fathers are important in the lives of their children and important sources of support for pregnant women. We encourage fathers to be involved in the pregnancy and at delivery. I recently accompanied our perinatal support specialist on a home visit to a pregnant mom who did not live with the father of her baby. The specialist and the mother were arranging for her to tour the hospital where she would deliver. The perinatal support specialist asked her if she would like to invite the father, and she said she would invite him. . . . Because it supports early bonding with the baby, we focus on making birth a very positive experience for both the mother and the father. We provide information and support, encourage families to speak to their health care provider, and support the use of doulas from the community, who are trained to support the actual birth experience" (Mary Bogle, personal communication, 2002).

When an expectant family is isolated or faces challenges that overwhelm their existing sources of support, EHS staff work to fill the gaps. For example, a prenatal diagnosis of disability for an unborn child may throw a family into a state of confusion or crisis. EHS programs will immediately link such families to their partner "Part C" providers, which are agencies that each state provides to meet the needs of infants and toddlers with disabilities. Early intervention from EHS and Part C provides expectant families with the peer support and expert resources they need to tap their child's many possibilities. For example, the Fresno EHS links families who receive a prenatal diagnosis of a congenital birth defect to the services and peer-support network of the local March of Dimes.

When necessary, EHS staff arrange for therapeutic mental health interventions for women during pregnancy, after delivery, and even beyond the first year postpartum in certain cases. Physiological and lifestyle changes, coupled with the stress of caring for a newborn, render many women especially vulnerable to depression after childbirth. Pregnancy is often a catalyst for bringing up a woman's "old history." An expectant mother may experience emotions related to the very early circumstances of her own life. Program staff seek to understand these feelings and how they contribute to the overall wellness of mother and unborn child, especially when women seem "noncompliant" in keeping scheduled prenatal appointments.

Because staff may struggle with concerns that are similar to those of the mother or family, EHS line workers also receive emotional support and guidance. Reflective supervision—during which the staff person and supervisor explore feelings and thoughts brought on by working with high-need expectant mothers—develops the support skills of the home visitor and helps him or her to become more self-aware (Gambi White-Tennant, personal communication to Mireille Kanda, August 2001).

Before and after birth, babies deserve the harmonized love, attention, and expertise of family, friends, and professionals. EHS supports low-income parents to give their infants the earliest and best start possible: a healthy pregnancy.

DISCLAIMER

The content of this chapter does not necessarily reflect the views or policies of the U.S. Department of Health and Human Services, nor does mention of trade names, commercial products, or organizations imply endorsement by the U.S. government.

REFERENCES

Administration for Children and Families. (2002). *Making a difference in the lives of infants and toddlers and their families: The impacts of Early Head Start.* Washington, DC: U.S. Department of Health and Human Services.

Centers for Disease Control and Prevention. (2000). Entry into prenatal care among women in the United States, 1989–1997. *Morbidity and Mortality Weekly Report, 49*(18), 393–398.

Delgado, J. L., Metzer, R., & Falcon, A. P. (1995). Meeting the health promotion needs of Hispanic communities. *American Journal of Health Promotion, 9*(4), 300–311.

Diemer, G. A. (1997). Expectant fathers: Influence of perinatal education on stress, coping and spousal relations. *Research in Nursing and Health, 20,* 281–293.

Durant, T., Colley Gilbert, B., Saltzman, L. E., & Johnson, C. H. (2000). Opportunities for intervention: Discussing physical abuse during prenatal care visits. *American Journal of Preventive Medicine, 19*(2), 238–244.

Early Head Start National Resource Center. (2000). *Giving children the earliest head start: Developing an individualized approach to high-quality services for pregnant women.* Technical assistance paper no. 3. Washington, DC: U.S. Department of Health and Human Services and ZERO TO THREE.

Expert Panel on the Content of Prenatal Care. (1989). *Caring for our future: The content of prenatal care.* Washington, DC: U.S. Public Health Service.

Florida State University Center for Prevention and Early Intervention Policy. (1999). *Partners for a healthy baby: Home visiting curriculum for expectant families.* Tallahassee: Florida State University.

Gazmararian, J. A., Adams, M. M., Saltzman, L. E., Johnson, C. H., Bruce, F. C., Marks, J. S., et al. The PRAMS Working Group. (1995). The relationship between pregnancy intendedness and physical violence in mothers of newborns. *Obstetrics and Gynecology, 85,* 1031–1038.

Gazmararian, J. A., Lazorick, S., Spitz, A. M., Ballard, T. J., Saltzman, L. E., & Marks, J. S. (1996). Prevalence of violence against pregnant women. *Journal of the American Medical Association, 275,* 1915–1920. [erratum: *Journal of the American Medical Association* (1997), *277,* 1125]

Head Start program performance standards and other regulations. 45 C.F.R. §§ 1301, 1302, 1303, 1304, and guidance. (Government Printing Office 2002).

Irish, K., Schumacher, R., & Lombardi, J. (2003). *Serving America's youngest: A snapshot of Early Head Start children, families, teachers, and programs in 2002.* Washington, DC: Center for Law and Social Policy.

National Center for Health Statistics. (2002). *Health, United States, 2002 With Chartbook on Trends in the Health of Americans.* Washington, DC: Government Printing Office.

Perkin, M. R., Bland, J. M., Peacock, J. L., & Anderson, H. R. (1993). The effect of anxiety and depression during pregnancy on obstetric complications. *British Journal of Obstetrics and Gynecology, 100,* 629–634.

Serwint, J. R., Wilson, M. E., Vogelhut, J. W., Repke, J. T., & Seidel, H. M. (1996). A randomized controlled trial of prenatal pediatric visits for urban, low-income families. *Pediatrics*, 98, 1069–1075.

U.S. Department of Health and Human Services. (2000) *Healthy people 2010: Vol. II (2nd ed.).* Washington, DC: Author.

Wadwa, P. D., Sandman, C. A., Porto, M., Dunkel-Schetter, C., & Garite, U. (1993). The association between prenatal stress and infant birth weight and gestational age at birth: A prospective investigation. *American Journal of Obstetrics and Gynecology*, 169, 858–865.

ABOUT THE AUTHORS

Mireille B. (Mimi) Kanda is deputy director of the National Center on Minority Health and Health Disparities, National Institutes of Health, U.S. Department of Health and Human Services. Formerly, she was director of the Division of Child Protection at Children's National Medical Center in Washington, DC. Also, for 5 years, she was chief of Health and Disabilities Services for the Head Start Bureau, Administration on Children, Youth, and Families, Administration for Children and Families, U.S. Department of Health and Human Services. In that role, she participated in the development of the Early Head Start initiative.

George L. Askew is founder and executive director of Docs For Tots, a nonprofit child advocacy organization in Washington, D.C., and an assistant clinical professor of pediatrics at the George Washington University School of Medicine. He recently served 1 year as chief of Health and Disabilities Services at the Head Start Bureau, succeeding Mimi Kanda. He was also medical advisor to the commissioner for the Administration on Children, Youth, and Families.

CHAPTER 5

READY FOR LIFE: HOW EARLY HEAD
START NURTURES EARLY LEARNING

J. Ronald Lally and Gambi White-Tennant

The experiences that a child has from birth through age 3 will affect him or her for a lifetime. Adults who rear and care for infants and toddlers have a solemn responsibility to fill those years with love and to nurture early learning experiences. Fortunately, as a result of research on the early development of children, we know a great deal about how babies develop and what they need. But sadly, throughout the country, what we actually do for babies continues to lag behind our rich knowledge base. As a national laboratory on early learning, Early Head Start (EHS) is changing all of that by effectively translating what we *know* about babies into what we *do* for them.

This bold claim is supported by promising results from EHS's first 5 years. The goal of EHS and Head Start is to increase the "child's everyday effectiveness in dealing with both his or her present environment and later responsibilities in school and life. [This goal] takes into account the interrelatedness of social, emotional, cognitive, and physical development" (U.S. Department of Health and Human Services, 1996). Results from the Early Head Start National Research and Evaluation Project (see Chapters 2 and 3) show positive effects across these domains of child and family functioning.

In Chapter 4, Mimi Kanda and George Askew make the case that EHS captures and translates the best knowledge about pregnancy into effective policy and practice on prenatal services for young families. This chapter picks up where they left off—at birth—and demonstrates why and how EHS is one of the nation's premier programs for nurturing the early learning of infants and toddlers.

WHAT DO WE KNOW ABOUT BABIES?

How do infants and toddlers think, feel, and develop? How should adults act to best facilitate early learning experiences? Effective programs such as EHS incorporate the answers to these questions into their very design. Fortunately, the amount of research on the first 3 years of life that supplies these answers has burgeoned during the past 20 years.[1] Recent studies demonstrate that, rather than being complete at birth, the human brain's "wiring" continues to grow and organize itself throughout childhood (Huttenlocher, 1979; Huttenlocher & Dabholkar, 1997). Particularly dramatic during the first year of life, brain development is driven by a mix of factors—some within the control of adults who care for babies, and some not.

First, positive and frequent exchanges between infants and adults bode well for the language, intellectual, emotional, and social skills that children will carry forward into adulthood. Research shows that young children who have experienced loving and consistent care from parents and other close caregivers will fare better than their less securely attached peers in

- forming relationships with others (Sroufe & Egeland, 1991; Sroufe, Carson, & Schulman, 1993; Thompson, 1998, 1999);

- demonstrating a balanced self-concept (Cassidy, 1988; Verschueren, Marcoen, & Schoefs, 1996);

- displaying advanced memory processes (Belsky, Woodworth, & Crnic, 1996; Kirsh & Cassidy, 1997);

- understanding emotions (Laible & Thompson, 1998); and

- developing a conscience (Kochanska, 1995, 1997).

In addition, studies of language have underscored the importance of early communication between adults and babies in the development of rich vocabulary and social competence (Hart & Risley, 1998). Adults who sing, talk, verbally label objects, and ask questions and wait for responses from infants directly affect the formation of their language (Shore, 1997). Conversely, limited or poor exchanges between babies and adults forebode poor outcomes: For example, studies in Romanian and Russian orphanages demonstrate that prolonged neglect can cause serious, long-term damage to a child's social, emotional, and intellectual health (Frank, Klass, Earls, & Eisenberg, 1996).

Second, environments have a powerful effect on the early development and learning of children. For example, the brain "expects" to receive some experiences from the environment. The development of a child's eyesight and her ability to interpret visual information depends on her being exposed to light and visual patterns (Black & Greenough, 1986; Greenough & Black, 1992). Although most environments typically provide sensory experiences in one form or another to the expectant brain, effective parents and caregivers play an important role in supporting and enhancing them. Parents and others also safeguard the infant's ability to use sensory information from the environment—for example, by identifying early signs of problems in seeing or hearing. In addition, exposure to hazards or toxins in the environment can have a significant deleterious effect on children's physical safety and physiological well-being. For example, excess lead in the blood can cause a host of neurobehavioral problems.

Third, loving and consistent basic care is the foundation on which an infant learns and grows. The human infant is completely dependent on adults for survival for almost the first 3 years of life—a much longer period than for other species. For example, malnutrition during the first 2–3 years of life can have a detrimental effect on brain development, including even the size of the brain (Georgieff & Rao, 2001; Morgan & Gibson, 1991; Morgan & Winick, 1985). Besides providing food, water, comfortable shelter, and protection from danger, adults also provide care to babies in ways that teach them the basic information they need to survive in the social and cultural world.

Fourth, many characteristics are delivered with the child at birth. For one thing, in addition to being born vulnerable, infants are born competent. Their brains are structured to make sense of things, to find meaning, to explore possibilities, to experiment. They are programmed to learn language and are genetically inclined to watch and learn how to do things from others. They are also strongly predisposed to form secure relationships with willing adults. Through these inborn competencies, babies themselves develop effective ways of thinking, feeling, and acting. Temperament is also an important component of a child's developing personality. Inborn characteristics such as mood, soothability, and adaptability affect young children's behavioral tendencies, their emotional qualities, and their capacities to tolerate stress (Thompson, 2001).

What About Babies From Low-Income Families?

How do factors such as family poverty, parental education, and poor neighborhood environments affect the development of infants and toddlers? The research discussed above is as applicable to a poor child as it is to a child whose family enjoys a higher level of income. However, what differs—sometimes dramatically—is the way in which factors such as income, parental education, and community environment influence the ability of parents and other individuals to respond to and meet their infants' and toddlers' many needs.

Of course, families from different socioeconomic strata demonstrate remarkably different capacities for securing safe housing, nutritious meals, good child care, and other supports for their children (Becker, 1981; Brooks-Gunn, Brown, Duncan, & Moore, 1995). Although the precise trade-offs that individual families make among employment, cash income, and time with their children are not yet well understood (National Research Council and Institute of Medicine, 2000), research shows that parenting is more likely to be compromised in families that have fewer resources and that poor developmental outcomes for children are strongly linked to economic hardship (Brooks-Gunn & Duncan, 1997). In addition, parents with more education tend to provide more early learning resources to their children—be it their parenting styles, home literacy environments, or access to resources such as high-quality child care and educational materials (Bradley et al., 1989; Laosa, 1983; Michael, 1972).

And although factors within families appear to have more influence on developmental outcomes than factors within neighborhoods (Klebanov, Brooks-Gunn, & Duncan, 1994; Klebanov, Brooks-Gunn, Gordon, & Chase-Landsdale, 1997), children who live in particularly impoverished environments such as the poor sections of inner cities are exposed to greater risks from their surroundings than their peers from less-distressed locales. For one thing, low-income children are more likely to witness a violent event (Buka & Birdthistle, 1997; Taylor, Zuckerman, Harik, & Groves, 1992) and to possibly suffer its negative psychological or behavioral consequences (Singer, Anglin, Song, & Lunghofer, 1995). Additionally, low-income children of color who live in inner cities have a disproportionate risk of exposure to physiological hazards such as lead poisoning (Brody et al., 1994).

Although families with low incomes may seem to face an increased amount of risk, the results of the Early Head Start National Research and Evaluation Project clearly indicate that such challenges do not automatically sentence children to low academic achievement and impaired development—quite the opposite, in fact. Research findings indicate that high-quality care and enriching environments provided by programs such as EHS promote the healthy development and achievement of low-income children throughout their first 3 years of life, in all the domains important to successful lifelong learning (see Chapters 2 and 3).

WHAT DO BABIES NEED FROM ADULTS?

Given what we know about early development and learning, what should we do to best support that process? Before answering this question, we should first underscore that babies are, by nature, active learners and explorers. Very young children are not blank slates on which caregivers write; nor are they impulsive, unsocialized beings whose urges and interests need to be constantly restrained. Adults who cast themselves as guides or partners in learning, rather than as trainers or teachers, will be more successful in encouraging infants to expand and adapt their built-in potential for happy, productive lives. This understanding is fundamental to answering the question, "What should we do for babies?"

The following 10 concepts inform our current understanding of how very young children think, feel, and develop and suggest straightforward ways by which adults can promote the healthy development and early learning of very young children.

1. Consistent, loving, and safe relationships are central to children's healthy development. This concept is critical to all aspects of child development. Safe and trusting relationships with consistent caregivers, particularly parents, give children the security they need to tolerate stress and the confidence they need to venture out and explore the world. As is true in much of infant development, no single recipe exists for forming loving, safe relationships with children. Rather, successful parents and caregivers use the "materials" at hand: holding, providing loving touches, sharing long gazes, and all the other verbal and nonverbal give-and-take of parent–child communication. Babies learn that they are important, safe, and loved by adults through everyday experiences—such as the way they are held, the gentleness of a touch, and the love of a long gaze. These experiences become the foundation on which children's futures are built.

2. Babies have distinct abilities and needs depending on their stage of development. Between birth and age 3, a child goes through three distinct developmental stages: young infancy, mobile infancy, and older infancy. Infants organize their thoughts and actions differently at each stage. Young infants, not yet crawling, primarily seek security and connection with caregivers who nurture them in loving and consistent ways, as described by the principle above. Mobile infants—from the time they begin crawling until about 16 months of age—use these feelings of security to venture off and explore the world. They need caregivers who don't overprotect them and who are always available to provide security, encouragement, and help as needed. Toddlers, beginning at 17–19 months, are consumed with issues of identity—"me," "mine," "I," and "you." Successful parents and caregivers support them to learn about themselves as separate individuals and how to act in relation to others.

3. Babies are individuals who have unique temperaments. Babies are not all alike. Each child has his own unique temperament, rate of development, and style of relating to others. Successful caregivers first educate themselves about the temperamental types—such as active, cautious, and easy—and then ask themselves, "How does this information help me to understand and respond to this child in this situation?"

4. Infants are active, self-motivated learners. Cognitive and learning research shows that children naturally bring motivation and competence to learning and that they do best when adults allow them to be active partners in setting the agenda for learning (Bloom, Russell, & Wassenberg, 1987; Bornstein, 1989; Bornstein & Tamis-LeMonda, 1989). Thus, effective parents and caregivers take advantage of the child's natural desire to learn and then expand, adapt, and encourage experiences that the infant finds most interesting. Caregivers who are not tuned in to a child's interest (e.g., learning about shadows) may preselect lessons or furnish environments (e.g., playing with blocks) that turn out to be of little interest or frustrating to the infant. By appropriately matching activities, equipment, and materials to the individual interest of the child, an adult can help a child learn and also feel good about herself as a learner.

5. Infants learn from the whole of any experience, not only the part on which the adult is focused. Infants do not experience social, emotional, intellectual, language, and physical learning separately. For example, a game about shapes and colors may also teach toddlers about the give-and-take of human interaction. Adults who consider all the ways in which the child may be learning from an experience are able to make the most of their interactions with very young children.

6. Infants learn through observation and imitation. Young children learn many things simply by watching adults. Not only do infants gather a sense of their own value by interpreting how they are treated, but they also learn how to survive in the world and how to function successfully within society and their culture by imitating their caregivers. Successful parents and caregivers conduct themselves in relation to their infant, others, and the world in ways that are worth emulating.

7. An infant's home culture is integral to the development of identity, self-esteem, and relationships with parents and extended family. A child's language, values, sense of self, and view of others all originate from her home culture and family. Caregivers who are not part of the child's home culture or family have a special responsibility here because they must learn about each child's home culture (and possibly even home language) in order to provide adequate care. The best approach is to acknowledge, ask, and adapt (Derman-Sparks, 1995). A successful caregiver will go to a child's family and

- acknowledge her own cultural beliefs and possible ignorance of the family's values;

- ask and observe how the family prefers to raise the child; and

- discuss with the family how their wishes might be adapted into her caregiving practice—or negotiate with parents and explain why she may not be able to adapt their wishes into her practice.

8. Children learn language in context, by interacting with those around them. Successful parents and caregivers comment on what their babies do, talk and sing to them, and encourage them to use words and sounds to express their emotions and guide themselves through their activities. Kuhl (2001) has shown that natural give-and-take exchanges are more effective than vocabulary drills, audio tapes, or video-cassettes in teaching language to babies. Effective support for language development includes providing verbally rich environments with books, pictures, music, and plenty of reciprocal communication between infants and tuned-in program staff and parents.

9. Safe and interesting environments promote healthy development. Infants and toddlers are strongly influenced by the environments and routines they experience every day—particularly very young infants who cannot move themselves from one environment to another. It is hard for an infant to focus if there are too many children, toys, or interruptions in the subtle give-and-take between the child and adult. Effective parents and caregivers support the infant's focus by creating safe, healthy, and interesting environments that are not cluttered, confusing, noisy, or chaotic. They pay careful attention to the impact of materials, equipment, and number of other people in the room.

10. Responsive caregiving by parents and others is critical. Plans and curricula are important tools in helping children learn. However, the younger the child, the more flexible these plans must be in order to support what that child needs, thinks, and feels. Effective caregivers for infants use observation techniques, parental input, and various assessments to see the big picture and develop responsive plans that are specific to each child. These plans help them answer questions such as

- How can the experiences I provide adapt to the temperament and interests of this child?

- Are these experiences appropriate to this child's level of development?

- What should be the goals for this child's development at this time, and if these goals are not already in a normal range, how might I intervene?

- Do these experiences address all of the child's emotional, social, intellectual, and physical needs and interests?

- Is the environment appropriate to the child's capabilities and for what she wishes to learn about?

The Parts: Support for Each Developmental Domain

The story of Margot and Stephen (see Box 5-1) is an example of how powerful daily interactions with adults are for very young children. Even an event as routine as a drop-off at the center can be an important vehicle for responsive, relationship-based care in EHS. Consider how different Stephen's concept of himself in relation to others would be if he were simply set down in a high chair on his arrival at the center rather than gently transferred from the arms of his mother to the embrace of his caregiver? He would feel diminished and ignored, rather than secure and loved.

Responsive care is particularly important to the emotional and social development of infants and toddlers. EHS caregivers are well-versed in the importance of attachment and the research findings mentioned early in this chapter. They also know that children learn from what they experience, and they imitate much of what they see. In

---

Box 5.1 : **Margot and Stephen**

Margot and her 10-month-old son Stephen approach the Friends of the Family Early Head Start child-care center. As Stephen gets closer to the building, he squeezes her arm. Margot says, "Oh Stephen, I bet Jasmine can't wait to see you!" They enter the building and exchange greetings of "Good morning!" with the staff and parents moving thorough the halls. When they arrive at Stephen's room, Margot looks for Jasmine, Stephen's primary caregiver. She sees Jasmine sitting on the floor in front of a mirror with Rory, 11 months old, and Tamara, 15 months old. The children squeal with delight as Jasmine holds a piece of paper over their reflected images and then pulls it away, exclaiming, "Ta-da!"

Margot says, "Good morning everyone. Stephen's here and he's feeling a little sad about leaving Mommy." Jasmine looks up and says, "Oh, Stephen, we're so happy to see you today! Look everybody, it's Stephen!" Tamara turns around to look at Stephen, claps her hand over her eyes, and giggles, "Da!" Everyone laughs, including Stephen, who has not yet released his mom's arm or allowed her to put him down. Jasmine says, "Margot, maybe you can sit with Stephen for a few minutes at the mirror while I put his things away."

Margot and Jasmine change places. As Jasmine and Rory put Stephen's belongings in his cubby, she hears Margot talking with the children. Jasmine comes back and sits on the floor. Stephen slides off Margot's lap and pulls himself up against the mirror, his nose pressed against the shiny surface. Jasmine asks, "Stephen, do you like how cool and smooth the mirror feels?" Stephen looks at Jasmine and smiles as he leans back against his mother's knees. Margot says, "I love starting the day here, it's great to know he will have such fun while I'm away." She then holds the paper in front of her son's image and

continued

---

addition, staff adapt their care to sensitively account for differences in the age, stage, and personality of every child.

For example, EHS caregivers search for babies' feelings by looking into their eyes, listening to their sounds, and observing their movements—and caregivers acknowledge these feelings in the ways that they act and verbally respond. Caregivers acknowledge that the social world of the infant is and should be very small in order to support a sense of safety and well-being that the baby can then convert into confident exploration of the world around her. This is why the performance standards speak to aspects of intimate daily care for infants, such as holding and making eye contact with them while they are fed. As the baby becomes a toddler, his social world expands. EHS caregivers and parents continue to literally and figuratively serve as the soft place to fall. In addition, experiences shared with peers—such as family-style meals—become

Box 5-1: **Margot and Stephen** *continued*

pulls it away again quickly. Stephen laughs, and Tamara and 16-month-old Jason beckon Margot to do the same for them.

Jasmine asks Margot when she needs to leave to make sure that she and Stephen have enough time to say good-bye to one another. Margot looks at her watch and says, "I think I would like to get a cup of coffee before I leave." Jasmine asks Margot whether it was a difficult morning for her and Stephen or whether it was just the weather. Margot laughs and says, "You know us best. When it's cloudy we just can't seem to get moving!" Margot asks whether Jasmine wants anything from the kitchen, and Jasmine says, "No, but don't forget to tell Stephen where you're going and that you'll be back." Margot tells Stephen, who continues to play at the mirror.

When Margot returns, she finds Stephen having breakfast. She kisses him on the forehead and says "ba-bye." Jasmine says, "Wait a minute, Mom; remember our special good-bye place that Stephen chose? Would you like to say good-bye from there? Jasmine wipes off Stephen's hands and mouth and says, "Come on Stephen, we're going to send mommy off to work and wish her a good day." As Jasmine picks up Stephen to go to the good-bye place, she calls to Brenda, another infant–toddler caregiver, to tell her that she's leaving to help Stephen say good-bye to Mom. When they reach the good-bye place, Margot reaches over to kiss Stephen. Stephen waves good-bye as he and Jasmine watch Margot cross the parking lot on her way to the bus stop. They gaze through the window until they can no longer see her. As Jasmine turns to go back to the room, Stephen clasps Jasmine's face in his hands and kisses her. Jasmine laughs and thanks Stephen for his juicy kiss.

Source: Based on a composite of Early Head Start programs by Gambi White-Tennant.

important to social development and also become opportunities to use rapidly growing vocabularies to interpret emotions (one's own and those of others).

To support cognitive growth, all EHS staff members receive training about how infants and toddlers learn about concepts such as causality, means-and-ends relationships, spatial relationships, thought and action learning schemes, the permanence of objects, and the use of imitation in learning (Lally, Mangione, Signer, Butterfield, & Gilford, 1992). The performance standards also require that programs promote early reading and math skills as appropriate to the developmental level of each child. EHS caregivers do not use flash cards or drills to achieve these aims. Rather, they skillfully create climates rich in written and numeric content appropriate to infants and toddlers. As guided by the interests of each child, caregivers support preliteracy and math skills through activities such as

- reading and discussing stories;

- offering age-appropriate reading and writing materials;

- telling stories from children's own and other cultures;

- showing toddlers the functional uses of print in the program or in the home (e.g., street signs, a shopping list, and names of helpers listed on a job chart);

- involving children in sequencing games;

- coaching parents about ways that the home environment can encourage literacy and numeracy development; and

- facilitating age-appropriate program and parent use of libraries, museums, and other community resources.

EHS staff members also support language development through activities and interactions that are individualized, are age appropriate, and include a spectrum of verbal and nonverbal communication, such as words, sounds, music, movement, and touch. Infants are born able to call attention to their needs and interests through cries, coos, babbles, and body movements. EHS caregivers reward and expand this skill by responding immediately to the need, repeating the baby's sounds, offering sounds to imitate, and explaining events (e.g., diapering) as they are taking place. For mobile infants who are beginning to jabber expressively, name familiar objects, and understand many words and phrases, EHS caregivers try to interpret their first attempts at words, repeat and expand on what they say, and tell them simple stories. For toddlers, who daily increase their vocabularies and use of sentences, EHS staff members encourage and expand language skills through songs, stories, directions, comfort, conversations, information, and play (Lally, Mangione, & Young-Holt, 1992).

EHS programs encourage the physical development of infants and toddlers by the way caregivers arrange the environment, the type of equipment that the programs use, and the nonintrusive support that caregivers provide for child movement. The performance standards require that there be adequate space for children to roll, crawl, walk, run, and play—inside and outside. A safe, well-cushioned environment that is free from toxins and other hazards is, of course, a priority. Infants in EHS can enjoy large and uncluttered floor space on which to roll. Toddlers are cared for apart from nonmobile infants and have plenty of space in which to experiment with their delightful, brand-new motor skills. Shelves and table tops are low to encourage child selection of toys and pushing up. Caregivers are usually found holding babies or on the floor engaged in eye-level activities and communication that captivate the crawler or new walker.

The Sum of the Parts: Support for the Whole Child

The preceding sections briefly summarize what EHS caregivers know about the specific emotional, social, intellectual, and physical learning needs of very young children. Because the child is much more than the sum of these parts, however, the sections that follow address how EHS policies and practices also help parents, caregivers, and home visitors to care for the whole child.

First, caregivers are taught that infants generally pick up social, emotional, and intellectual information simultaneously and that they frequently switch focus from one domain to another. Say, for example, that a center-based EHS program sets up a corner outfitted with hanging swaths of fabric where mobile infants can initiate hide-and-seek games with one another, caregivers, and parents. What is the staff's purpose in creating such a structure? Physical development will occur as infants crawl, grasp, and seek bright colors and soft textures. Intellectual development will occur as infants experiment with the disappearance and reappearance of others. Social and emotional development will be supported through the exuberant, surprise encounters between caregiver and child. To the untrained observer, the joyful simplicity of this "child's play" will belie the sophistication that went into designing it.

Second, curriculum in EHS is a delicate balance of infant interests, parental input, and planned activities and developmental goals. As required by the performance standards, EHS programs must use curricula that cover: (a) goals for children's development and learning, (b) experiences that will promote achievement of these goals,

(c) steps that staff and parents will take to help children achieve these goals; and (d) materials needed to support the implementation of the curriculum.

Third, programs conduct early screenings for sensory, behavioral, and developmental concerns and ongoing assessments of development to set learning goals for each child and to intervene early, if necessary. An assessment in EHS is not a "test"; rather, it is an ongoing discovery of the whole child (Meisels, 2000)—it measures the child's strengths and needs as well as the resources that he will need from his family and community. The performance standards clearly state that the assessment process can be both formal and informal, blending results from respected tools and structured observations with input from those who best know the child's typical behavior and capacities. Thus, the assessment of very young children in EHS is always a collaborative process that involves parents deeply and helps to differentiate and expand parents' and providers' perceptions of the baby or toddler. Timely screening and assessment also promote early identification of infants with delays or disabilities that may require special intervention. (See Chapter 9 for more examples of how EHS serves children with disabilities and their families.)

Fourth, EHS staff members support and monitor the medical, dental, and mental health needs of each infant and toddler in the EHS program. For one thing, timely and ongoing observations and documentation of children's physical and emotional well-being are part of the assessment process described above. Additionally, staff members screen each child for health problems in the child's person (e.g., medical, dental, or mental health concerns) or environment (e.g., lead in the home and safety hazards, such as an inadequate car seat). Families who do not have access to regular care will often put off obtaining preventive appointments. EHS staff members help families establish an ongoing source of accessible medical care for each family member. In addition, a consistent pediatrician is important to ensuring that the infant's growth, immunizations, and other primary health care needs are kept on track. EHS programs also support, complement, and supplement the nutrition that children receive at home through diet assessment, parental education, and nutritious meals and snacks in child-care settings. Each program also strongly encourages and supports breast-feeding for babies. (See Chapter 4 for more details about this subject.)

RESPECT FOR CULTURE AND LANGUAGE

EHS is an extremely diverse program. A range of ethnicities—from Central American to West African, Western European to Hmong—might be found in a single program. Because home culture and home language have a profound influence on how and what a child learns about the world, others, and him- or herself, EHS staff acknowledge each child's home culture and home language as the context in which that child will learn best.

EHS caregivers and home visitors support home culture as the context for early development by first learning about and acknowledging each family's values, beliefs, and preferred child-rearing practices. Then, staff members align caregiving and home visit content as closely as possible with the family's cultural practices. This approach not only strengthens the work of and respect between the adults but also ensures more congruent in- and out-of-home experiences for the child. Learning flourishes under such circumstances. Additionally, the child's vital link to home and family is not harmed.

For example, EHS caregivers often encounter differences between the way an infant is fed at home and the way she is fed at the program. In EHS caregiving settings, meal time is offered as an experience of taste, texture, sight, smell, and social interaction. Older infants and toddlers are encouraged to select their own portion sizes and to feed themselves as independently as possible. However, allowing an older infant to use her hands to explore food may seem overindulgent to families from cultures in which spoon-feeding a child is encouraged for the first several years. Or perhaps a refugee family, who has experienced food scarcity, may grow concerned that a child is being encouraged to waste food. Rather than shrug off such viewpoints, EHS caregivers actively seek to understand the sources and strengths of the family's practice, explain how typical EHS practice encourages development and good eating habits, and then negotiate an arrangement that moves the program and the family to a place of mutual comfort.

EHS caregivers and home visitors also incorporate the language spoken at home into their visits with families and their care for children. Any enrolled child and family will, of course, be exposed to a great deal of English. However, EHS staff members always seek to meet the family halfway, even if only one family in a program speaks a fairly uncommon language. For example, caregivers who are not fluent in the child's home language often learn commonly used words, phrases, or songs to create the safe and comforting "sound of home" for the baby. To support emerging literacy skills, staff members often include home language on print materials that the child may encounter—for example, signs around the room or a labels on puzzles. A home visitor who is not language-congruent with one of the families with whom he works is often accompanied by a paid or volunteer translator and will frequently bring to the home visit EHS materials that are translated into the family's original language.

EHS program managers often hire staff members and use volunteers who mirror, in many important respects, the populations they serve. EHS programs regularly offer staff members opportunities to learn about the cultures represented by program families, and some staff members are trained to speak other languages, when necessary. To help staff members serve families of varied cultures, EHS programs often form strong partnerships with other community organizations that support members of particular ethnic communities, such as translation agencies and mutual aid societies. In addition, EHS staff members frequently offer enrolled families opportunities to share stories, songs, food, and ideas from their culture with other families, children, and program staff.

Because such a significant gap still exists between what we know about babies and what we actually do for them, EHS offers the nation a historic opportunity to raise the bar on the level of care provided to our country's infants and toddlers. The EHS program is our largest laboratory for applying up-to-date research to infant–toddler learning and home visiting. To date, the program's results are promising: In a country where less than 10% of infant–toddler child-care programs were rated as being developmentally appropriate in 1995 (Cost, Quality, and Child Outcomes Study Team, 1995), the EHS program represents a remarkable step forward.

ACKNOWLEDGMENTS

The authors of this chapter are indebted to Jack P. Shonkoff, Deborah A. Phillips, and the Committee on Integrating the Science of Early Childhood Development for cogent and exhaustive presentation of the science that does and should support effective policies and practice for very young children.

NOTE

1. For a thorough review of research on early development and learning, see *From Neurons to Neighborhoods: The Science of Early Childhood Development*, edited by Jack P. Shonkoff and Deborah A. Phillips (National Research Council and Institute of Medicine, 2000).

REFERENCES

Becker, G. S. (1981). *A treatise on the family.* Cambridge, MA: Harvard University Press.

Belsky, J., Woodworth, S., & Crnic, K. (1996). Infant attachment security and affective–cognitive information processing at age 3. *Psychological Science, 7,* 111–114.

Black, J. E., & Greenough, W. T. (1986). Induction of pattern in neural structure by experience: Implications for cognitive development. In M. E. Lamb, A. L. Brown, & B. Rogoff (Eds.), *Advances in developmental psychology, Vol. 4* (pp. 1–50). Hillsdale, NJ: Lawrence Erlbaum Associates.

Bloom, K., Russell, A., & Wassenberg, K. (1987). Turn taking affects the quality of infant vocalizations. *Journal of Child Language, 14,* 211–227.

Bornstein, M. H. (Ed.). (1989). *Maternal responsiveness: Characteristics and consequences.* San Francisco: Jossey-Bass.

Bornstein, M. H., & Tamis-LeMonda, C. S. (1989). Maternal responsiveness and cognitive development in children. In M. H. Bornstein (Ed.), *Maternal responsiveness: Characteristics and consequences* (pp. 49–61). San Francisco: Jossey-Bass.

Bradley, R. H., Caldwell, B. M., Rock, S. L., Ramey, C. T., Barnard, K. E., Gray, C., et al. (1989). Home environment and the cognitive development in the first three years of life: A collaborative study involving six sites and three ethnic groups in North America. *Developmental Psychology, 25*(2), 217–235.

Brody, D. J., Pirkle, J. L., Kramer, R. A., Flegal, K. M., Matte, T. D., Gunter, E. W., et al. (1994). Blood lead levels in the U.S. population: Phase 1 of the Third National Health and Nutrition Examination Survey (1988–1991). *Journal of the American Medical Association, 272,* 277–283.

Brooks-Gunn, J., & Duncan, G. J. (1997). The effects of poverty on children. *The Future of Children, 7*(2), 55–71.

Brooks-Gunn, J., Brown, B., Duncan, G. J., & Moore, K. A. (1995). Child development in the context of family and community resources: An agenda for national data collection. In National Research Council and Institute of Medicine, *Integrating federal statistics on children: Report of a workshop* (pp. 27–97). Washington, DC: National Academy Press.

Buka, S., & Birdthistle, I. (1997, Winter). Children's exposure to violence: Extending the research frontier. *The Chicago Project News, 3*(1). http://www.hms.harvard.edu/chase/projects/chicago/news/newsletters/win97/nlwin97.htm

Cassidy, J. (1988). Child–mother attachment and the self in six year olds. *Child Development, 59,* 121–134.

Cost, Quality, and Child Outcomes Study Team. (1995, January). *Cost, quality, and child outcomes in childcare centers: Public report* (2nd ed.). Denver: University of Colorado at Denver, Economics Department.

Derman-Sparks, L. (1995). Developing culturally responsive caregiving practices: Acknowledge, ask, and adapt. In P. L. Mangione (Ed.), *Infant/toddler caregiving: A guide to culturally sensitive care* (pp. 42–44). Sacramento: California Department of Education.

Frank, D. A., Klass, P. E., Earls, F., & Eisenberg, L. (1996). Infants and young children in orphanages: One view from pediatrics and child psychiatry. *Pediatrics, 47*(4), 569–578.

Georgieff, M. K., & Rao, R. (2001). The role of nutrition in cognitive development. In C. A. Nelson & M. Luciana (Eds.), *Handbook of developmental cognitive neuroscience* (pp. 491–504). Cambridge, MA: MIT Press.

Greenough, W. T., & Black, J. E. (1992). Induction of brain structure by experience: Substrates for cognitive development. In M. R. Gunnar & C. A. Nelson (Eds.), *Developmental behavior neuroscience* (Minnesota Symposia on Child Psychology, Vol. 24, pp. 155–200). Hillsdale, NJ: Lawrence Erlbaum Associates.

Hart, B., & Risley, T. R. (1998). *Meaningful differences in the everyday experience of young American children.* Baltimore: Paul H. Brookes.

Huttenlocher, P. R. (1979). Synaptic density in human frontal cortex: Developmental changes and effects of aging. *Brain Research, 163,* 195–205.

Huttenlocher, P. R., & Dabholkar, A. S. (1997). Regional differences in synaptogenesis in human cerebral cortex. *The Journal of Comparative Neurology, 387*(2), 167–178.

Kirsh, S. J., & Cassidy, J. (1997). Preschoolers' attention to and memory for attachment-relevant information. *Child Development, 68,* 1143–1153.

Klebanov, P. K., Brooks-Gunn, J., & Duncan, G. J. (1994). Does neighborhood and family poverty affect mothers' parenting, mental health, and social support? *Journal of Marriage and the Family, 56*(2), 441–455.

Klebanov, P. K., Brooks-Gunn, J., Gordon, R., & Chase-Lansdale, P. L. (1997). The intersection of the neighborhood and home environment and its influence on young children. In J. Brooks-Gunn, G. J. Duncan, & J. L. Aber (Eds.), *Neighborhood poverty:*

Context and consequences for children (Vol. 1). New York: Russell Sage Foundation.

Kochanska, G. (1995). Children's temperament, mothers' discipline, and security of attachment: Multiple pathways to emerging internalization. *Child Development, 66,* 597–615.

Kochanska, G. (1997). Multiple pathways to conscience for children with different temperaments: From toddlerhood to age 5. *Developmental Psychology, 33,* 228–240.

Kuhl, P. K. (2001, July). *Born to learn: Language, reading, and the brain of the child.* Address to the White House Summit on Early Childhood Cognitive Development, Washington, DC.

Laible, D. J., & Thompson, R. A. (1998). Attachment and emotional understanding in preschool children. *Developmental Psychology, 34*(5), 1038–1045.

Lally, J. R., Mangione, P. L., Signer, S., Butterfield, G. O., & Gilford, S. (1992). *Discoveries of infancy: Cognitive development and learning* [Videotape]. Sacramento and Sausalito, CA: The Program for Infant/Toddler Caregivers (developed collaboratively by the California Department of Education and WestEd).

Lally, J. R., Mangione, P. L., & Young-Holt, C. L. (Eds.). (1992). *Infant/toddler caregiving: A guide to language development and communication.* Sacramento: California Department of Education.

Laosa, L. M. (1983). School, occupation, culture, and family. In E. Sigel & L. Laosa (Eds.), *Changing families* (pp. 79–135). New York: Plenum.

Meisels, S. J. (2000, October). Readiness and relationships: Issues in assessing young children, families, and caregivers. *Head Start Bulletin, 69,* 5–6.

Michael, R. T. (1972). *The effect of education on efficiency in consumption.* New York: Columbia University Press.

Morgan, B. L. G., & Winick, M. (1985). Pathological effects of malnutrition on the central nervous system. In H. Sidransky (Ed.), *Nutritional pathology: Pathobiochemistry of dietary imbalances* (pp. 161–206). New York: Marcel Dekker.

Morgan, B., & Gibson, K. (1991). Nutritional and environmental interactions in brain development. In K. R. Gibson & A. C. Petersen (Eds.), *Brain maturation and cognitive development: Comparative and cross-cultural perspectives* (pp. 91–106). Hawthorne, NY: Aldine de Gruyter.

National Research Council and Institute of Medicine. (2000). *From neurons to neighborhoods: The science of early childhood development.* Committee on Integrating the

Science of Early Childhood Development. J. P. Shonkoff & D. A. Phillips (Eds.). Board on Children, Youth, and Families, Commission on Behavioral and Social Sciences and Education. Washington, DC: National Academy Press.

Shore, R. (1997). *Rethinking the brain: New insights into early development.* New York: Families and Work Institute.

Singer, M. I., Anglin, T. M., Song, L., & Lunghofer, L. (1995). Adolescents' exposure to violence and associated symptoms of psychological trauma. *Journal of the American Medical Association, 273,* 477–482.

Sroufe, L. A., & Egeland, B. (1991). Illustrations of person–environment interaction from a longitudinal study. In T. D. Wachs & R. Plomin (Eds.), *Conceptualization and measurement of organism–environment interaction* (pp. 68–86). Washington, DC: American Psychological Association.

Sroufe, L. A., Carson, E., & Schulman, S. (1993). Individuals in relationships: Development from infancy through adolescence. In D. C. Funder, R. D. Parke, C. Tomlinson-Keasey, & K. Widaman (Eds.), *Studying lives through time: Personality and development* (pp. 315–342). Washington, DC: American Psychological Association.

Taylor, L., Zuckerman, B., Harik, V., & Groves, B. (1992). Exposure to violence among inner city parents and young children. *American Journal of the Diseases of Children, 146,* 487–494.

Thompson, R. A. (1998). Empathy and its origins in early development. In S. Braten (Ed.), *Intersubjective communication and emotion in early ontogeny.* Cambridge, England: Cambridge University Press.

Thompson, R. A. (1999). Early attachment and later development. In J. Cassidy & P. R. Shaver (Eds.), *Handbook of attachment: Theory, research, and clinical applications.* New York: Guilford.

Thompson, R. A. (2001). Development in the first years of life. *The Future of Children, 11*(1), 21–33.

U.S. Department of Health and Human Services. (1996). *Head Start regulations and program guidance for parts 1301–13011.* Washington, DC: Author.

Verschueren, K., Marcoen, A., & Schoefs, V. (1996). The internal working model of the self, attachment, and competence in five-year-olds. *Child Development, 67,* 2493–2511.

ABOUT THE AUTHORS

J. Ronald Lally is co-director of the Center for Child and Family Studies at WestEd, an educational research and development laboratory in San Francisco. Much of his research deals with two topics: social–emotional development in infancy and the effect of early intervention on adult functioning. He, his staff, and a faculty of national experts conducted Program for Infant Toddler Caregivers (PITC) intensive training and certifying events for the more than 700 Early Head Start and Migrant Head Start programs in various states.

Gambi White-Tennant is the infant–toddler specialist at the New York University Head Start Quality Improvement Center. She has extensive experience in developing, implementing, and operating programs for infants, toddlers, and their parents in various settings (e.g., child care, substance recovery programs, boarder baby programs, HIV programs, and adolescent parent programs).

CHAPTER 6

DADS AND BABIES: EARLY HEAD START AND FATHERS

Jeffery M. Johnson

I n recent years, awareness about the important role that fathers play in the overall well-being of their children has been growing (Lamb, 1976; Pruett, 1997). We now know that fathers can, and often do, become as attached to their infants as mothers do and that the father's active involvement with his infant can lead to better developmental outcomes for the child (Horn, 2000). Father involvement can affect children's cognitive and social development and their academic achievement. Unfortunately, during the past few decades, the number of children growing up in homes without fathers has increased dramatically. In 1960, fewer than 10 million children in the United States lived in homes without their fathers; in 2002, the number was nearly 25 million (U.S. Department of Health and Human Services, 2002a).

Fortunately, since the 1990s, interest among policymakers in promoting the active involvement of fathers in the lives of their children and families has been widespread. The U.S. Department of Health and Human Services (2002a) has developed a special initiative to support and strengthen the roles of fathers in their families, guided by the following principles:

- all fathers can be important contributors to the well-being of their children;

- parents are partners in raising their children, even when they do not live in the same household;

- the roles that fathers play in families are diverse and related to cultural and community norms;

- men should receive the education and support necessary to prepare them for the responsibility of parenthood; and

- government can encourage and promote fathers' involvement through its programs and through its own workforce policies.

Early Head Start (EHS) programs are on the forefront of these efforts to reach out and involve fathers. The findings from the national evaluation indicate that EHS can have an important effect on fathers (Administration for Children and Families, 2002). This chapter briefly discusses some of the emerging research on fathers of young children and the initial efforts of EHS to assist fathers in forming relationships capable of enhancing the development of their infants and toddlers.

FATHERS' CARE

Most research on fathers' involvement with their children has been conducted with middle-class families. Because of the limitations of this research, attitudes toward low-income fathers often have been based on stereotypes rather than data. The media, social service agencies, and even friends and family members may reinforce these beliefs that have guided national policy and program practices for poor families. More recently, however, researchers are providing fresh insight into the lives of low-income families and fathers' involvement with their children, particularly their babies. For example, the Fragile Families and Child Well-Being Study, which is being conducted in cities across the United States, follows a new birth cohort of children and their parents in an effort to learn more about unmarried, low-income mothers and fathers and their biological children (McLanahan et al., 2001).

According to the study's initial analysis of data on 2,760 unmarried couples, collected in 16 cities from April 1998 through November 2000, unwed parents appear committed to each other and to their children at the time of their children's birth.[1] For example, 83% of unmarried mothers and fathers were romantically involved at the time their child was born, and 50% of the couples were living together. More than 70% of mothers who participated in the study, who were interviewed in the hospital within 48 hours of their children's birth, said that their chances of marrying the baby's father were 50% or greater. Eighty percent of the unmarried fathers were involved in helping their baby's mother during pregnancy. About 83% of mothers in the survey indicated that the father provided financial help during the pregnancy, and 80% of the mothers and 90% of the fathers reported that he contributed in other ways (such as providing transportation) during pregnancy. The overwhelming majority of mothers want the father involved in raising the child. Furthermore, two thirds of mothers and three fourths of fathers agreed with the statement, "It is better for children if their parents are married" (McLanahan et al., 2001).

The Fragile Families and Child Well-Being Study also found that despite high hopes for their families, most unmarried parents are poorly equipped to support themselves and their children. For example, although 84% of the mothers and 90% of the fathers worked at some time during the year in which pregnancy occurred, nearly 30% of the fathers were out of work prior to the interview. Furthermore, about one third of the mothers and fathers lacked high school degrees. Limited human capital and earning potential are likely to hamper the efforts of these new parents to maintain stable families (McLanahan et al., 2001).

These and other findings contribute to a picture of low-income parents and their children that challenges long-held beliefs. Many poor fathers do care about their families and want to take on the task of parenting. Many talk about how they love their children and want to provide them with a home, stability, and discipline—gifts that these often young, unprepared, and inexperienced fathers might not have received from their own fathers. Many poor fathers say they welcome their children and see fatherhood as a way of erasing the mistakes of the past, a chance to prove that they can become the men their fathers failed to be.

This new research can be used to design programs that, among other things, teach men how to become better parents. It suggests that social service practitioners and educators—including EHS staff—can help families strengthen their fragile bonds and promote better outcomes for their children rather than succumb to the stresses threatening to crack those brittle ties.

In sum, many young, low-income fathers appear to take their roles as dads quite seriously. They see fatherhood as the "growing-up" part of manhood, a time when the ability to be a provider and nurturer is paramount. Their willingness to take on the daunting role of parent, even when they are ill equipped to do so, is heartening, but timely support is of the essence.

Based on a study of several hundred programs with promising approaches to working with fathers and families, Levine and Pitt (1997) identified several ways to promote responsible fatherhood. They include, among others, preparing men for the legal, financial, and emotional responsibility that come with becoming a father; encouraging establishment of paternity at childbirth; and reaching out to men who are fathers to foster their emotional connection to and financial support of their children. Emerging research findings indicate that it is critical to build on the early interest that low-income fathers show in their young children, particularly in their babies, to encourage more sustained involvement as the child grows older.

INVOLVING FATHERS IN EARLY HEAD START

Since EHS began in 1995, this program has encouraged a strong and continuous focus on the promotion of father involvement through research, demonstration programs, and technical assistance. EHS research on fathers has been supported by the

Administration for Children and Families, the Office of the Assistant Secretary for Planning and Evaluation, the National Institute of Child Health and Development, and The Ford Foundation. These studies include surveys with fathers, including qualitative and quantitative questions when children are 2 and 3 years old, conducted at 12 EHS sites; videotaped assessments from a limited number of sites; a study of fathers of newborns; and a practitioner study that included focus groups and surveys of father involvement in EHS.

Along with these research efforts, the Head Start Bureau, in collaboration with the Office of Child Support Enforcement, has funded 21 EHS fatherhood demonstration programs (Raikes et al., 2002). In addition, the Early Head Start National Resource Center, the National Head Start Association, and the National Center for Strategic Nonprofit Planning and Community Leadership have provided training and technical assistance to help EHS programs engage and support fathers.

Information from all of these activities indicates that many EHS programs are working hard to develop their capacity to serve and involve fathers. These programs can already point to important accomplishments.

Information From the Early Head Start Practitioner Survey and the Early Head Start Impact Study

In late 1999 and early 2000, a survey was sent to 422 EHS programs across the country to collect information about the ways that programs were reaching out to involve fathers; 62% of the programs responded. The results indicated that

- In the typical EHS program, almost one half of the children have a resident father (44.6%), and about one quarter have an involved nonresident father, although there is considerable variation across programs in the population of fathers of EHS children.

- Nearly all EHS programs try to involve resident biological fathers (98.8%) and resident father figures (94.8%). Most programs also attempt to involve nonresident biological fathers (77.2%) and nonresident father figures (57.9%).

- Programs seem to pass through stages (early, mid-stage, and mature), becoming increasingly sophisticated in their efforts to involve fathers.

- EHS programs that are "mature" in terms of father involvement hire and train a father involvement coordinator, hire male staff, rely on men for outreach to fathers, involve nonresident as well as resident fathers, reach out to fathers who are in prison, and involve fathers in employment and education activities as well as in spending time with their children (Raikes et al., 2002).

At the time of the survey, most EHS programs (72%) considered themselves in the "early" stages of involving fathers. Twenty-one percent rated themselves as "mid-stage," and 7% rated themselves as "mature."

According to the EHS impact study (Administration for Children and Families, 2002), the overall program is already having an effect on fathers. Interviews with fathers and videotaped interaction data gathered in the father study sites indicated that fathers whose families participated in the EHS program spanked less, were less punitive in disciplinary practices, and were less intrusive in interactions with their infants and toddlers than fathers in the control group.

Information from Early Head Start Demonstration Programs

The 21 EHS demonstration programs, funded for 3 years, are expected to establish partnerships with their local child support agency and other community resources. According to an interim report on the projects, most of these programs had little or no experience providing services directly to fathers before they received the demonstration grant. Discussions with program leaders and a review of grant applications revealed six common goals related to fathers (Bellotti, 2002):

1. expanding fathers' knowledge of child development, confidence in parenting, and overall involvement in their children's lives;

2. increasing fathers' participation in EHS;

3. enhancing staff sensitivity to the needs of fathers;

4. encouraging strong parenting partnerships;

5. promoting fathers' self-sufficiency and financial responsibility for their children; and

6. helping fathers better understand and navigate the child support system.

As early as 1 year after their establishment, these demonstration programs had made progress toward the goal of involving fathers. To earn a "father-friendly" reputation, the demonstration programs provided activities that are interesting and relevant to men, hired male staff, and trained other staff members to be sensitive to fathers' needs.

At this stage, programs were finding nonresident fathers in general and teen nonresident fathers in particular, difficult to identify, locate, and engage. In addition, cultural beliefs about the role of fathers, scheduling conflicts with work, and lack of transportation limited fathers' participation in EHS.

Despite these challenges, the EHS demonstration projects are providing a wealth of new ideas and promising practices (Bellotti, 2002).[2]

Recruitment and Outreach

The coordinator of the Fathers-in-Training (FIT) program in Indianapolis, Indiana, has hosted continental breakfasts for fathers ("Donuts for Dads") at which he promotes the program and leads fathers through a focused discussion of fatherhood issues. He also reaches out to student-parents at two area high schools and appears as a regular guest on a local radio show that airs a segment on fatherhood issues. EHS programs also reach out to fathers during home visits, connect with them when they pick up their children from the program, develop fliers aimed at fathers, or hold special events (such as fishing trips and baseball games) to create an atmosphere that welcomes fathers.

Engaging Fathers at the Time of the Child's Birth

Fatherhood program practitioners maintain that a father's enthusiasm—and thus his incentive to remain and deepen his involvement—is highest at the "magic moment" of the child's birth. EHS programs work to engage fathers during the pregnancy and at the hospital and to follow up with help negotiating the child support system, employment training, and other services as needed.

The Sacramento Employment and Training Agency (SETA) EHS program in California uses the *Partners for a Healthy Baby Home Visiting Curriculum for Expectant Families* (Florida State University Center for Prevention and Early Intervention Policy, 1999) to talk with expectant fathers about their role before, during, and after delivery. SETA EHS staff members encourage fathers to attend their baby's delivery and addresses their fears (Catherine Goins, personal communication to Mary Bogle, 2002).

Ongoing Involvement

Providing ongoing opportunities to involve fathers in the various stages of their child's development takes special programming and creative ideas (see the story of Tallie, Carla, and Ne'Talia in Box 6-1).

Box 6-1 Tallie, Carla, and Ne'Talia

Young men in their teens and twenties gather around a table in the meeting room of the county Head Start. Tallie, a tall, slim young man, leads the discussion: "You don't know what tomorrow brings. Tomorrow may be gone, so you have to know that you left today doing what you can for your child. Your child is defenseless, but one day they will want to fend for [themselves], and you're going to want to know that you've done everything to your best ability to prepare them for life. So what that requires you to do now is prepare yourself."

He knows of what he speaks. A few years earlier, Tallie graduated from high school with much to be proud of—student government president, national recognition for his academic achievements, and voted "Most Likely to Succeed" by classmates. He and his high school sweetheart, Carla, ventured off to college with high hopes.

Then Carla became pregnant, and everything changed. She relocated to their hometown to give birth to and raise their new baby girl, Ne'Talia. Tallie eventually followed, but the adjustment was painful. Says Tallie, "The minute that happened with her, I totally took the downside of life. I got discouraged.

"I really [began] to wonder what was going on. It was a turning point in my life." The male involvement staff of the EHS program already had been reaching out to Tallie. Carla and Ne'Talia were active participants, and repeat phone and house calls from male social workers finally brought Tallie into the fold as well. Today, the young father credits EHS with helping him to revive some of his old dreams and assume a positive new identify as a doting dad.

Carla agrees. "I think the chance to spend time with Ne'Talia and to have people supporting [him] helped him to realize his role as a father and how important it is to take part in your child's education and life. Early Head Start has opened doors for us and opened our eyes to see what truly happens in a family."

When Ne'Talia was 2 years old, Tallie and Carla wed. Both parents now attend college. Tallie's commitment to EHS has grown along with his dedication to his family. He is now a leader in the program's male mentoring program, which gathers to share the male perspective on child development, financial planning, and the importance of setting goals in life. Members also encourage one another to engage in special projects to enhance the lives of their children—for example, Tallie persuades small businesses to reach out to young fathers so that they can support and be role models for their children. The positive example provided by other men was what sealed Tallie's bond with his daughter and EHS. "Seeing [other] guys with [their children] and seeing them with Head Start and how much love and caring that [they're] sharing with other people's kids—it kind of hit me, 'What are you doing?'" (Early Head Start National Resource Center, 2001).

To help provide fathers with skills and knowledge in parenting and a support system to help them with challenging times, the Red Cliff Band of Lake Superior Chippewa EHS program in Wisconsin is using T. Berry Brazelton's *Touchpoints* curriculum (Brazelton, 1992). The EHS program is incorporating into its *Touchpoints* curriculum lessons about the roles that men have played in raising children in traditional Native American families.

In 2002, the EHS program of the New York Foundling Society called Parenting Activities for Papi's Involvement (PAPI), operating in Puerto Rico, planned to start selecting padrinos (godfathers) to serve as father figures for children in EHS who did not have a father figure in their lives.

Empowering Fathers

Many EHS programs are helping empower fathers by including them in decision making—encouraging them to serve on program committees and to become parent representatives on the policy council. In 2002, the Denver-based Family Star EHS program in Colorado planned to establish El Concilio, a steering committee for the project with seats reserved for fathers or father figures of EHS children.

Improving Job Skills

Several of the fatherhood demonstration programs are working to improve fathers' job skills. The fatherhood coordinator in the Bridgeport, Connecticut, EHS program has established a collaborative project with the Sheet Metal Workers Union to provide trade union apprenticeships. He has also worked with other local organizations to provide training in construction, copier repair, and driver education. In Alice, Texas, the Community Action Corporation of South Texas fatherhood demonstration, the Compu-Dad Project, emphasizes computer training as a way to help fathers become financially self-sufficient as they also become more involved in their children's lives.

Although it is still too early to evaluate the effectiveness of the EHS fatherhood demonstration programs formally, participating parents and staff already perceive important accomplishments. Some programs report that staff members are now more likely to ask fathers to participate in events, and they have been surprised at how interested the fathers are in becoming involved. They report that the fatherhood coordinator has played a crucial role in helping staff members better understand the value of increased father involvement. In other programs, fathers who were reluctant to participate are now talking freely to the teaching staff and to the fatherhood advocate.

Still other programs report that fathers are coming to classrooms more frequently and staying longer than before. As one program put it, "Before the demonstration . . . fathers believed the program was for babies and mothers and that no one was helping them be a father. Now . . . fathers and father figures believe they are an important part of the program and feel that staff members, especially the father involvement partner, is there to meet their needs" (Bellotti, 2002, p. A77).

EFFECTIVELY INCLUDING FATHERS

Although many EHS programs have reached out to fathers, it is clear that much more remains to be done to fully involve fathers in the programs. To assist Head Start and EHS programs to welcome and include fathers, the National Center for Strategic Nonprofit Planning and Community Leadership has developed a father-friendly assessment. This assessment helps programs evaluate how they are currently working with fathers and where they may need to improve buy-in from the agency administration, commit resources, and revise communications or marketing materials.

EHS and other programs that seek to include fathers in a meaningful way must ensure that planned activities are truly father friendly. Such activities should be relevant and appropriate; simply issuing invitations is not enough. To involve fathers effectively, programs should

- believe in the value and importance of both parents' involvement in the lives of their children;

- recognize that there is no "one-size-fits-all" approach to working with and involving fathers;

- implement a father-friendly atmosphere, which may include something as simple as a welcome banner at open house that says, "Welcome Moms and Dads";

- hire male staff members and solicit ideas and suggestions from men and fathers regarding how the program can work best for them;

- involve fathers "holistically" in the program—assume they want to be there and that they want and expect to be consulted about the status and progress of their children;

- develop a community resource list for men that offers information on topics such as child support enforcement and mediation, employment resources, and parenting training;

- document and maintain good records regarding work with men and fathers;

- form strong partnerships and community collaborations that seek to strengthen fragile families and sustain father involvement, and network with social service agencies that offer a range of resources to families, including social welfare agencies, welfare-to-work offices, child support enforcement offices, and faith-based and community-based organizations that support families' and children's well-being; and

- use safety measures to prevent any form of abuse (from verbal abuse to possible violence), judge the feasibility of efforts to promote father involvement on a case-by-case basis, and identify counseling resources for families—including drug and alcohol treatment, if warranted, and crisis counseling, such as domestic violence services for women and batterer's education for men.

As alluded to earlier, women working with men in early childhood settings can be difficult, especially when parental relationships are tense. These EHS services for men have proven to be more successful than EHS fatherhood coordinators had hoped, particularly in instances where peers are part of the counseling process. Peer disapproval against domestic violence is a powerful tool in rehabilitating men who have never been taught that hitting is never an appropriate response in any situation.

Finally, the importance of partnerships in this work cannot be overstated. Public- and private-sector groups concerned with social welfare issues traditionally have had little meaningful interaction. Historically, welfare agencies did not talk to child support enforcement officials, who often did not talk to community-based family support groups or child development or educational institutions. Yet, each entity oversaw, instituted, or administered some aspect of policy or undertook work on behalf of families. Now that welfare benefits are ending, the money that dads can contribute to families is absolutely critical, particularly to boost their children's well-being. New efforts are needed to work creatively across agencies, particularly with Child Support Enforcement, Temporary Assistance for Needy Families agencies, employment services, and early childhood programs.

CONCLUSION

We need to create new policies and a system that supports the role of fathers by fostering productive working agreements between government and community-based organizations, including faith-based and educational institutions. We must move beyond the stereotypes that presume that families are self-supporting units and that children do as well without fathers as they do with them. We commit a grave injustice against children and contradict commonly held notions of family values if we do not build new systems—systems that understand and respond to the desires and needs of real families with basic family support.

Children lose out when they do not have the active involvement of loving fathers or other adult males in their lives. Children need as many positive role models as we can give them. Fathers and other responsible men should be viewed as assets to any EHS program. Programs that address the needs of fathers and promote their involvement in the lives of their children are an important step in the right direction.

NOTES

1. The researchers interviewed nearly all the mothers but were able to interview only 75% of the fathers.

2. Unless otherwise specified, examples of promising practices from the Early Head Start Fatherhood Demonstration Programs were taken from the site profiles in *Reaching Out to Fathers: The Early Head Start Fatherhood Demonstration* (Bellotti, 2002).

REFERENCES

Administration for Children and Families. (2002). *Making a difference in the lives of infants and toddlers and their families: The impacts of Early Head Start.* Washington, DC: Author.

Bellotti, J. (2002, October 18). *Reaching out to fathers: The Early Head Start fatherhood demonstration.* Interim report. Princeton, NJ: Mathematica Policy Research.

Brazelton, T. B. (1992). *Touchpoints.* New York: Perseus Books.

Early Head Start National Resource Center. (2001). *Families speak: The Early Head Start experience* [Videotape shown at the 2001 Head Start and Child Care Birth to Three Institute]. Washington, DC: U.S. Department of Health and Human Services and ZERO TO THREE.

Florida State University Center for Prevention and Early Intervention Policy. (1999). *Partners for a healthy baby: Home visiting curriculum for expectant families.* Tallahassee: Florida State University.

Horn, W. (2000). Fathering of infants. In J. D. Osofsky and H. E. Fitzgerald (Eds.), *WAIMH handbook of infant mental health* (Vol. 3, pp. 269–298). New York: J. Wiley & Sons.

Lamb, M. E. (1976). *The role of fathers in child development.* New York: John Wiley and Sons.

Levine, J. A., & Pitt, E. W. (1997, August/September). Community strategies for responsible fatherhood: On-ramps to connection. *Zero to Three, 18*(1), 36–41.

McLanahan, S., Garfinkel, I., Reichman, N. E., Teitler, J., Carlson, M., & Audigier, C. N. (2001). *The Fragile Families and Child Well-Being Study baseline report.* Princeton, NJ: Princeton University.

Pruett, K. D. (1997, August/September). How men and children affect each other's development. *Zero to Three, 18*(1), 3–10.

Raikes, H., Boller, K., van Kammen, W., Summers, J., Raikes, A., Laible, D., et al. (2002). *Father involvement in Early Head Start programs: A practitioners study.* Lincoln, NE: University of Nebraska, and Princeton, NJ: Mathematica Policy Research, Inc.

U.S. Department of Health and Human Services. (2002a). *Fatherhood initiative.* Retrieved from www.fatherhood.hhs.gov/index.shtml on May 17, 2004.

U.S. Department of Health and Human Services. (2002b). *Promoting responsible fatherhood.* HHS fact sheet. Retrieved from www.fatherhood.hhs.gov/index.shtml on May 17, 2004.

ABOUT THE AUTHOR

Jeffery M. Johnson is president and CEO of the National Center for Strategic Nonprofit Planning and Community Leadership. He is an expert in the areas of leadership, employment training, urban poverty, and youth employment, with a particular focus on the plight of African American men and families. He is the author of several publications, including *Fatherhood Development: A Curriculum for Young Fathers* (Wilson & Johnson, 1994) and writes a monthly column called "Father's Corner" for *The National Head Start Association Magazine.*

Turning a "Me" Thing Into a "We" Thing: Early Head Start and Teen Parents

Nick Wechsler

Teenage parents are, first and foremost, teenagers. Adolescence is a period that is charged with rapid physical, emotional, intellectual, and social growth and change—it is about becoming and defining oneself. When adolescents become parents, who they will be has, in part, been answered: Mommy or Daddy. How each individual will act as a parent and grow as a young adult is part of the focus of programs such as Early Head Start (EHS).

Even though teen pregnancy rates are at their lowest in 20 years, the United States still has the highest rates of teen pregnancy and teen birth in the industrialized world. Four in every 10 girls become pregnant at least once before age 20. Every year, more than 900,000 teens become pregnant in the United States. Nearly half a million teens give birth every year (The National Campaign to Prevent Teenage Pregnancy, 2002). We know that teen childbearing puts adolescents at risk for poor health, difficulties in school, abuse and neglect, welfare dependency, and a range of other social problems that affect the well-being of their children.

EHS can help change these odds. What distinguishes EHS from many other child development and family support programs that serve teen parents is the program's recognition of the need to serve both the child and the parent within the context of their family, community, and culture. The Early Head Start National Research and Evaluation Project (see Chapters 2 and 3) documents the effect of this program design. Teen parents headed slightly more than one third of the families enrolled in the EHS research sites; the percentage of teens in each program ranged from 19% to 90% (Administration for Children and Families, 2002). Even though the EHS program was not designed specifically to work with teen parents, the results of the evaluation were promising. EHS programs had a positive effect on the social–emotional development of children of teen parents, teen parents' supportiveness, and teens' participation in educational activities. The EHS evaluation suggests that when programs put a high priority on providing intensive services that focus on child development along with teens' education, employment, and other issues, they can have a significant effect on the progress of both children and parents (Administration for Children and Families, 2002).

This chapter provides a glimpse into the lives of teenagers who have become parents and the challenges they face in raising their infants and young children while undergoing intense growth and development themselves. It outlines the various approaches used by EHS to reach out and support teen parents and raises additional issues that should be explored as EHS builds on its promising beginning.

THE MULTIPLE WORLDS OF TEEN PARENTS

To effectively aid teen parents and their young children, EHS and similar programs must work in four worlds at once: the world of the child, the world of the teen, the world of the parent–child relationship, and the world of the extended family and community.

The World of the Child

Adolescence is a period of experimentation in which teenagers determine whom they want to be. In large part, they do this by judging how the world reacts to and interacts with them. When teens become parents, their children are thrust into the center of the experiment.

In Chapter 5, Lally and White-Tennant provide a picture of what children need during their first years of life. They emphasize the importance of repeated experiences that allow babies and toddlers to develop a sense of security and trust, feelings that they are safe in the world and fortified for the adventures ahead. Positive early experiences teach babies and young children that they can direct their own care by communicating with their caregivers in a manner that leads to responsive interactions, appropriate stimulation, and nurturing care (Ramey & Ramey, 1999).

Children live for experiences that bathe them in safety and encourage them to master interactions with people and objects. The toddler's mantra of "mine," "me do," and "my way" are all expressions of this natural drive to be competent and do for oneself. Teenagers share this same mantra.

In the early years, children discover through experience how they fit into the world. The quality of the attachment that babies establish with their primary caregivers becomes a powerful theme in what will become the child's life story. Early emotional experiences and the manner in which a child's needs, temperament, and interests match and coexist with those of her parents affect the lives of child and parent alike.

The developmental "dance" between parent and child is a critical part of early experience, whatever the age of the parent. The parent's "steps" in the dance are most beneficial when they are dependable, well timed, and sensitively matched to the baby's. In considering children of adolescent parents, one must wonder how a teenager's typical way of being—often the antithesis of the parental styles just described—can satisfy the primary needs of a child. Yet adolescent parents have the capacity to be just what their children need. Support and positive interventions can make the difference for these young families.

The World of the Teen

> When I was in school and stuff, I wanted to be the best. I was always at the top of my class. When I got pregnant I felt low, you know, I felt like I wasn't going to be nothing. I started looking down. I wouldn't comb my hair and all that other stuff. Physically I was ready, but you know, mentally I really didn't want it. I wish I could go back and rewind time and be a child again. It has been up and down for me, but right now I am back on track. I want to be a psychiatrist. My mother said I would never be no psychiatrist, and I said yes I will. If it takes me the rest of my life, I will do it.—Casandra, 15-year-old mother

Teenage parents who enroll their babies in EHS programs enroll themselves as well. Like most teenagers, adolescents who are parents have a hard time keeping themselves on an emotional even keel. The health and well-being of teenage parents and their infants and toddlers depends in part on the quality of nurturing that is given and received in a context of extreme contradictions. "Typical" teenagers may exude energy or wallow in lethargy. They may be passionate or apathetic. They may demonstrate great care and concern for others yet be extremely self-centered. When teenagers are organized internally—able to pull themselves together—they can be attuned to others. Their success at staying regulated affects their ability to be emotionally balanced, aware of their own and others' feelings, and engaged enough in what they are doing to gain positive reinforcement for their participation. Their babies depend on this.

Although extremes of emotion characterize even a healthy adolescence, poverty and isolation from family and other important adults threaten teenagers' healthy development. Left without consistent and dependable adult relationships, adolescents turn to their peer group to serve as a social conscience (Blum & Rinehart, 2001).

How a teen mother experiences relationships—specifically, those with her own parents and those with the father of the baby and other men in her life—influences how she relates to her own child. The staff members of programs that serve teen parents have an important opportunity and a critical responsibility to provide mothers with positive experiences of being in a relationship with others. An adolescent who feels secure and trusting, loved and loving, competent and successful brings those feelings to her role as a mother. She is only able to give to her child what she herself has experienced.

Teenagers' bodies, attitudes, and experiences often make them hyperaware of their own growing sexuality. The culture in which they live, especially the media, normalizes and idealizes messages about sexual behavior and intimate relationships. From a biological standpoint, girls are entering puberty at progressively earlier ages (Hermann-Giddens et al., 1997; Kipke, 1999). However, early physical maturation is not accompanied by cognitive and emotional maturation, which typically remains childlike.

Psychologically, adolescence has been viewed as a time of separating from the adults in one's family of origin and forging one's own identity. This identity struggle is similar to that of the young toddler. Both are striving for autonomy, both want to do things their own way, and neither can appreciate the enormity of the challenges ahead. Teenagers can feel overwhelmed, helpless, or out of control as they are caught up in an internal struggle to establish their identity in the face of all of the contradictions and role confusion they experience. This struggle can literally take on life-and-death proportions. Rates of adolescent depression, eating disorders, and suicidal ideation and attempts are alarmingly high (Blum, Beuhring, & Rinehart, 2000).

With the advent of brain scanning, scientists have learned more about the physical structure of the adolescent's brain during the years spanning puberty to young adulthood. During this period, the frontal lobes that are responsible for functions such as self-control, judgment, emotional regulation, organization, and planning are going through a transformation. While the brain reorganizes this circuitry for adult processes, the functions performed by the frontal lobes are compromised in the short term (Begley, 2000; Giedd et al., 1999; Kipke, 1999). For teenagers who also happen to be parents, this phenomenon can interfere with the parental traits and behaviors that are most critical for a baby's healthy development.

The World of the Parent–Child Relationship

My daughter was 2 months old before I got into the program. I had postpartum depression. I was so disgusted and aggravated with her, she wouldn't stop crying and she wouldn't sleep. I was constantly under pressure. I just wasn't ready to have a baby. I know I let my parents down. And it hurt because I couldn't do

anything to make them acknowledge me. When I was little, no one acknowledged me. I was never acknowledged as a human being, and it carried on to my
daughter . . . . Now I am so proud to show her [off]. It's like, "Yeah, this is my
baby," and now our relationship is close. I see her as God watching me and
another child, a double child.—April, 16-year-old mother

It is essential that the world inhabited by a teen mother and her child provides the
kind of experiences and emotional nurturing each needs for their own survival and
growth. Parent and child enter the relationship with their own developmental imper-
atives, their own neurological growth to complete, and their own emotions. Each is in
the throes of his or her own life journey, charging ahead, determined to assert an individual identity and compelled by individual needs. Their relationship is, indeed, that
of a double child (Cardone, Gilkerson, & Wechsler, 1998; Wechsler, 1998).

Connected 24/7

Teen parents' relationships with their children offer them the opportunity to "start
over." The idealism that often is a part of the adolescent consciousness can help
teenagers believe that no matter what life has been like for them, they can make it
better for their children. This belief also may enhance their sense of feeling valuable
and important to their children, building a sense of personal worthiness and self-
esteem. Becoming a parent may, in fact, invigorate a sense of purpose in teens.

Numerous studies document difficulties in teenage parent–child communication.
Teen mothers experience greater stress as parents and, in turn, are less sensitive, less
patient, less positive, less verbal, and less able to accurately interpret their child's cues;
they also maintain inappropriate expectations concerning their children's abilities
(Bernstein, Percansky, & Wechsler, 1996). But despite all of this, young parents still
dream of the best for their children. It is a powerful motivating factor and gives parents and programs a place to start.

The desire to do the best for their baby is a motivation that can be galvanized and used
to help direct teen parents' behaviors. But direction alone cannot sustain teen parents
through the highs and lows of parenting. Positive recognition, accurate information
about child development, and consistent reinforcement serve to keep parents
engaged. Young parents especially require repeated, strong reminders that they are
needed by their children and are being effective with their children. Feeling competent allows young parents to experience the joy and gratification of parenting. It can
keep them on track.

Turning a "Me" Thing Into a "We" Thing

I found out when I was 5 months pregnant. I was going through a lot of problems. I was being a really bad girl, a very bad girl. I didn't care, not until I went to the hospital and they told me I was pregnant. Then they let me hear the baby's heartbeat and I said, 'Oh my God.' It's like you have another heart in you. That's when it really clicked in, 'You have a baby in you. Stop it, stop your little running, stop your fooling around, grow up!' Now, I feel good. I learn new things every day from her. Now, when she cries I know what she needs. I feel good. I'm her mom and I know what my baby needs.—Tina, 17-year-old mother

Teenage parents and their babies yearn for similar experiences to spur their individual development. They both need repeated experiences of feeling worthy, capable, understood, and successful in getting what they need. Within the relationship they share, teenage parents and their babies have the potential to experience an essential ingredient for positive development.

Developmental psychologist Susan Goldberg observed that the experiences that adolescent parent and the young child share—and the way in which they communicate—can enhance their mutual feelings of security, value, success, and happiness during a period of rapid development and change for parent and child. Goldberg (1977) identifies the repeated positive interactions that emerge organically from the parent–child relationship as "moments of mutual competence" (Bernstein, Percansky, & Wechsler, 1996). These moments strengthen the parent–child relationship because during such moments, parent and child are having a primary need fulfilled. The more time they spend connected in this way, the greater the opportunities for each of them to give and to get.

In the Frame or Out, the Father Is Always Part of the Picture

A lot of fathers, they don't hang around. They're taking off and forgetting their babies. I don't want to be that kind of father. I want to be there for my daughter. —Cedric, 17-year-old father

Young fathers often come to their new role as ill prepared as young mothers, but the feeling of being needed and loved by one's baby is as profound for a young man as for a young woman. The father–child attachment is a powerful force, one that can support the development of a young man's identity, responsibility, and resilience as a father.

However, many strong forces can begin to pull a father away from his baby, including his relationship with the mother of his child, her extended family, his family and peers, and community pressures (Pruett, 2000). Of these forces, the young father's changing relationship with the mother of the baby is clearly the most influential component in the father's continuing relationship with his child.

A teenage father who is involved at the birth of his child or in the immediate days after the child's birth seems to be enthralled with the baby and how that baby makes him feel. He, too, experiences the birth of himself as a parent. Similar to many parents, he believes that parenting is an opportunity to start over, do better, and right the wrongs in his own life. Early experiences with their babies seem to be profound ones for many young fathers; research has established that the earlier a young dad begins to participate with his child, the longer he participates (Cardone, Gilkerson, & Wechsler, 1998; Pruett, 2000). This finding suggests that even though social policy (as expressed through legislation) assigns specific responsibilities to fathers, it is fathers' loving relationships with their children that gives them reasons to act responsibly.

The World of the Extended Family and Community

Robert Blum's analysis of the National Longitudinal Study of Adolescent Health data led him to recognize that "what emerges most consistently as [a] protective [factor] is the teenager's feeling of connectedness with parents and family. Feeling loved and cared for by parents matters in a big way" (Blum & Rinehart, 2001, p. 31; Kipke, 1999).

As teens become parents, many remain living with their immediate and extended family; others find themselves isolated and alone. Grandparents, aunts, and uncles can provide a tremendous source of support for young parents; however, they can also present challenges. Teen parents have to integrate their new role as parents with the fact that they remain children themselves. They have to find a balance between wanting to be on their own and remaining dependent on their own parents for financial and emotional support.

For a young mother, finding a balance is influenced by her family's beliefs and attitudes, her relationships with the teen father and his family, and her relationships with friends and neighbors, who have their own expectations and opinions. EHS programs must reach out and nurture all of the relationships that encircle the teen parent. They have to send clear messages of support for teen parents attempting to care for their newborns, encourage those who seem to be avoiding this responsibility, and respect the cultural traditions of the families. It is often the EHS staff member who is called on to help all sides navigate tense moments but also to recognize and celebrate young families' successes and achievements.

REACHING TEEN PARENTS THROUGH EARLY HEAD START

A recent national benchmark study, *What Grown-Ups Understand About Child Development* (ZERO TO THREE, CIVITAS, & BRIO Corporation, 2000), raises concern regarding adults' information gaps about children's development and capabilities during the first 3 years of life. Particular attention is drawn to adult parents' inaccurate understanding of how children experience their world, their misguided expectations of children's developmental abilities, and their confusion related to discipline and spoiling. Only one third of the adult parents surveyed stated that they felt prepared for parenthood; another one third felt very unprepared. Parenting is difficult for all mothers and fathers. Without support, experience, knowledge, and resources, teenage parents face even greater difficulties. Programs such as EHS that serve young families can guide young parents and their children safely along the pathways of development.

EHS uses a strengths-based approach to promote individual and relational development. It is focused on education; services are designed to enhance children's learning and development and to improve their long-term academic outcomes. Teenagers' needs in these areas are frequently equal to their young children's needs.

EHS programs provide family support as they bolster family relationships and broaden parents' network of community relationships. The program's approach is intended to enhance, empower, and enable parents' abilities to act in their infants' and their own best interests. Because adolescents' development is driven by the need to do things their own way, this is an ideal match.

At the same time, EHS is a prevention program, promoting the existing protective factors in a family as a strategy to prevent developmental vulnerability later in life. This focus on observed capacities and existing strengths can become a lifeline as teens and their children confront risks during life's ups and downs. This inner sense of "I can do it," "I am worthy," and "I am cared for" becomes a protective factor for infants as well as their teenage parents (Bernstein, Percansky, & Wechsler, 1996).

Programs such as EHS that are successful in supporting parents in their efforts to support their young children provide a working model of positive interactions. In recent years, these programs have shifted from working to prevent or fix problems facing teenage parents to promoting young parents as the most influential and vital resource in their children's as well as their own development (Roth & Brooks-Gunn, 2000). The types and range of services that EHS programs provide encompass a teenage parents' basic needs: nurturing and well-informed one-on-one relationships with adults; accessibility to child care and respite care; positive connections with peers; and access to education, health, employment, and other resources.

Effective programs such as EHS create opportunities that satisfy adolescents' developmental needs, especially the need to see themselves as competent and successful. These programs protect the teenager by providing respectful program structure and clear limits. Ultimately, these programs draw adolescents into meaningful participation with their babies and help lead parents in creating (or enhancing) a positive self-definition not only as parents but as human beings. This approach to program design—built around supportive, meaningful, and respectful relationships and interactions—helps to inform and shape teens' lives.

When an EHS program recruits a teenage family, it must expect, accept, and engage the full range of emotions and behaviors that teenagers bring to programs—"the charming and the alarming." When a teen mother and her young child enroll in a program, they step into a world of opportunities that ideally meets their most pressing needs. As EHS's experience shows, it can be accomplished through home visits or a child-care situation and through positive peer-to-peer interaction.

Connecting Through Home Visits

Consumers identified four themes that together create a picture of what families value in home visitor:

- the ability to offer encouragement and hope;
- being caring and committed to the job;
- teaching skills; and
- the provision of resources.

Parents described a successful home visitor as someone who knows a lot of things, but "doesn't act like she knows everything (acts superior)" (Keim, 2000).

The EHS child development specialist and the family support specialist, both of whom visit families at home, provide teen parents a singularly powerful connection: someone to talk to who truly cares. In addition, program staff members bring critical information to parents and deliver it an accessible manner. Being a parent is a big responsibility for anyone; it is uncertain, ever changing, always challenging, and sometimes overwhelming. Parenting makes you happy, sad, proud, and scared. The teen years evoke the same feelings. Having a helpful adult nearby really matters.

Teenage parents experience many stresses—biological, emotional, economic, social, educational, and parental—that may lead them to experience a periodic sense of disequilibrium. The EHS staff members who visit help to keep these young parents together. They provide some structure and consistency in what may sometimes feel like a chaotic world. They may also help to regulate teen parents so that they can best care for themselves as well as their babies (Robinson & Graves, 1996).

The most effective tool that EHS staff members have is the secure attachment that they establish with the parent. The task is made more difficult in light of teens' past experiences, which may lead them to mistrust those who say they care. EHS staff members who are able to establish a close, collaborative relationship with parents find that this bond is a necessary prerequisite for working together effectively. To prepare staff members for this aspect of their work, EHS home visitors are trained to be patient, focused, and ready to navigate the unpredictable change, chaos, and crisis that often characterize young parents' lives. Staff members approach each front door with the hope that they will make a connection—with the belief that parents care about their children and the knowledge that good relationships can make a difference.

Once inside, home visitors usually begin their visit by asking something akin to, "How have you been since I last saw you?" Often the response is a litany of the stressors affecting parents and children. Staff members hear stories concerning boyfriends, girlfriends, school, work, parents, gangs, violence, and other disappointments. Hearing what is on the teen's mind, staff are presented the opportunity to demonstrate their concern and interest in understanding what life is really like for the young person before them.

Home visitors confront a challenge at this juncture: Can they hear and empathize about these experiences without being driven to direct or fix the situations? This moment is made more challenging by the contradictions that teens often express in talking with adults: "Leave me alone . . . I can take care of myself . . . I don't need you telling me how to live my life," while in the next breath acknowledging "I want you to take care of me . . . I need you to understand what I'm going through . . . If you really cared about me you would know what to do."

Staff members may, quite normally, experience their own contradictions: "I care so much about this young person that I need to make things OK" versus "These are tough times, but I know she has the ability to make it through." Communicating with teens has its own inherent challenges. Teenagers can easily feel violated when adults attempt to direct their lives or "tell them what to do." They can also easily feel abandoned if the adults in their lives don't seem to want to know or care about what is on their minds and in their hearts. Staff members often walk a tightrope when partnering with young families, working hard to be neither too directive nor too detached.

Few experiences are more meaningful than being cared for—and cared about—by another (Pawl, 1995). Teenagers thrive in situations where they are able to express themselves independently while concurrently maintaining a "safe home base"—a supportive relationship in which they feel loved and cared for by someone who believes that these teenage parents are able to do the right thing, for themselves and for their babies. A teenager, then, seeks relationships with caring adults who will "watch my back" but "not be in my face."

When home visitors are able to hear and empathize with the teen's experiences without being drawn into the tumult of her life, they are better able to understand the teen's needs and can ultimately be more available as a resource and guide. Home visitors are challenged to attend to the teenager's present state and circumstances while also focusing on the child's needs. Typically, home visits are organized to focus on promoting the growth and development of the child, which opens up many opportunities for the young parent to feel successful.

This need to feel successful has important implications. When teenage parents provide the kind of care and nurturing that meets their children's needs and promotes their children's development, they are building their own sense of self-confidence, self-esteem, and competence. When home visitors use a strengths-based approach (i.e., shifting the focus from the parents' limitations to the parents' accomplishments and abilities), teenagers experience moments of mutual competence with their children. It is an approach that encourages long-term positive changes in parent–child relationships.

Extending Goldberg's mutual competency model, one might ask what kind of relationship between home visitors and parents is good for the development of the teenager and her child. The answer seems to be that when home visitors engage young parents in a way that results in teens feeling secure, valued, successful, and happy, the experience encourages and supports families' positive development. It becomes the home visitor's most important function during every encounter to articulate and amplify the positive behaviors and personal strengths that they see in the parent, particularly in relation to how the parent nurtures her child. When this is the nature of the working relationship between home visitors and parents, teenagers develop a sense of "I can do it . . . I am worthy . . . I am able . . . someone believes in me." Home visitors, too, return to their program filled with a sense of hope and promise.

Teenagers live a much too busy and dynamic life to limit their program activities to the home. Consequently, EHS and similar programs have a multitude of opportunities to enter into teens' lives in a supportive and nurturing manner. Embracing the adolescent parent as a multifaceted member of society opens up the possibility of diverse avenues of program involvement.

Connecting Through Child Care

For many teenagers, the need to complete high school or start college initiates what may be a teen parent's first separation from her child. Furthermore, welfare reform involves new pressure to participate in work or work-related activities, even when children are under age 1. These expectations force young parents to decide who will care for their children in their absence (Alan Guttmacher Institute, 1994; Congressional Budget Office, 1990).

EHS programs help young parents find and maintain high-quality extended family care, family day care, or center-based care for their children. Regardless of the setting in which care takes place, EHS has an obligation to ensure that child-care arrangements are of good quality and help promote child development. For teens, this care often is provided in alternative high schools, which are established by school systems to meet the educational needs of young people in challenging circumstances (see Box 7-1). Accessible and high-quality care for infants allows teens the time to do what is important to them and their futures. It also allows them to experience the pride that comes from knowing their young children are receiving safe, loving, stimulating, and nurturing care.

There is another reward as well. Over time, EHS-quality care that supports the mutual competence of children and their parents becomes one more positive and formative relationship for the teenager. When teens believe that their children are well cared for, and when they themselves feel cared for by EHS staff, they learn that relationships with others can be a source of joy, satisfaction, and personal growth.

EHS child-care providers recognize that when they care for children, they must partner with parents. When parents are adolescents, providers are often called on to support the teenagers as well, so they can effectively work together in the best interests of the children. EHS caregivers may be counted among the most meaningful adults in a teen parent's expanding world of relationships.

BOX 7-1 Meeting Teens Where They Live and Where They Learn: Shasta Early Head Start

Shasta Early Head Start in northern California operates two Infant Parenting Centers in alternative high schools: one at North Valley High School in Anderson, and one at Mountain Lakes High School in Shasta Lake City. Stephanie Barrett, supervisor of the Mountain Lakes High School site, says that often the solution to poor teen-to-baby communication is demonstrating its opposite: "We really role model for parents. We talk to children through everything, 'OK, I'm going to change your diaper. Does the wipe feel wet? Isn't it good to feel clean?' Parents hear us talking to them, and we educate them on the importance of talking lovingly to a child. We also notice all the positives, 'Wow. Look at the way she smiled at you when you said that. She wants to make eye contact with you. She really loves you.' Believe me, every positive thing that a teen mom does, we are going to notice it. We do weekly staffings and a training on adolescence, and it comes up all the time: 'Have we praised the parents enough? Are we doing enough to encourage them?' Sincere, positive reinforcement is a big part of working with teens. You can offer the best infant care in the world, but if not you're not helping the parent, you're not helping the child."

Jill Brenner, supervisor of the Shasta EHS North Valley High School site, concurs: "We have one parent who has power and control issues with her child, who is an emerging toddler and knows what she wants to do. One of the hardest things was feeding, because the child wants to feed herself and the mom wanted to do it for her. Our caregivers addressed this by inviting the mom to sit next to the child and just watch her during a meal—looking for cues when she wants to be helped. This child opens her mouth and says 'Ah' when she wants to be fed by Mom. She also holds a fork in one hand and eats with the other. When she puts the fork down, you know she is done feeding herself and may want help to continue eating. Mom has come a long way. You can read the success on her face when she and her child enjoy a meal together."

Each Shasta Early Head Start center serves 16 children—8 infants and 8 toddlers. Parents drop off their tots before classes, returning frequently during the day for meals and playtime. Both centers are flexible about parents' comings and goings, and the high school teachers help their students carve out convenient times during the day to be with their children. When an infant is nursing, teachers are accustomed to a mom departing algebra at will for a loving one-plus-one session with baby.

Parents and grandparents alike are invited to drop by, volunteer in the center, and attend parent meetings. Shasta staff members also encounter grandparents during visits to teen homes, which generally occur three times a year. Barrett acknowledges that the program must walk a fine line in supporting the entire household and promoting positive identity formation in the teen: "After all, the parents are coming from homes where they are still the child. It's hard to manage the different roles. If parent–grandparent tension is an ongoing issue, we'll send a family worker on a home visit to address the problem. For example, sometimes grandparents will be holding to old rules

continued

on child-proofing that say children have to learn not to touch breakable or dangerous things. The family worker can work with the parent and the 'parent's parent' to brainstorm a toy corner filled with Tupperware or to child-proof the house together."

Although Shasta staff members often work with both parent and grandparent, they also give the teen parent time alone. Barrett explains, "It's important to say to the teen, 'We want to know what you think,' because sometimes grandmas will already have information they want to share, and we want to validate the teen mom's ideas and knowledge about parenting."

Source: Mary Bogle, personal communication, March 2002.

Respite care, a place where parents can find temporary shelter for their children, is invaluable to young parents as a haven of safety in times of crisis. It can also prevent a crisis by providing a safe place for parents to temporarily leave their children during difficult periods when they may need time to care for themselves.

All of these caregiving settings create expanded social circles for very young children as they make new friends. The depth of these first friendships becomes apparent as toddlers play, learn, and grow together. The same can be said for parents' relationships with providers and other parents in the EHS environment.

Connecting Through Positive Peer-to-Peer Interactions

Adolescence is often lived as a group experience. Involvement and acceptance by peers is a driving force in the lives of teenagers. Programs that offer positive peer activities provide indispensable opportunities for teenage parents to develop meaningful peer relationships that fulfill a primary social and developmental need—to be understood and accepted. Parenting groups and parent–child playgroups are a valuable service in EHS and other family support programs. They keep teenagers involved, in a social sense as well as in their own ongoing discovery of themselves as parents.

Programs can become an even more integral part of the lives of young parents when they address other needs and interests—for example, through tutoring, mentoring, and General Educational Development (GED) services that match the adolescent's individual learning style with his learning needs. In addition, group activities that call for creative expression, physical movement, and community involvement all build on the natural enthusiasm of teenagers. Health care for children and parents that is sensitive to the unique needs of adolescents also helps to keep these young families safe and healthy.

BOX 7-2 Welcoming the Next Generation of Parents: The Confederated Tribes of Warm Springs Early Head Start

The Confederated Tribes of Warm Springs in Oregon honors the communitarian needs of the young parent in its teens-only, home-based Early Head Start program. Under the guidance of program staff, the young people who are enrolled develop relationships with key adults who teach them about the culture of the four tribes represented on the reservation. In the process, the culture and rituals of child rearing are passed on to the next generation, and each teen parent's place in the circle of life is accepted and honored.

Says Julie Quaid, director of the Early Childhood Education Department, Confederated Tribes of Warm Springs: "We believe that we all were created by and connected to the mother. The grandmothers have a special role because they keep the connection to the mother alive. She will save the baby's umbilical cord stump after it dries off. She may craft it into a special good luck charm, a connection from where we came. Grandmothers also make the baby's first baby board, and they are the first to place the infant on the board for sleep. The relationships and connections we help build here are the foundation of our work, and we hope they become the foundation for the lives of the teens and their babies."

Source: Julie Quaid, personal communication, August 2001.

LOOKING TOWARD THE FUTURE

Although EHS's work with teen parents is promising, many challenges remain in serving this unique population. Additional research and discussion among programs is needed to learn more about questions such as

- What specific activities appear to be providing the best results with teen parents, for overall family functioning as well as child development?

- Are there differences between programs that serve a large percentage of teen parents and programs that serve only a few teens?

- In what ways can EHS programs serve as a national laboratory to ensure effective services in all programs that serve teen parents?

- What programs or activities work best in reaching teen fathers? in serving a range of cultural groups? in supporting the grandparenting role as well as the role of the young parent?

Box 7-3 Missy, Travis, and Jade

Missy waves to everyone as she strolls into the Discovery High School Early Head Start Infant/Toddler Center, also known as "the Lab." To the casual observer, the sight of Missy may at first seem incongruous. Maybe it's the spiky, bright blond hair and baggy track suit vying with the sweet-16 grin on her face. Maybe it's the toddler balanced on Missy's hip in that pose so common to confident moms everywhere—a woman's posture struck by a girl.

On the wall behind Missy is a large collage titled "My Life Before and After Jade." On one side is a patchwork of photos of Missy in the years prior to the birth of her daughter—not the images of her enjoying football parties and wedding receptions with other young adults that one might expect, but mostly pictures of a child in hair ribbons and Halloween costumes. On the other side is a collection of newborn photos surrounding the words "Sweet Life." Missy points to the glittery winged child holding up Jade's half of the collage, "That's the Fairy of Pure Joy. It's really cute 'cause she also has Down Syndrome." Just like Jade.

After engaging in an extended bye-bye wave and peek-a-boo routine with her child, Missy scoots out to class. Jade's primary caregiver, Linda, who has been with the baby since she was 3 days old, calls out "See you at lunch" as she settles Jade in for breakfast. Later, around nap time, Travis (Jade's father) comes to visit. Hands with wrists wrapped in chain-and-leather bracelets cuddle Jade as he lulls her to sleep in an enormous rocking chair. Although Dad's eyes, ears, nose, and mouth are pierced with fierce-looking studs, the faces of him and his daughter are peaceful. When Jade's sighs signal full slumber, a Lab caregiver guides Travis in the art of wrapping the child in a blanket and laying her gently down, without waking, on a sleeping pad.

Toward the end of the day, Missy returns to the Lab to work on developmental goals with Jade and the children of her classmates—gaining competence as a mother while earning vocational preparation credits as a student. The Lab's physical therapist demonstrates how she can support Jade's trunk and legs in the toddler's efforts to pull up on a carpeted cube. Low muscle tone, a problem common to children with Down Syndrome, is a challenge that Jade must struggle against to achieve enough stability and strength to walk. Walking is a big goal for mother and child.

The day will end with a support group during which the young moms compare notes on their children's eating habits and cold patterns and discuss the latest triumphs and travails with parents and boyfriends. At 3:30 p.m., it's home to dinner with Jade's grandparents, homework, and a few lullabies before lights out. Tomorrow they'll do it all over again.

Source: Early Head Start National Resource Center, 2001.

- How can EHS build on its efforts to promote education and long-term self-sufficiency?

- How can community resources be maximized to develop effective full-day services for teens in school or in the workforce?

Many teenage parents work hard to balance attention to their own needs and those of their children. In programs such as EHS, they learn how to provide loving and responsible care while coping with the relentless demands of being a parent, a teenager, and more often than not, a student as well as an employee. They do this in a world that may or may not be loving and supportive, a world that often holds powerful stereotypes of what "teen parents" are all about. Young mothers and fathers face these challenges and more. But they also retain a joyous energy and powerful optimism for the future. These young people, like all parents, share a dream for their children: that they will grow up to be happy and healthy and enjoy a life filled with opportunity and success. EHS helps parents ensure that this dream is one that comes true.

REFERENCES

Administration for Children and Families. (2002). *Making a difference in the lives of infants and toddlers and their families: The impacts of Early Head Start.* Washington, DC: U.S. Department of Health and Human Services.

Alan Guttmacher Institute. (1994). *Sex and America's teenagers.* New York: Author.

Begley, S. (2000, May 8). Mind expansion: Inside the teenage brain. *Newsweek,* p. 68.

Bernstein, V., Percansky, C., & Wechsler, N. (1996). *Strengthening families through strengthening relationships: The Ounce of Prevention Fund Developmental Training and Support Program.* Mahwah, NJ: Lawrence Erlbaum Associates.

Blum, R. W., & Rinehart, P. M. (2001). *Reducing the risk: Connection that makes a difference in the lives of youth.* Minneapolis: University of Minnesota, Division of General Pediatrics and Adolescent Health.

Blum, R. W., Beuhring, T., & Rinehart, P. M. (2000). *Protecting teens: Beyond race, income, and family structure.* Minneapolis: University of Minnesota, Division of General Pediatrics and Adolescent Health.

Cardone, I., Gilkerson L., & Wechsler, N. (1998). *The community-based FANA teen mothers, fathers, and their infants: Promoting attachment and mutual growth.* Chicago: The Ounce of Prevention Fund.

Congressional Budget Office. (1990). *National Longitudinal Survey of Youth (1979–1985)*. Washington, DC: Author.

Early Head Start National Resource Center. (2001). *Families speak: The Early Head Start experience* [Videotape shown at the 2001 Head Start and Child Care Birth to Three Institute]. Washington, DC: U.S. Department of Health and Human Services and ZERO TO THREE.

Giedd, J. N., Blumenthal, J., Jeffries, N. O., Castellanos, F. X., Liu, H., Zijdenbos, A., et al. (1999). Brain development during childhood and adolescence: A longitudinal MRI study. *Nature Neuroscience, 2*(10), 861–863.

Goldberg, S. (1977). Social competence in infancy: A model of infant–parent interaction. *Merrill-Palmer Quarterly, 23*, 163–177.

Hermann-Giddens, M. E., Slora, E. J., Wasserman, R. C., Bourdony, C. J., Bhapkar, M. V., Kock, G. C., et al. (1997). Secondary sexual characteristics and menses in young girls seen in office practice: A study from the Pediatric Research in Office Settings Network. *Pediatrics, 99*(4), 505–512.

Keim, A. L. (2000). *Finding and supporting the best: Using the insights of home visitors and consumers in hiring, training, and supervision*. Washington, DC: ZERO TO THREE.

Kipke, M. D. (Ed.). (1999). *Adolescent development and the biology of puberty: Forum on adolescence*. Washington, DC: National Academy of Sciences.

National Campaign to Prevent Teenage Pregnancy, The. (2002). *Not just another single issue: Teen pregnancy prevention's link to other critical social issues*. Washington, DC: Author. Retrieved from www.teenpregnancy.org in May 2004.

Pawl, J. (1995). The therapeutic relationship as human connectedness: Being held in another's mind. *Zero to Three, 15*(4), 1–5.

Pruett, K. D. (2000). *Fatherneed: Why father care is as essential as mother care for your child*. New York: Tree Press.

Ramey, C. T., & Ramey, S. L. (1999). *Right from birth: Building your child's foundation for life*. New York: Goddard Press.

Robinson J. L., & Graves, L. (1996). Supporting emotional regulation and emotional availability through home visiting. *Zero to Three, 17*(1), 31–35.

Roth, J., & Brooks-Gunn, J. (2000). What do adolescents need for healthy development? Implications for youth policy. *Social Policy Report, 14*(1), 1–19.

Wechsler, N. (1998). *Hand in hand: Teen parents and their babies.* Washington, DC: National Organization on Adolescent Pregnancy, Parenting and Prevention Network.

Wechsler, N. (2004). *Teen mothers, fathers, and their infants: Promoting attachment and mutual growth.* Chicago, IL: Ounce of Prevention Fund.

ZERO TO THREE, CIVITAS, & BRIO Corporation. (2000). *What grown-ups understand about child development: A national benchmark survey.* Danbury, CT: Authors.

ABOUT THE AUTHOR

Nick Wechsler is assistant director for program development for The Ounce of Prevention Fund in Chicago. He has written or coauthored several articles on working with adolescent parents in an effort to promote their infants' and their own development. He coauthored the training manual, *The Community-based FANA, Teen Mothers, Fathers, and Their Infants: Promoting Attachment and Mutual Growth* (1998).

CHAPTER 8

FIRST RELATIONSHIPS: INFANT MENTAL HEALTH IN EARLY HEAD START

JoAnne E. Solchany and Kathryn E. Barnard

"Can I trust you?"

"Will you keep me safe?"

"Will you be there for me?"

"Can you take care of me?"

These are the questions that babies might ask as they leave the womb and enter the arms of their parents. Babies come into this world completely dependent on their caregivers—for safety and protection, for food and physical care, and for love and nurturance. For babies to flourish—indeed, even to survive—they need loving human interaction and stimulation as much as physical care. They need mothers and fathers who can say "Yes!" to their newborn's first question, and "I'll try my best" to the others.

Children develop in the context of relationships. The Advisory Committee on Services for Families With Infants and Toddlers summarized more than 3 decades of research in its 1994 statement, which provided the rationale for Early Head Start (EHS): "The child–caregiver relationships with the mother, father, grandparent, and other caregivers are critical for providing infants and toddlers support, engagement, continuity, and emotional nourishment necessary for healthy development, and the development of healthy attachments. Within the context of caregiving relationships, the infant builds a sense of what is expected, what feels right in the world, as well as skills and incentives for social turn-taking, reciprocity, and cooperation" (U.S. Department of Health and Human Services, 1994).

Similarly, in *From Neurons to Neighborhoods*, the Committee on Integrating the Science of Early Childhood Development of the National Research Council, Institute of Medicine (2000), concluded, "A vast store of research . . . has confirmed that what young children learn, how they react to the events and people around them, and what they expect from themselves and others are deeply affected by their relationships with parents, the behavior of parents, and the environment of the home in which they live" (p. 226).

For babies and toddlers, the relationship with their primary caregiver—usually the mother—plays an especially significant role in their mental well-being. This is why a mother's ability to keep her mind on her baby (rather than on her own troubled past or present) is such a powerful indicator of strength or fragility in a child's caregiving environment. A mother who can put her child's needs before her own is able to provide the nurturance that a child needs to establish a healthy sense of well-being. As the baby enters the mother's arms, that baby should also move to the forefront of the mother's mind.

This chapter looks at infant mental health from a relationship perspective. It describes, in some detail, patterns of interaction between babies and their mothers; these interactions, repeated over time, create unique relationships. It also discusses how adult relationships in EHS—between staff members and parents, and between home visitors and their supervisors—can protect and strengthen mother–infant relationships. In addressing these issues, the chapter refers to the growing body of clinical and scholarly research on infant mental health that underlies sound program design and practice in EHS and other infant–family programs.

Within this chapter are examples of women, babies, and program staff from EHS programs and other community-based intervention programs serving infants, toddlers, and their families. These stories demonstrate a range of risk scenarios and interventions that one might encounter in an EHS program. They also exhibit many of the challenges, as well as the successes, found throughout the programs.[1]

THREE PATTERNS OF INTERACTION

The stories of Sylvia and her son Rocko, of Erin and her daughter Katie, and of Marla and her children Lisa and Philip show how different patterns of interaction develop and come to characterize mother–child relationships as well as how babies' development proceeds within these relationships. All three mothers were pregnant and single when they enrolled in an EHS program that offered weekly home visits and group "socializations" twice a month. Each mother worked with a single home visitor during her pregnancy and her baby's first year.

Sylvia and Rocko

Sylvia was 24 years old, single, and pregnant with her first baby when she enrolled in EHS. Her apartment, though sparsely furnished, was quiet, clean, and organized; she was gradually accumulating a stock of baby toys and equipment. During her pregnancy, Sylvia would invite Gretchen, her home visitor, to sit with her at her clean, uncluttered kitchen table; she eagerly examined the materials about pregnancy, childbirth, and child development that Gretchen brought.

Rocko was born a healthy 8-pound, 6-ounce baby with no difficulties. He was quiet, seeming to cry only when hungry—often not even coming to a full cry as Sylvia responded quickly to his little fusses, groans, and grunts. When Gretchen came to visit, Sylvia always had Rocko in her arms, either sitting on the sofa or in a rocking chair. As she talked with Gretchen, Sylvia would intermittently speak to Rocko in a cooing voice, asking him if he was hungry or telling him she loved him.

Rocko grew steadily and had no medical problems. By 6 months of age he was bright, alert, and interactive. He would frequently burst into laughter over a playful look from his mother or Gretchen. By 12 months of age he was walking, playing with toys on his own for short periods, following his mother around the apartment, and dancing to children's music she played regularly on the stereo.

Erin and Katie

Erin, the mother of five children, had been diagnosed and treated for depression several times before she became involved in EHS. When Erin's youngest child, Katie, was born, she had a great deal of difficulty breast-feeding, which was extremely important to Erin. Her struggle to breast-feed her daughter quickly led Erin into another bout with depression. Erin was not able to sleep—she lay awake worrying and ruminating all night—mostly about Katie's not being as close to her as her other children because of the breast-feeding problems. Erin's appetite nearly vanished; she seemed unable to take care of herself, rarely washing her hair; and she stopped cleaning her home.

Yet despite the problems Erin was experiencing, Katie was thriving. So were Erin's other children. Erin seemed to use all of her available energy to care for her children. They were clean, well fed, involved in school activities, and actively engaged in mental health treatment around issues related to the domestic violence they had witnessed between Erin and their biological father. In observing their interactions, the home visitor noted that Erin seemed to be able to "pull it together" for her baby. Her interactions were loving, nurturing, gentle, and focused. She talked frequently to Katie, describing what was happening within their interaction ("Mommy's going to change your diaper now"), as well as describing her daughter's emotions ("What are these tears about Katie, are you sad? Did you miss Mommy?").

Marla, Philip, and Lisa

Marla was the mother of Philip, 30 months, and Lisa, 14 months. Each child was delayed in several domains of development. Marla had a long history of homelessness, disconnection with her family, and a pattern of depression. Her personal hygiene was extremely poor. Her home was cluttered with fast-food bags; food was smeared on the walls and floor; and soiled diapers and half-full bottles were scattered throughout the small apartment that she had only recently acquired. Marla seemed unable to interact with her children. She seemed frozen in one particular easy chair, focused on the television. The EHS home visitor would often find Marla in her pajamas, her children strapped into their high chairs, and the television on, regardless of the time of day. Marla seemed oblivious to what was going on with her children.

Philip abused himself by biting himself and hitting his head on walls. He was often aggressive in his interactions with people—spitting at them or kicking their legs. He seemed to have no concept of "another child" when in potential play situations and would engage with toys only fleetingly, soon disengaging by throwing or beating the toy. Lisa, 14 months old, seemed essentially "empty." She made only fleeting eye contact, demonstrated signs of tactile defensiveness (splaying her fingers, refusing to touch things, unable to grasp certain objects), and seemed emotionally flat, with no sense of joy.

As different as Sylvia, Erin, Marla, and their children are from one another, their circumstances are equally common in EHS and other community-based programs serving families with infants and toddlers. Indeed, on an enrollment form for a service program, the mothers might look almost identical—single mothers in their twenties, high school graduates, who live in a low-income neighborhood and have few sources of informal social support. But what is it about the feelings and connections between these mothers and their babies? For Marla, trying to take care of her children as well as herself is a struggle. She manages to provide a bare minimum in food and shelter, but she seems unable to provide the nurturance, protection, and stimulation that her children should be able to count on. Her thoughts are far from her children.

Sylvia, in contrast, thinks about and plans for Rocko all the time—she did so even before he was born. She responds to her baby quickly, easily, and creatively, providing Rocko with the nurturance he needs to grow and develop into a healthy, interactive, happy toddler. Erin struggles successfully to focus on Katie's needs. Her children thrive even though her mental health continues to deteriorate.

These stories also suggest the ways in which babies' development reflects the mothering they receive, which is a large component of infant mental health. Lisa is lethargic and is beginning to avoid—rather than seek—human interaction. Philip exhibits significant delays in his social development, alternating between bouts of external aggression and self-abuse. Katie is thriving despite her mother's mental health problems, most likely due to the mediating influence of maternal protective factors such as knowledge of baby's needs, good social and verbal skills, and a strong commitment to her children. Katie remains at risk for future problems, however, without intervention. Rocko, on the other hand, shows pleasure in interaction, seeks it out, is physically active, and shows a range of emotion from his first days onward. He is solidly connected to his mother and responds joyfully to the emotional warmth and richness of experience that she offers.

RISK FACTORS AND WAYS OF INTERVENING

Home visitors—as well as child-care providers, primary health care workers, and other community-based infant–family practitioners—must constantly consider how best to support positive parent–infant relationships (like that of Sylvia and Rocko), shore up situations that may become problematic later (like that of Erin and Katie), and intervene in troubled relationships (like that of Marla, Philip, and Lisa). They ask themselves

- What can we do to prevent the development of mental health problems?

- What can we do to intervene when we identify the potential for development of infant mental health problems?

- How do we handle a problem that is already present?

Infant mental health practice encompasses a continuum of activities and services designed to respond to these questions. Several ways to approach infant mental health have been used. These programs can be viewed in terms of their focus: parent-based, focused on the teaching of parenting and caregiving skills; child-based, working directly with the child on developmental issues; and relationship-based, working within the context of the relationship.

Many individual risk factors—and, more importantly, perhaps, the cumulative effect of multiple risks facing a child and family—may contribute to problems in infant mental health. However, a disturbed relationship between the primary caregiver and the child has been identified as one of the most significant risk factors and one of the pathways most amenable to intervention. Several recent studies lend support to this view (Carter, Garrity-Rokous, Chazan-Cohen, Little, & Briggs-Gowan, 2001; DelCarmen-Wiggins & Carter, 2001; Keren, Fledman, & Tyano, 2001; Pawl &

Lieberman, 1997; Reznick & Schwartz, 2001; Shaw, Owens, Giovannelli, & Winslow, 2001; Spieker, Solchany, McKenna, DeKlyen, & Barnard, 1999; Thomas & Guskin, 2001; ZERO TO THREE, 1994). In addition to relational risk factors, Keren et al. (2001) found parental psychopathology to be a leading risk factor in the development of infant mental health problems.

Maternal depression has been identified as a major factor leading to infant mental health problems. However, mothers with depression provide a range of caregiving experiences—even good ones—to their young children, and the developmental outcomes among these children vary. Although science does not yet understand all the mechanisms at work, researchers know that depression can be expressed differently in each person; that individual life circumstances are important to consider; and that many women who are diagnosed with depression may have additional, sometimes unidentified, psychopathology that may worsen the experience for them (Carter et al., 2001).

Mothers who face multiple challenges typically need individualized, multilayered interventions so that they can successfully nurture their infants and toddlers. When progress is slow, children need support to protect their developmental progress. Home visitors can help coordinate the meeting of the family's immediate needs, they can steadily work with the baby or child with the goal of keeping development on track, and they can serve as a source of support for the mother and other family members. When the mother is facing major mental health issues herself, she may need intervention outside the realm of any single program or individual home visitor. Referrals to persons or programs specializing in treating depression and other mental health disorders are important. The child's developmental needs may require referral to centers treating developmental delays.

For the mother who cannot seem to connect with mental health services for herself or her child, a therapeutic day care or child development center—where the child is in the care of others for a portion of each day or week—may provide support to the child and parent. Out-of-home care may also provide alternative avenues to support and enhance the child's developmental progress. Fathers should be strongly encouraged and supported to be there for both mom and baby. Coaching fathers in ways that they can be most helpful is an important program component. Despite program staff's best efforts, however, some families have difficulty accepting and using the services offered—leaving home visitors and caregivers with the taxing role of lending support and encouragement until such time as the families are ready to accept more intensive help.

The stories of Marla and Erin illustrate many of these points. For Marla, intervention consisted of getting her children into a full-time, therapeutic child-care setting, getting periodic respite care, and providing in-home physical and occupational therapy for the children. Marla was offered counseling and was encouraged to begin a course of antidepressant medication but refused both. She did accept a home aide, who helped her set up a cleaner home and a regular schedule for the family. The children improved greatly, even though Marla remained "stuck."

Intervention for Erin initially involved twice-weekly respite care for the children so that she could begin therapy. Initially, Erin was not comfortable leaving her children with someone else—even for 2-hour blocks—but agreed to try it for 2 months. She began psychotherapy and was also placed on medications. Several weeks later, Erin told her home visitor that she "didn't know people could feel this good." Her energy increased, her interactions with friends and other adults increased, and she joined the parent council of her EHS program. Keeping her home clean was still a struggle, but all of her children were doing well. Katie seemed well connected with her mother.

To work effectively with Marla, Erin, and their children, the home visitor needed to be aware of relationship-based, parent-based, and child-based intervention approaches; to mobilize a wide range of community services as needed; and to use her own positive relationship with the mothers as the context within which all interventions occurred. She needed to find a match between the strengths and needs that she observed in the families, the resources that were available in the community, and the mothers' readiness to avail themselves of services.

EARLY HEAD START AND INFANT MENTAL HEALTH

Infant mental health is emerging as a central focus of preventive and early intervention programs for children in the zero-to-three years, particularly within EHS. Responding to the needs of program staff and at the behest of the Early Head Start Technical Work Group, the Head Start Bureau convened a national meeting in October 2000 to bring together EHS parents, staff and technical assistance providers, federal staff and partners, and experts from the infant mental health field to talk about the role of EHS, Migrant Head Start, and their child-care partners in supporting the mental health needs of children and families (Administration on Children, Youth, and Families, 2000). The Head Start Bureau used input gathered at the meeting to launch the Early Head Start Mental Health Initiative, which encompasses programmatic as well as research components. The goal of the initiative is to improve the quality and availability of comprehensive mental health supports for very young children and their families—those served by EHS and their community partners.

The initiative is guided by a task force of 29 individuals from the infant–family field, including EHS program staff and parents as well as federal representatives from the Child Care Bureau, Head Start Bureau, and Office of Special Education Programs (Rachel Chazan-Cohen, personal communication to Mary Bogle, August 2002; Chazan-Cohen, Jerald, & Stark, 2001). The task force participates in work groups to conduct the various activities of the initiative and to build consensus on infant mental health issues and needs throughout the field. The Early Head Start National Resource Center supports three activities of the initiative:

- gather and share data on family perceptions of the emotional well-being of infants and toddlers;

- provide a battery of resources—including guidance documents, intense training, and follow-up consultation—to program caregivers and administrators on how to meet the comprehensive mental health needs of infants, toddlers, and families; and

- raise awareness among state and local stakeholders, and among a range of helping professionals at large, regarding the mental health and emotional development needs of very young children.

In addition, the Administration on Children, Youth, and Families (ACYF), Head Start's umbrella agency, is sponsoring a range of research projects designed to study the mental health needs of children under age 5 and to improve programmatic efforts to prevent and intervene in mental health problems (Rachel Chazan-Cohen, personal communication, September 2002). Particular to EHS are program-wide research efforts, such as the collection of indicators on child and family social–emotional well-being in the Early Head Start National Research and Evaluation Project. Local study efforts linked to the national study are also focused on mental health issues, including depression, attachment, and antisocial activities.

The Early Promotion and Intervention Research Consortium, funded in September 2002, seeks to develop and test approaches for supporting the mental health of infants and toddlers and their families within the EHS program. It builds on prior efforts in preschool Head Start, including the Head Start Mental Health Research Consortium, a collaboration between ACYF and the National Institute of Mental Health that was designed to develop and test state-of-the art techniques for preventing, identifying, and treating children's mental health disorders within a Head Start context.

EHS programs are translating the technical assistance and research described above into a wide variety of promotion, prevention, and treatment strategies to address the mental health needs of infants, toddlers, and families. Supported by a host of requirements found in the Head Start Program Performance Standards (*Head Start program performance standards and other regulations*, 2002), promotion and prevention efforts largely focus on supporting and enhancing the parent–child relationship and the care-giver–child relationship through strategies such as regular home visits, low teacher-to-child ratios, screening procedures that ensure early identification, and practices that build trust between caregiver and infant. (For more details about these standards, strategies, and practices, see Chapters 1 and 5.)

In addition, many EHS directors are focusing on the creation of organizational environments that support infant mental health. Most prevalent among the strategies (Emde, Bertacchi, & Mann, 2001) are

- reflective supervision, which is the process by which supervisors spend significant one-on-one time with supervisees to help them share dilemmas, see alternatives, plan activities, extend empathy, and build their capacity to support infant and family mental health;

- access to an infant mental health specialist who can provide reflective supervision, train staff, engage in parental guidance and developmental counseling, or occasionally offer relationship-focused therapy to parent and child; and

- in-service trainings or support for continuing education for EHS staff people, particularly home visitors, so that they can be better able to recognize and meet the mental health needs of very young children and their families.

In sum, infant mental health is best thought of as an integral part of EHS and other comprehensive community programs, rather than as individual referrals to outside agencies or providers. To promote and protect infant mental health, EHS and other community program staff members learn to recognize what a mentally healthy relationship between a parent and an infant looks like, to observe and assess the interactions between parents and young children, and to work with parents to strengthen or repair their relationships with their babies and toddlers. Such relationship-based work occurs during moment-by-moment opportunities for creating attunements between parent and child in feeding, play, and caregiving. Home visitors also need to be aware of parent-based and child-based intervention approaches and be able to mobilize a wide range of community services as needed. To these ends, child-care staff, home visitors, and family advocates work in concert with mental health professionals as co-architects of the growing infant mental health component of EHS and other community programs.

The Parent–Child Communication Coaching Program

What EHS staff and other well-trained intervention providers know is that the essence of the work lies within the parent–child relationship. The baby must develop trust with the primary caregiver. The baby must feel confident enough to explore the world, and safe and secure as a part of the world. To provide security for a baby, the parent must see the baby as a priority—the baby's needs should come first. This happens only when the parent can keep the baby in mind throughout the daily routines of life.

We (the authors of this chapter) have developed and used a multilevel program approach in an EHS program, the Parent–Child Communication Coaching (P-CCC) Program. The P-CCC Program is designed to focus on mental health promotion and prevention from pregnancy through the first 3 years. It involves "coaching" the parent–child relationship and interaction through the use of specific activities and videotape intervention.

In the context of efforts to help staff of EHS and other community-based programs enhance parent–child interaction and parent–child attachment as well as optimal mental health, we identified caregiving behaviors during pregnancy and four periods of early development that we believe, based on child development literature and our experience, promote positive interaction between parent and child and thereby promote good mental health for both. We designed P-CCC as an intervention approach that was anchored in specific, developmentally appropriate, and scientifically grounded activities that would appeal to participants and that home visitors could be expected to implement during each period of development.

Pregnancy

It is desirable that the pregnant woman be aware of the physical presence of her unborn child. Acknowledgment that a child is growing inside her womb is the beginning of a lifelong connection between a mother and her child (even if the child does not survive or if someone else raises the child). Acknowledging the unborn child is, however, only the beginning of the psychological work of pregnancy; the woman must also begin to imagine what the baby will be like and what becoming a mother will require of her. These maternal behaviors significantly affect the relationship that she will establish with her child after birth. If a mother has difficulty connecting with her baby before birth, she is highly likely to continue experiencing difficulties within her relationship—in other words, she will have a difficult time keeping the baby "on her mind."

Other issues also come into play during pregnancy that may relate to the development of the mother–child relationship. For example, the type and amount of support available to the woman during her pregnancy has a significant effect on the mother's capacity to relate to her baby. A woman with little or no support becomes at high risk for difficulties transitioning into motherhood and in relating to her child (Rubin, 1975; Solchany, 2001). Among the mothers in our EHS study, fewer than 3 in 10 said they had a supportive partner or husband during their pregnancy.

This low percentage is most likely related to several issues, including the difficulties that these mothers may have in identifying what they need, asking for what they need, or accepting the help and support they desire—as well as the difficulties that fathers may have in figuring out how to be supportive and how to provide the necessary help. EHS programs address some of these issues by promoting the significance of fathers in the family and by actively encouraging the participation of fathers in the program. (For more details about father involvement in EHS, see Chapter 6.) Such strategies can support children and families in the long and short run. In comparing two groups of EHS mothers—equal in terms of childhood history of trauma, loss, and chaos— those whose fathers were involved throughout their childhoods tended to develop better coping and interaction skills within the program. This study suggests that the presence of their own fathers served as a buffer from these mothers' early negative experiences (Solchany, Spieker, & Barnard, 1999).

Some of the behaviors we like to see in women during their pregnancy and the supports we believe are important to them and their unborn children include

- being aware of the presence and activity of their unborn child;

- having emotional support;

- imagining or fantasizing about motherhood and the baby;

- beginning some type of communication (such as singing) with the unborn child;

- feeling connected or bonded to the child before birth; and

- making plans or preparing for the birth and arrival of the baby.

In the P-CCC approach, the home visitor encourages the mother to use specially designed activity sheets to keep track of the baby's "kicks and wiggles" in the second and third trimester of pregnancy and to think about the baby's activities in relation to her own activity. Exploring present support systems, strengthening them, and filling in any gaps is also a major task during this period. These activities are designed to help the mother lay the foundation for attachment by connecting with her unborn child.

From Birth to 3 Months

In the first 3 months after birth, mother and baby must make significant transitions. The baby must adjust to living outside the womb and establishing feeding and sleep rhythms that provide a foundation for physical, cognitive, and social–emotional growth and development. The mother must begin to think of herself as a mother and must put the baby foremost on her mind. She must learn how to recognize, understand, and meet the baby's demands as well as find a balance and synchrony in her relationship with her baby. Keeping the baby close at hand is a behavior that seems to be good for both parent and child during this period.

Other important maternal behaviors during this period include finding ways to connect with the baby (e.g., eye contact, games), getting comfortable with the role of a mother, and understanding babies' capacities for experiencing and expressing emotion. In our community of mothers, we found that almost one half found it hard to take care of their babies (46%). More than three out of five (61%) found motherhood to be different from what they had imagined. Tragically, 20% of women felt their babies had the ability and motivation to become angry with them—thoughts that often lead to feelings of rejection and inadequacy on the mother's part.

Mothers' behaviors and attitudes that we believe promote healthy social and emotional development—or optimal mental health—of babies during the first 3 months of life include

- understanding the baby's patterns and transitions (e.g., stages of sleep);
- understanding the baby's behaviors, actions, and emotions;
- developing healthy and fun interactive times with the baby;
- being close to the baby (e.g., holding the baby during feedings, making eye contact, or using a soft baby carrier);
- being able to adapt to the unexpected parts of motherhood; and
- having a support system that is readily available.

In the P-CCC approach, home visitors focused on supporting the mother's use of a soft baby sling. They also used several materials and strategies to help parents learn about their babies and use what they learned in daily routines, such as feeding.

From 4 to 8 Months

During this period, babies become experts in social responsiveness. They typically enjoy social games, make eye contact, and burst out in smiles when they find a partner who is fun to be with. During this period, babies begin to develop the capacity to experience a wide range of emotions and ways to express and communicate them; however, they still need their parents to help them modify and regulate those emotions. Babies who receive soothing and comfort when distressed begin to learn how to manage difficult feelings, whereas babies who receive no support can become overwhelmed and despondent around difficult emotions. Parents must be able to handle their own emotions in a healthy way if they are to be able to assist their babies effectively.

Babies also become powerful communicators at this age, so the goals for parents include being able to interpret babies' communications accurately and to respond sensitively to the baby's emotional needs of the moment. Each time the parent can respond appropriately to the baby, their connection strengthens—the parent feels more satisfied that she can meet the baby's needs, and the baby feels more secure that his parent(s) can be trusted and will be there when he needs them.

When a mother's mind is on her 4- to 8-month-old baby, she is often anticipating the fun of interacting with her baby at this age. We have identified several abilities and behaviors in mothers that contribute to positive mental health:

- understanding the baby's developing abilities and range of emotion;

- understanding the baby's attempts to communicate and connect;

- understanding the effect of experiences and environment on the baby;

- keeping the baby close through use of a soft baby carrier, sling, or backpack;

- allowing and supporting opportunities for the baby to succeed in independent activities (e.g., playing with toys, falling asleep on her own, and beginning self-feeding).

P-CCC activities at this stage encourage self-exploration of feelings about mothering and about the baby—especially the baby's emerging range of emotions and the way he expresses different emotions. Activities also encourage communicating and connecting with the baby through interaction that is based on imitation.

From 9 to 18 Months

During the last part of the first year, children begin to spontaneously use gestures for communicating—for example, waving "bye-bye." The child's ability to communicate, along with the parents' attempts to understand the child, become important benchmarks of mental health within the parent–child relationship. Ideally, parents actively help the child develop nonverbal and verbal expression and respond to the child's words and questions, reinforcing attempts to communicate. A child who is responded to and encouraged to communicate is one who feels powerful in the world and significant in the life of his parent(s). Children who are not spoken to or interacted with will often develop delays in the ability to communicate, leading to decreased interactions, impaired ability to communicate their needs clearly, and difficulty in being social or relating to others—dysfunctional mental health.

In the P-CCC program, parents were encouraged to try and understand their baby's unique style of communicating wants, needs, and emotions—that is, the baby's gestures, sounds, and words. Parents often found that when they began to understand their baby's signs or gestures, conflict naturally lessened. Parent and baby enjoyed interactions more. Parents were then asked to teach the baby specific signs or gestures to increase their developing communication abilities. Having gestures for "poopy diaper" and "I want to sit on your lap" simply makes things easier for both parent and baby. The parenting behaviors we found most significant included

- increasing understanding of the baby's attempts to communicate wants, needs, thoughts, and emotions (using gestures, signs, sounds, and words);

- interacting with the baby using the baby's own signs or gestures; and

- reading with the baby.

At this stage, the P-CCC approach focuses on helping parents identify the baby's own emerging way of using signs and gestures to communicate as well as teaching the baby specific signs and gestures to fill communication needs.

As the child approaches the age of 15 months, a greater emphasis is placed on developing the relational behaviors needed for reading. For example, we found that many of the parents with whom we worked had difficulty just sitting with their babies—a behavior necessary for reading activities. Therefore, home visitors worked with the parents using other "sitting with" activities such as playing with a homemade toy and interactive games. This preparation helped parents be more ready for the use of reading to enhance the parent–child relationship during the last stage of early development that we targeted.

From 18 to 30 Months

Talking, talking, talking. Reading, reading, reading. As a child grows and her social world expands, the ability to communicate with others takes on a greater focus.

Toddlers and preschoolers begin to rely on a larger vocabulary and an increased ability to use these words to communicate concepts and to question the workings of the world. Words and language help children to make sense of their world and also give them the tools to be able to understand their emotions and thoughts on a deeper level. A child who can say to an adult, "I'm hungry" or "I am mad that Kimmy took my doll" is generally able to interact on a more positive level than the child who "falls apart" when hungry or hits or bites when angry over a typical peer conflict. A child who can communicate clearly can interact well with others and express herself effectively; both skills contribute to healthy emotional development.

Reading is one of the most effective ways to provide children with these important skills and abilities. Reading with a parent provides shared interaction, shared attention, attentional focus to an activity, patience, anticipation, expression of emotion, practice in emotional regulation, body contact, nurturance, cooperation, and joy. In addition, conversation with adults and reading to young children has been shown to support the development of language and cognition—both of which are also foundational to the child's future reading ability.

The behaviors that we found supportive during this period are the same as those we found during the stage of 9–18 months.

Using Videotaping in Interaction Guidance

Another component of the P-CCC program is interaction guidance. Many families who participate in EHS and other community-based programs may benefit greatly from this component. Interaction guidance can be described as a combination of education and coaching—teaching the parent how to interact in more productive and positive ways with the infant, then supporting and coaching the parent in interactions with the child.

Home visitors in community-based programs can learn to use interaction guidance, including videotaping in the home. The practitioner uses the video with the parent as a point of departure for the identification and reinforcement of the parent's strengths in nurturing the child.

Using a video of a normal routine event, such as feeding or a diaper change, the practitioner and parent can observe and think about the child's responses and bids for connection. With the proper support, the parent may also examine what he might have done differently in certain instances. The video allows the parent to observe his own behavior and the infant–parent interaction from a different vantage point—that of an outside observer. Videotaping within a community-based program can also serve as a vehicle for building practitioners' skills in understanding a developing mother–child relationship and facilitating well-focused interventions. The following example illustrates this interaction guidance process.

Jennifer and Rory

Kara, an EHS home visitor, came to her five-member group supervision session with a videotape of 20-year-old Jennifer feeding her 18-month-old son, Rory. Kara had always regarded Jennifer very highly and often described her as "one of the best" mothers in the program. Even as she taped the interaction, Kara felt positive and excited at the prospect of talking to her colleagues and supervisor about this mom and baby. But, as Kara told the group, when she reviewed the tape on her own, she was surprised by worrisome aspects of the interaction between Jennifer and Rory—things she had never noticed before.

Jennifer could not seem to read Rory's signals that he was full; she forced food into his mouth regardless of what he did. Interestingly, she did this with a very loving and concerned voice and way of being: As Jennifer force-fed Rory, she simultaneously talked to Kara about how her son loves his food and loves to eat. Before presenting each spoonful of food, Jennifer banged loudly on the high-chair tray with the spoon, presumably to orient the child to the food. However, Rory seemed to startle in response to the noise. Kara had not noticed the banging at all until she viewed the video. She suggested it was because there were several other people in the home and the noise level was fairly high anyway.

Watching the video with Kara was a learning experience for everyone in the group. The video revealed a mother who seemed "under pressure." She was tense, and her interactions with her baby were tense and pressured. Her kind demeanor and positive, cheerful tone masked the underlying tension. The difficulty in the interaction was not easy to identify until everyone was able to step back and observe. Once EHS staff members were able to recognize the level of tension and misunderstanding in the feeding situation, they could see this pattern in some of the other interactions between mother and child.

Kara used the video with Jennifer to show her how important she was in her son's life. Watching the video together, Kara showed Jennifer the many good things she did with Rory, as well as how Rory really paid close attention to his mother. She was also able to provide examples to Jennifer of how Rory sometimes wanted more time to explore his meal and go slower. Looking at the strengths Jennifer had, as well as providing her with some assistance in developing a better understanding of her interactions with Rory, helped to promote more thoughtful interactions between mother and baby.

Four months later, Kara brought the supervision group a new video. This showed a much calmer interaction between Jennifer and Rory. Mother and child interacted with words and gestures. Rory's pattern of response had shifted as well. He now easily ate his meal, remained focused, and was able to laugh and enjoy his mother.

STILL MUCH TO BE DONE

Given the mental health challenges that families face, the paucity of resources available in the community, and prevailing attitudes about infant mental health, it is often a major accomplishment for a home visitor to maintain a connection with a mother through continuing home visits. The home visitors described in the examples in this chapter are among the best in the field. They tried diligently to understand each family, made necessary referrals, and remained dedicated to the well-being of the children and the parents. However, program staff members such as these individuals often face enormous obstacles to achieving effective practice, including

- lack of response from Child Protective Services to reports of neglect;

- lack of knowledge or reluctance of medical providers to identify or diagnose infant mental health issues;

- lack of community resources to address identified infant or maternal mental health needs;

- program cultures that emphasize keeping mothers or families enrolled, sometimes leading to staff reluctance to raise difficult issues; and

- societal unwillingness to acknowledge infant mental health problems (Emde, 2001) and support community-wide responsibility for young children's mental health.

As Emde (2001, p. 24) notes, "If we can overcome our denial of infant suffering and problems of adaptation and development—as advances in infant mental health theory, research, and practice can help us to do—we may be able to design and establish community-based systems of care to achieve the twin goals of strengthening pathways to healthy development and preventing developmental compromises and serious mental health disorders."

The staff of EHS and other community-based providers can protect and strengthen mother–baby relationships in many ways, making it easier or possible for mothers to feel well and keep their minds on their babies, and for babies to be able to trust in the care that their mothers and other loving adults provide. Locally and nationally, EHS is making important contributions to the field of infant mental health, but changes throughout the currently fragmented system of services for vulnerable families with infants and toddlers are necessary, as well.

ACKNOWLEDGMENTS

Much of this chapter, particularly the information about the Parent–Child Communication Coaching Program and the examples of women, babies, and program staff, is based on research conducted by the authors and supported by grants from the Administration on Children, Youth, and Families to the University of Washington (0-YF-0013–01) and to the Children's Home Society of Washington (904C0036/01).

NOTE

1. The pregnancy activities used in this program, plus an additional 53 activities, have been published as *Promoting Maternal Mental Health During Pregnancy: Theory, Assessment, and Intervention* (Solchany, 2001).

REFERENCES

Administration on Children, Youth, and Families. (2000). *A commitment to supporting the mental health of our youngest children* [Informal follow-up report on the Infant Mental Health Forum of October 23–24, 2000, prepared by Deborah Roderick Stark]. Washington, DC: Author.

Carter, A. S., Garrity-Rokous, F. E., Chazan-Cohen, R., Little, C., & Briggs-Gowan, M. J. (2001). Maternal depression and comorbidity: Predicting early parenting, attachment security, and toddler social–emotional problems and competencies. *Journal of the American Academy of Child and Adolescent Psychiatry, 40*(1), 18–26.

Chazan-Cohen, R., Jerald, J., & Stark, D. R. (2001, August/September). A commitment to supporting the mental health needs of our youngest children. *Zero to Three, 22*(1), 4–12.

DelCarmen-Wiggins, R., & Carter, A. S. (2001). Assessment of infant and toddler mental health: Advances and challenges [Special Section]. *Journal of the American Academy of Child and Adolescent Psychiatry, 40*(1), 8–10.

Emde, R. N. (2001, August/September). A developmental psychiatrist looks at infant mental health challenges for Early Head Start: Understanding context and overcoming avoidance. *Zero to Three, 22*(1), 21–24.

Emde, R. N., Bertacchi, J., & Mann, T. L. (2001, August/September). Organizational environments that support mental health. *Zero to Three, 22*(1), 67–69.

Head Start program performance standards and other regulations. 45 C.F.R. §§ 1301, 1302, 1303, 1304 and guidance, 1305, 1306, and 1308 and guidance. (Government Printing Office 2002).

Keren, M., Fledman, R., & Tyano, S. (2001). Diagnoses and interactive patterns of infants referred to a community-based infant mental health clinic. *Journal of the American Academy of Child and Adolescent Psychiatry, 40*(1), 27–35.

National Research Council, Institute of Medicine (2000). *From neurons to neighborhoods: The science of early childhood development.* Committee on Integrating the Science of Early Childhood Development. J. P. Shonkoff & D. A. Phillips (Eds.). Board on Children, Youth, and Families, Commission on Behavioral and Social Sciences and Education. Washington, DC: National Academy Press.

Pawl, J. H., & Lieberman, A. F. (1997). Infant–parent psychotherapy. In J. Noshpitz (Ed.), *Handbook of child and adolescent psychiatry* (pp. 339–351). New York: John Wiley and Sons.

Reznick, J. S., & Schwartz, B. B. (2001). When is an assessment an intervention? Parent perception of infant intentionality and language. *Journal of the American Academy of Child and Adolescent Psychiatry, 40*(1), 11–17.

Rubin, R. (1975). Maternal tasks in pregnancy. *Maternal–Child Nursing Journal, 4*(3), 143–153.

Shaw, D. S., Owens, E. B., Giovannelli, J., & Winslow, E. B. (2001). Infant and toddler pathways leading to early externalizing disorders. *Journal of the American Academy of Child and Adolescent Psychiatry, 40*(1), 36–43.

Solchany, J. E. (2001). *Promoting maternal mental health during pregnancy: Theory, assessment, and intervention.* Seattle: University of Washington, NCAST Publications.

Solchany, J., Spieker, S., & Barnard, K. (1999, April). *Variability in engagement: Easy versus difficult-to-engage families.* Presented at the 63rd Biennial Conference of the Society for Research in Child Development, Albuquerque, NM.

Spieker, S., Solchany, J., McKenna, M., DeKlyen, M., & Barnard, K. (1999). The story of mothers who are difficult to engage in prevention programs. In J. Osofsky and H. E. Fitzgerald (Eds.), *WAIMH Handbook of Infant Mental Health* (Vol. 3). New York: John Wiley and Sons.

Thomas, J. M., & Guskin, K. A. (2001). Disruptive behavior in young children: What does it mean? *Journal of the American Academy of Child and Adolescent Psychiatry,* 40(1), 44–51.

U.S. Department of Health and Human Services. (1994). *The statement of the Advisory Committee on Services for Families With Infants and Toddlers.* Washington, DC: Author.

ZERO TO THREE. (1994). *Diagnostic classification of mental health and developmental disorders of infancy and early childhood.* Washington, DC: Author.

ABOUT THE AUTHORS

JoAnne E. Solchany is an assistant professor in the Department of Family and Child Nursing and in the Infant Mental Health Program at the University of Washington in Seattle. She is also a clinical specialist in child and adolescent psychiatric nursing, a child psychiatric nurse practitioner, and a child psychotherapist focusing on infant–parent psychotherapy. Solchany is the author of *Promoting Maternal Mental Health During Pregnancy: Theory, Assessment, and Intervention*.

Kathryn E. Barnard is a professor of nursing and psychology and affiliate of the Center for Human Development and Disability at the University of Washington in Seattle. She is the author of *Nursing Child Assessment Feeding and Teaching Scales*. She has conducted research in the general areas of child health assessment, early intervention with at-risk infants and families, and parent–child interaction. She is also the director of the Center on Infant Mental Health and Development at the University of Washington Center for Excellence in Developmental Disabilities. She also served as a member of the Advisory Committee on Services for Families With Infants and Toddlers.

CHAPTER 9

SUPPORTING CHILDREN'S POSSIBILITIES: INFANTS AND TODDLERS WITH DISABILITIES AND THEIR FAMILIES IN EARLY HEAD START

Linda Brekken

The Guido family emigrated from El Salvador in 1986. Most of the year, they live with their five children in Florida. Minerva is 10, Ernesto is 8, Marvin is 6, Katia is 5, and Osvaldo is 27 months. Katia and Osvaldo have Down syndrome.[1]

When Mr. and Mrs. Guido came to the United States, they spoke an indigenous Salvadoran dialect. Because Spanish is the language spoken by Mr. Guido's coworkers and in their neighborhood, the Guidos are now proficient in Spanish. Mr. Guido works in the fields—often 7 days per week—and travels from Florida to New Jersey to follow the picking season of crops such as gladiolas and blueberries. In addition to supporting his family in the United States, Mr. Guido regularly sends money to his elderly parents and his three older children in El Salvador. Mrs. Guido used to work in the fields with Mr. Guido but now remains at home to care for the needs of her two youngest children.

When Mrs. Guido became pregnant with Osvaldo, the family enrolled in Early Head Start (EHS). Because Katia attended Head Start, Mrs. Guido already had a close, trusting relationship with Maria, the Head Start disabilities coordinator, who had helped them access supports such as Social Security to cover some of the medical costs of Katia's condition. Through prenatal testing, the Guido family learned that Osvaldo also had Down syndrome. Maria—herself a former migrant worker and mother of a child with special needs—provided emotional support, information, and resources to Mrs. Guido after the prenatal diagnosis.

Because Osvaldo was born with a heart condition associated with Down syndrome, EHS initially helped the Guidos arrange for their son to receive Early Intervention services at a hospital 90 minutes away. Later, when EHS opened a center-based program, the Guidos enrolled Osvaldo there, where he could receive Early Intervention services in his classroom, very close to home. Osvaldo receives physical therapy, occupational therapy, and speech and language services at the EHS center. Although he is thriving, his heart condition requires careful monitoring. Often his hands have a purple or bluish tinge.

Mr. Guido is proud of his family. Despite still keen memories of the stress he suffered while caring for Katia and Osvaldo when they were seriously ill newborns, he says now, "Katia is growing up; she's beautiful. She's got her life going. And

Osvaldo, too, he's learning to walk. [Our three older] kids, they study, it's good for them. They speak English. When you don't speak English, you struggle" (*Hilton/Early Head Start Training Program*, 2000).[2]

M ost of us will never encounter the overwhelming obstacles faced by the Guido family. Imagine what it would be like to face learning not one, but two new languages while enduring the harsh economic and lifestyle consequences of the migrant worker's way of life—all while raising five children, two of whom have disabilities and other medical problems. How would you do it? The answer is, with vision—and with help. By envisioning a better life for their family and gaining the support of others (such as EHS staff members) who believed in that vision, Mr. and Mrs. Guido have forged a better life for themselves. Says Mrs. Guido through a translator, "My dreams have come true . . . because in this country [my children] get medical care and help. If they were in El Salvador, I think they would not have survived."

The visions and expectations of families, friends, and professionals shape the futures of infants and toddlers with disabilities. It is important to recognize that one cannot know exactly what is possible for any individual child. When professionals or others predict that a child "cannot" or "will not" achieve a developmental goal or master a particular task, they fail to imagine many possibilities. By offering quality services and supportive relationships instead, people involved in the lives of very young children with disabilities can set the stage for promising futures.

Inspired by the vision that all babies can grow up to be productive citizens, EHS provides the kind of leadership, information, and human caring that is so essential to infants and toddlers with disabilities and their families. EHS staff members also understand that myriad factors—child characteristics, family supports, community resources, life experience, strength of will, and "plasticity" of brain development—influence developmental outcomes for infants and toddlers with disabilities. EHS strives to make the most of these factors for all children.

In 2002, an estimated 13% of EHS children had a disability or developmental delay (Irish, Schumacher, & Lombardi, 2003). Nationally, slightly more than 2% of all children from birth to age 3 receive Early Intervention services for disabilities (Office of Special Education Programs, 2001). Thus, EHS is reaching deep into the pool of families who have infants and toddlers with special needs.

This chapter discusses EHS's approach to serving these children and families by exploring the roles of context, relationships, information, and leadership as key elements in providing high-quality early childhood services.

THE CONTEXT

To understand disability services in EHS, one must know about the Part C Early Intervention system as well as the science that supports the inclusion of children with disabilities and their families in "natural environments" (i.e., settings that serve typically developing children).

Policy: A Partnership That Delivers

Early Intervention services for infants and toddlers with disabilities and their families are available in every state through Part C of the Individuals With Disabilities Education Act (IDEA; Individuals With Disabilities Education Act, 1997). To receive federal dollars under Part C, each participating state designs a comprehensive, interagency, interdisciplinary system of Early Intervention services. Each state also determines the agency that will manage the Part C system and the eligibility criteria for the children whom the system will serve.

Head Start, a nationwide federal program, has a long-standing commitment to children with disabilities and requires programs to make at least 10% of their enrollment opportunities available to young children with disabilities (*Head Start program performance standards and other regulations*, 2002a). As a result, Head Start has become the nation's largest community-based program that provides services to children with disabilities and their families (Head Start Bureau, 1997).

EHS programs meet their disability enrollment obligation by working closely with the Part C system. This partnership works well because the IDEA legislation requires that Early Intervention services be provided in natural environments such as EHS settings. In addition, EHS defines an infant or toddler with a disability using the same definition that the state Part C program has adopted (*Head Start program performance standards and other regulations*, 2002b). Because child eligibility criteria vary from state to state, infants and toddlers with various disabilities and varying degrees of developmental delay are served in EHS programs throughout the country.

EHS's welcoming environment for families of infants and toddlers with disabilities, combined with the natural environments mandate of the Part C system, provides the basis for an ideal federal–state partnership that supports children on a local level. Families of children with disabilities who are eligible for EHS can access the program's comprehensive child health, development, and family support services in tandem with the specialized Early Intervention services and supports provided by the Part C system.

Research: So Much to Gain—for Everyone

It's very rewarding to see our children [with disabilities] go on to preschool. The children have confidence in their abilities [because] they've been in a setting with their peers. The teachers also grow. They're sad to see their children move on, but yet at the same time they feel very good. They feel, "Wow! I did this. I can do this!"—EHS administrator[3]

Research on the plasticity of the brain is particularly relevant to children with disabilities. A diagnosis of disability describes a condition that has been caused by heredity, the environment, or other factors, but it tells little about the future of any one child. The child's brain development will, of course, be influenced by the disability, but it will also be influenced by her unique experiences. In other words, the brain adapts to experience (Nelson, 1999). Thus, well-designed and successfully implemented interventions can promote significant short-term gains in the cognitive and social performance of young children with disabilities (Casto & Mastropieri, 1986; Farran, 2000; Guralnick, 1998; Shonkoff and Hauser-Cram, 1987). In the subsequent sections, three other sets of research findings that have influenced EHS policy and practice for children with disabilities and their families are described.

First, Early Intervention services that are embedded in everyday routines and practices offer children opportunities to practice new skills in functional settings with their family members, peers, professional staff, and others in the community (Bruder & Dunst, 2000). After all, if everyone who interacts with the child emphasizes language learning—not only the speech and language pathologist during weekly therapy sessions—the child's language learning opportunities are greatly expanded. Research has also found that services provided in natural contexts enhance children's ability to transfer this learning to other situations (McWilliam, 1996; Rainforth, York, & MacDonald, 1992).

Second, high-quality natural environments that support all children's development create a climate in which children are respected and valued as important members of the group. Both infants with disabilities and their typically developing peers develop a sense that they belong in the group when they fully participate in everyday activities (Bruder, 1993; Kunc, 1992; Odom & Diamond, 1998). Also, intervention provided in a community context reduces the stigma associated with services in segregated settings and helps children with disabilities gain social acceptance (Guralnick, 2001).

These findings are important because the negative attitudes of others pose one of the greatest barriers that children with developmental challenges face in achieving their full potential. Even professionals may forget that young children with disabilities are more like their typically developing peers than they are different. Adults who work with children need to understand that their own attitudes about disabilities shape how children interpret and react to differences among people. By creating environments that emphasize respect and belonging for all children, EHS staff have the potential to change the negative attitudes that are so debilitating for individuals with disabilities in our society.

Finally, inclusive environments that benefit infants and toddlers with disabilities benefit all children (Odom & Bailey, 2001). For one thing, typically developing children in inclusive settings are exposed to and become more accepting of differences in others from an early age. For another, the sophisticated strategies that support the successful inclusion of infants and toddlers with disabilities also build caregiver skills that enhance the overall quality of EHS for all children. These skills include relationship building, observation, individualization, adaptation, planning, collaboration, and reflective practice.

RELATIONSHIPS MATTER

> We see typically developing kids who are learning empathy and compassion and making friends with kids with varying abilities. We see parents who are making friendships with other parents, supporting each other. We see staff who love to work together, who are learning from each other, who are energized by each other.—Early Intervention administrator

A disability or other special need must be understood by professionals in the context of an individual child, the child's family, and the child's development. When service providers are able to shift their focus from a child's disability to the unique gifts and joys that he brings to his family, program, and community, they set the stage for positive developmental outcomes. By focusing on establishing collaborative, supportive relationships with families, professionals reduce families' feelings of isolation and, instead, create a web of support for parents and children.

Family Ties

Because family context and culture shape a child's development, EHS providers seek first to develop positive relationships with and within families. A practitioner who understands each child's strengths, temperament, learning style, interests, and needs in the context of that child's family can better assist the child to adapt to her unique challenges, whether in the areas of language, behavior, or motor skills (Hanson, Gutierrez, Morgan, Brennan, & Zercher, 1997).

A child's culture is a particularly important context for learning and development. Says one EHS administrator, "It is impossible to separate the infant or toddler from their family culture. . . . Different cultures have different ways of dealing with infants and toddlers with disabilities; that has to be acknowledged and respected." The best means of navigating complex cultural issues is through respectful listening and nonjudgmental negotiation. Values and expectations may vary within families. For example, in one EHS program, the family's culture ascribed a child's disability to fate. Older family members believed that it was their duty to accept the child as she was—without intervention. The child's mother, however, also valued education and wanted her child to have opportunities to develop. After learning how Early Intervention and EHS services could benefit her child, she became the driving force within the family for her child's enrollment.

Services to a child with special needs emerge from a partnership with the family and must include every member—not only the mother, who is often the primary focus of services. EHS staff members involve fathers, grandparents, extended family members, and other significant people in a child's life. This extended inclusion is especially important when adapting services to family norms and culture because in some communities, the elders—rather than the parent—may make decisions for the family or community. As EHS providers listen to families articulate their values and expectations, they learn more about the deeper interpretations attached to the disability. With this knowledge, providers are better able to offer individualized services that reflect a family's beliefs and culture.

Networking with other families—talking with others who have similar experiences—is often the most important support that a family can receive. Each state has resources for parent-to-parent support; EHS and Early Intervention staff members are experts at linking families to these support systems. Says one parent of a child with a disability, "Ten years ago a friend of mine and I started a Spanish-speaking family group [for] families [who have a child with a disability]. . . . What I learned about parent-to-parent support is that it has a ripple effect. You throw a stone out in a little pond and then watch the effect. We provided support to other families, and now those families support other families. The effect continues. Now, rather than call it parent-to-parent support, we call it a family network of support."

Reaching the Staff Who Reach the Children

One of the biggest barriers to relationship building with families is the fear and discomfort that new staff members sometimes feel in working with infants and toddlers with disabilities (Buysse, Wesley, Keyes, & Bailey, 1996; Gallagher, 1997). This problem is compounded by staff shortages in the early childhood field in general. Caregiving staff may lack experience in the care of children with special needs. However, comfort and confidence usually build over time, as staff members have positive experiences with children with disabilities and are able to access support from colleagues, families, and Early Intervention partners. Says one EHS teacher of a toddler in her care, "I was a little afraid at first. I was afraid of hurting him—everybody was. He was so fragile. But it turned into a special relationship that stays and stays." Allowing staff to express such feelings and fears in a safe, supportive environment promotes the successful inclusion of children with disabilities into programs such as EHS.

Says one EHS administrator, "Many people have not been around children with disabilities, and there's a certain fear that's involved to anything that is new or unfamiliar . . . . So I say to new staff, 'It's OK. It's natural to have fears and apprehension.' . . . . The fear is from wanting to do a good job and feeling like one might not be able to do the best possible job . . . . When you work with infants and toddlers with disabilities, the wonderful thing is that there are so many people working together. There are the families and the Early Intervention and support staff. So you're not out there alone."

Agency-to-Agency Support

EHS programs and their Early Intervention partner agencies must work hard to build relationships among staff that focus on the needs of the child rather than the "turf" of each agency. Proper coordination of the many services needed by children with disabilities takes time—especially when philosophies differ between agencies or when clarity about roles and responsibilities is lacking (see Box 9-1).

If they are enrolled in the Part C system, infants and toddlers with disabilities and their families will have an Individualized Family Service Plan (IFSP) developed by Early Intervention service providers and the family. If the child is also enrolled in EHS, then EHS staff members are often invited by the Early Intervention Program or by parents to attend the IFSP planning meeting for the children in their care. The IFSP is the road map for all specialized services and guidance about how staff can adapt routines and activities to meet a child's needs within the natural environment—whether at home, in child care, or as part of EHS or other programs and services.

BOX 9.1 **A Special Partnership for Special Children: Fresno County Economic Opportunities Commission EHS and Exceptional Parents Unlimited**

The evolution of the partnership between the Fresno County Economic Opportunities Commission Early Head Start (Fresno EHS) and Exceptional Parents Unlimited (EPU) tells a lot about how children and families benefit when EHS programs work closely with their Part C neighbors.

Kathleen Shivaprasad, program manager of the Fresno EHS, invited EPU Infant–Family Program Manager Laurie Clark to be the Part C representative on the Fresno team for a SpecialQuest training. The Fresno team returned from the first training with strategies and materials on building bridges between the two agencies. A potluck lunch, presentations at staff meetings, and collegial friendships soon followed. Five years later, joint home visits, play groups (also known as parent–child socializations), and training are now the norm between the two partners.

Clark also returned from the first SpecialQuest with a stronger sense of EHS's commitment to children with disabilities. "I was so impressed that they had parents of children with disabilities there to share their stories to help others gain insight. I came back saying, 'Gosh, Early Head Start really gets it, they really understand what families with special needs go through and what they need.' I still use a lot of the materials I received at SpecialQuest on subjects like dealing with change and team building with the staff of EPU. SpecialQuest gave us the tools that we needed to make the collaboration successful."

Of the collaboration, Shivaprasad says, "Our agencies complement each other. We enhance EPU's ability to provide families [who have] children with disabilities with a natural environment that includes families of typically developing children, and they enhance our expertise on Early Intervention." For example, EPU staff train EHS staff on how to participate effectively in IFSP meetings. In addition, EPU and Fresno EHS home visitors often team up to conduct developmental assessments on infants and toddlers with disabilities.

Both agencies hope to pursue funds to jointly open an EHS center in a new EPU building. The facility would serve the full-day care needs of children with disabilities in a natural environment with typically developing children. Co-location with EPU offers many tangible benefits, such as reduced transportation barriers for children whose families may have to haul equipment such as oxygen tanks aboard vans in order to access EPU's specialized services, and easy access to the expertise of EPU speech, language, and occupational therapists (Mary Bogle, personal communication, November 2002).

Because the IFSP is such a critical part of providing quality care to children, a strong partnership between the EHS provider and the Early Intervention provider is essential to its success. Also, in collaboration with parents, EHS staff members develop Family Partnership Agreements for all families to outline the services and supports that families need from the EHS program. For families whose children have disabilities, these agreements should be closely coordinated with families' IFSPs as well. One EHS disabilities coordinator says that her program and their Early Intervention partner ensure an effective IFSP by asking, "How can we minimize those differences [between agencies] and [create] one document so that the family doesn't perceive this as two sets of paperwork and two sets of services working in isolation—so [it's clear] that there is one service plan for their family?"

Many EHS and Early Intervention programs implement the IFSP together. Often, families enjoy shared Early Intervention and EHS home visits, complete with the combined activities and input from both service providers. In addition, EHS and Early Intervention partnerships often include shared referral mechanisms, collaborative screening and assessment processes, co-located staff, and a host of other innovations that significantly streamline and improve services for children.

INFORMATION MATTERS

> We have [children for] a short time, while parents have them for a lifetime. We hope that the techniques and skills that we have, we can share with the families . . . . By the same token, what the parent knows will enhance us as caregivers and administrators in caring for their children.—EHS administrator

Families need information, resources, and support to address the concerns and questions that often arise after the diagnosis of a disability in their infant or toddler. Programs such as EHS fill this gap by educating families on their children's developmental challenges and by offering insight into the systems and processes that are in place to support the child, such as Part C.

Information and Support for Families

> It's important to be able to hear the stories of those veteran families. Young families who are just starting out need to hear the stories. . . . From there, their imaginations can go wild on what the potential life of their child can be.—Parent

Early identification of a disability can occur in several ways in EHS. Some families may receive a prenatal diagnosis from a physician. In other cases, EHS may identify the problem and work with the family to access Early Intervention services. Families may bring concerns to EHS or to their Early Intervention or health care providers that result in a diagnosis. Or, Early Intervention staff may assess the infant's disability and refer the family to EHS for intervention in a natural environment.

Regardless of how the identification process is initiated, families typically describe this period as an emotional and stressful time. EHS and their early intervention and other community partners help families cope by providing reliable, accurate information about each child's disability and unique needs—as well as resources to meet those needs.

Information and Training for Staff

> Early Head Start staff [may come to] know a whole lot about cerebral palsy, or spina bifida, or a number of disabilities, but they will learn that [information] relative to a real little child, learning the practical strategies [of how to] integrate the child into an activity, play group, child care center, or home visit.
> —EHS disabilities coordinator

In caring for a child with special needs, information about that child's disability is often the first thing most people want to know, but the best place to start is with the child. Getting to know a child as a child first—her interests, strengths, and abilities—helps ensure that the staff member's focus is on what the child can do (not limited to what the child cannot do).

Conversations with families can help caregivers to better appreciate children's strengths and gifts as well as to understand the context of children's everyday lives. As a field, Early Intervention is making a critical shift away from a "deficit model" to focus more on what young children can do and how adaptations can be designed to help them do more. Rather than expectations being based on a child's diagnosis, each child's developmental trajectory is seen as unique. Thus, EHS staff members become experts on each individual child first, then familiarize themselves with the disability.

Sensitively designed screening and assessment tools, careful observations, and learning about each unique infant and family serve as the foundation for specialized services and supports. This approach also helps staff members select the right mix of resources and services that best meet the individual needs of each child in their care.

These resources include people such as the EHS disabilities coordinator; his team members; Early Intervention partners; the child's family; and local, state, and national training and technical assistance providers. Information from sources such as scholarly journals and reliable Internet sites is also valuable.

Ongoing training and professional development are critical to overall program quality. Of particular relevance to the EHS community is the Hilton/Early Head Start Training Program, a public–private partnership between the Conrad N. Hilton Foundation and the Head Start Bureau. First funded in 1997, the program's mission is to support staff from EHS and Migrant and Seasonal Head Start (MSHS), family members, and community partners to develop skills and strategies for accessing and using services, resources, and technology to provide appropriate services to infants and toddlers with significant disabilities and their families.

Participating EHS and MSHS programs send teams of five people to intensive training events called SpecialQuests. The teams include a parent of a child with a disability, an Early Intervention partner, an EHS/MSHS administrator, the disabilities services manager, and another staff member. The training sessions last 3 to 4 days, and teams return for 4 consecutive years. The SpecialQuest curriculum covers state-of-the-art inclusion practices drawn from research literature and best practices.

Each team works with a learning coach who supports them during SpecialQuest and provides 3 days of in-person consultation at the home site. While on site, SpecialQuest learning coaches identify progress toward the team's goals and outcomes, work with the team, and provide support and problem solving. For example, the team might help the local Early Head Start Policy Council develop enrollment criteria to ensure that children with disabilities receive preference for enrollment, or help EHS and Early Intervention programs develop effective interagency service delivery.

During a SpecialQuest, each team sets goals for the coming 4 years. These might include general objectives, such as increasing the number of children with significant disabilities enrolled in their program, providing more support to families, or enhancing family leadership. Teams also work on specific strategies, such as the development of integrated therapy models within EHS classrooms and ways to advance family skills in using the Internet to obtain information and access resources for children with disabilities. EHS and Early Intervention staff use SpecialQuests to forge stronger alliances among their agencies. The interagency teams seek outcomes including joint training, shared home visits for families, and more coordinated transition plans for children with disabilities who are leaving infant–toddler-oriented services for the world of preschool services.

Between 1998 and 2002, SpecialQuest trained 259 teams that were supported by 140 learning coaches (Hilton/Early Head Start Training Program, 2001). In addition, materials from the SpecialQuest training have reached more than 67,000 additional family members and staff (Hilton/Early Head Start Training Program, 2002). A new cohort of teams began training in 2003.

The experience of SpecialQuest and other effective training and technical assistance efforts suggests that families and staff who work with children with special needs require access to learning experiences that are sufficiently intense over time to produce change and that include follow-up support for implementing new strategies. Change-producing training is grounded in principles of adult learning—relating specifically to the needs of the learner, employing a variety of learning modalities, providing exercises in problem solving, and supporting practice in the program setting. Offering training to teams that include representatives from intervention programs and the larger community ensures that a range of key players will share responsibility for creating change (Knapp-Philo, Corso, Brekken, Bair-Heal, 2004).

How training is delivered is as important as its content. For example, to understand thoroughly the principle that cultural beliefs and values influence the way a family perceives their child's special needs, staff need an opportunity during the course of training to reflect on their values and beliefs about disability. How might these influence work with families whose cultures are different from their own? Most early intervention training points out that an understanding and appreciation of cultural values is an essential aspect to developing relationships with families and creating service plans. When working with a family from a particular culture, staff need to learn about the culture's views of the child's disability, theories of causation of disability, and beliefs about traditional and contemporary health practices. Yet trainers must also help staff learn how to avoid cultural stereotyping and the mistaken assumption that all members of a culture maintain the same values. Only well-tuned training and supervision can help staff members achieve this difficult balance.

Self-awareness is perhaps the most important area of competence that staff members can bring to work with children who have special needs. It is not enough to simply understand the child, the culture, and the values of each family. Through supervision and training, caregivers must also become aware of how their own personal values, experiences, and organizational culture affect their attitudes toward individuals with disabilities. Well-trained staff members know that perceptions of disability and its consequences influence the life paths of children with special needs—negatively or positively.

Information and Training Resources From Partners

> You stand behind the environment that you provide. You look at all the players that will be involved in delivering services to the child, and you give them the information that they need to work with that child. Then you develop the questions: How will we reassess? At what point will we reevaluate? What are we doing to monitor the environment and that child's progress in that environment?—EHS administrator

Working with community partners, staff members can advocate for infants and toddlers with disabilities and their families, link with community resources, and provide ongoing support to families and other team members. Inclusion means effective, responsive, individualized adaptations of services within the context of family life and child care. No one-size-fits-all manual can describe exactly what to do.

EHS staff members often expand their knowledge and skills on how best to support children with disabilities through training provided by Early Intervention and other community partners. State, regional, and national training opportunities also can enhance learning across agencies. Joint training activities such as these also meet requirements for EHS and the Child Find provisions in Part C of the IDEA.

The Community Partnerships for Child Development (CPCD) EHS, based in Colorado Springs, Colorado, shares several training arrangements with its local Part C partner. CPCD serves 135 infants and toddlers, of whom about 22% have special needs. In addition to offering joint training to the child care community at large, CPCD and its Part C partner plan a biennial community conference that addresses issues concerning children with disabilities. And, as needed, Part C staff members train CPCD staff in special techniques such as sensory integration activities. CPCD parents of children with disabilities often share their experience and expertise with staff members during training sessions, which "emphasize the philosophy of the person first and the disability as one aspect of the child's life" (Early Head Start National Resource Center, 1999; Noreen Landis-Tyson, personal communication to Mary Bogle, November 2002).

LEADERSHIP MATTERS

Leaders of programs serving very young children with special needs and their families need a plan of action and a commitment to implementing it. Without strong leadership, programs are likely to waste precious time—a profound loss for children with disabilities for whom Early Intervention is so vital. EHS places a premium on developing the leadership potential of all its stakeholders—children, families, staff, and partners.

Follow the Child

> I did not choose to have a child with Down syndrome. This was a shock to us. And when [health care providers] told us that she wouldn't be able to walk or do this [or that], it was all "don't, don't, don't." They were already putting up barriers . . . . When she had her open heart surgery, they said she would never stand, [but] she started pulling out her IV at the hospital and stood up on the rail of the crib. I thought, "This is a feisty little one, and if she's going to fight, I'll fight with her. I'm going to be with her."—Parent

Ideally, the families of infants and toddlers with disabilities are partners with providers in determining the services that their children need. For this to happen, providers must be willing to listen to and learn from families. On the surface, the concept of child and family leadership may appear to devalue professional training and insight. But, quite to the contrary, respectful observation, listening, and responding to the cues of the child and his family—skills that are the essence of professionalism—are precisely the skills required in family-centered service delivery.

Modes of service delivery that are now considered outdated treated families and children as the passive recipients of prescriptive help. Most service providers today understand that they are likely to be much more effective if they follow the lead of very young children and their families. This is true for children with developmental challenges as well as typically developing children.

As discussed in Chapter 5, responsive care is a principal feature of the program's care for infants and toddlers. Through careful observation, staff members learn about children's interests and needs. Through careful listening, staff members learn about families' needs, concerns, existing resources and support systems, and dreams for their children. EHS staff members also teach parents and other family members to follow their children's lead—specifically to read infants' cues, understand their temperaments, and respond in ways that meet the babies' needs.

Even the most well-meaning caregiver can fall into the trap of defining her role as fixer of a child's deficits rather than supporter of a child's possibilities. In addition, young children with disabilities may face greater challenges in providing cues to their caregivers than their typically developing peers. For example, a child with cerebral palsy may have motor skill challenges that interfere with his ability to express his intent clearly and may need more time in responding to interactions. A child with visual impairments may not be able to read her caregivers' facial cues, and her family may need additional support in developing responsive, reciprocal interactions.

Together, staff members and parents can learn more about how a child's disability may influence his development and can begin responding in ways that meet the unique needs of the unique child.

Parent Power

> We have to figure out how to help parents find that faith in themselves that will help them take care of themselves, take care of their baby, take care of their family, and grow from there.—Early Intervention coordinator and parent

Parents and other family members are in their children's lives for the long haul. They will love and support their children for a lifetime, whereas programs such as EHS will assist in their care for only a few years. In validating that parents know their children best, high-quality programs implement practices that support meaningful family decision making and leadership—not only for each family with regard to its child, but also program wide. This is why the Head Start Program Performance Standards require joint trainings for parents and staff members. And customized training programs such as SpecialQuest assume that parent involvement will result in a more effective learning experience for all participants.

Family leadership is embedded in the concept of family-centered services in EHS. Families provide valuable leadership in guiding programs, serving on advisory boards, sharing peer support, and advocating for their children and families locally, statewide, or nationally. Time and again, professional caregivers discover that families can offer important expertise in helping staff members learn specialized procedures and strategies. For example, holding a child with Down syndrome—who may seem "floppy" due to low muscle tone—may cause a caregiver to become anxious or uncomfortable. Often, seeing the father of that child casually cradle and snuggle the child is the best means of resolving this anxiety. Through word and deed, many families can tell the professionals, "I wasn't trained in this, I just had to learn it. And if I can learn it, so can you!"

Decision making on a program level is another important way that parents can and do lead. Head Start has always had a strong commitment to this kind of leadership. For example, each EHS program is governed by a policy council, which has 51% family representation and makes decisions about program priorities, hiring, budgets, and enrollment criteria. It is important to ensure that the voices of families of young children with disabilities are represented on the policy council. However, this does not happen without conscious efforts to promote opportunities for family leadership through ongoing mentoring and support.

The benefits of promoting parent leaders extend well beyond EHS. For decades, families of children with disabilities have been the driving force behind legislation and policies in special education and developmental disabilities, including Part C. Children with disabilities simply would not have the civil rights and services that they benefit from today without their families' advocacy.

Program Leadership: Philosophy, Staff Support, and Collaboration

> When the home visitor told me that the mom needed to go back to work and needed child care in our center, my first thought was, "Is the mom ready?" What was really going on was that we weren't ready. Sometimes I think, as administrators, we put up smoke screens. We should be able to stand behind the quality of our programs for all children. Just try it. Of course you plan. Take it in little pieces, but you can do it!—EHS administrator

Effective program leadership helps staff members understand not only what to do, but why to do it. First, good leaders create and maintain program philosophies that articulate how children learn and develop, the role of family and culture in development, and the role of staff members in promoting development. The most effective philosophies address the importance of serving all children and explicitly state their commitment to the inclusion of young children with disabilities.

Second, good leaders ensure that staff members receive supportive supervision and time for reflection. EHS directors give their staff members ample opportunities to express their thoughts and feelings about serving infants and toddlers with disabilities in a safe, supportive environment. Leadership practices such as these not only have a direct effect on staff's capacity to function in demanding jobs; they also have a systemic effect on the entire program and the quality of the experience for children and families. A good program director or supervisor will model a climate of support and belonging in which children with disabilities and their families will thrive.

Third, good leaders ensure joint planning among collaborative partners. Together, EHS and Early Intervention leaders create coordinated systems of care that recognize each others' methods, reflect current laws and regulations, clarify roles and responsibilities, advocate that families receive the services they need, build relationships among direct service providers, and build a common philosophy and set of values. Effective program leaders craft joint training on community resources and the services of other providers, conduct site visits to each others' programs, hold regular interagency planning meetings, and design shared vision statements for the children and families served.

Many EHS and Early Intervention leaders work together to adopt common screening and assessment instruments and processes. For example, Kathleen Shivaprasad, program manager of the Fresno County Economic Opportunities Commission EHS, serves on and is the former chairperson of the Fresno Early Childhood Coalition, an interagency group set up to coordinate Part C activities. The coalition has sponsored training for Fresno-area early-care providers to use the Infant–Toddler Developmental Assessment, a tool that meets the criteria for assessment established by the IDEA.

Good leaders recognize that uncoordinated services can be a major barrier to inclusion. For example, when EHS was first funded, there was confusion in the field about whether EHS and Early Intervention were actually competing services. Leaders from the federal, state, and local levels cut through this haze by pointing out that the law—and common sense—clearly require that services be collaborative, not either/or.

An EHS director and Early Intervention administrator emphasize the importance of partnership when they explain, "We needed each other. We needed to come together, to achieve common ground, a common voice. We had to reach out to each other to achieve our vision, to help all children grow and learn" (Head Start Bureau, 1997).

CONCLUSION

EHS uses respectful relationships, individualized services, and visionary leadership to adapt programs to the unique needs of very young children with disabilities and their families. A parent sums it up best: "My daughter said, 'Oh yeah, my brother was born with possibilities, and he showed us how special we are.' So my first reaction was to say, 'Sweetheart, the word isn't *possibilities*, its *dis-* . . . *dis-* . . .' and I couldn't even finish the word. I listened to what she said, and I realized how much more positive it was—so much more life affirming."

NOTES

1. The first and last names of the Guido family have been changed to protect their privacy.

2. Unless otherwise noted, all quotes from parents, administrators, caregivers, and partners used in this chapter are taken from training videotapes developed for the Hilton/Early Head Start Training Program (2000).

3. Unless otherwise cited, all quotes from parents, administrators, caregivers, and partners used in this chapter are taken from training tapes developed for the Hilton/Early Head Start Training Program (2001).

REFERENCES

Bruder, M. B. (1993). The provision of Early Intervention and early childhood special education within community early childhood programs: Characteristics of effective service delivery. *Topics in Early Childhood Special Education, 13*(1), 19–37.

Bruder, M. B., & Dunst, C. J. (2000). Expanding learning opportunities for infants and toddlers in natural environments: A chance to reconceptualize early intervention. *Zero to Three, 20*(3), 34–36.

Buysse, V., Wesley, P., Keyes, L., & Bailey, D. B., Jr. (1996). Assessing the comfort zone of child care teachers serving young children with disabilities. *Journal of Early Intervention, 20*(3), 189–203.

Casto, G., & Mastropieri, M. A. (1986). The efficacy of early intervention programs: A meta-analysis. *Exceptional Children, 52*(5), 417–424.

Early Head Start National Resource Center. (1999). *Early Head Start program strategies: Staff development.* Washington, DC: U.S. Department of Health and Human Resources and ZERO TO THREE.

Farran, D. C. (2000). Another decade of intervention for children who are low income or disabled: What do we do now? In J. P. Shonkoff & S. J. Meisels (Eds.), *Handbook of early childhood intervention* (pp. 501–539). New York: Cambridge University Press.

Gallagher, P. A. (1997). Teachers and inclusion: Perspectives on changing roles. *Topics in Early Childhood Special Education, 17*(3), 363–386.

Guralnick, M. J. (1998). The effectiveness of early intervention for vulnerable children: A developmental perspective. *American Journal on Mental Retardation, 102,* 319–345.

Guralnick, M. J. (2001). *Early childhood inclusion: Focus on change.* Baltimore: Brookes Publishing.

Hanson, M. J., Gutierrez, S., Morgan, M., Brennan, E. L., & Zercher, C. (1997). Language, culture, and disability: Interacting influences on preschool inclusion. *Topics in Early Childhood Special Education, 17,* 307–336.

Head Start Bureau. (1997). Leading the way: Disabilities services and the management team. In Head Start Publications Management Center, *Training guides for the Head Start learning community.* Washington, DC: U.S. Department of Health and Human Services.

Head Start program performance standards and other regulations. 45 C.F.R. § 1305.6(c). (Government Printing Office 2002a).

Head Start program performance standards and other regulations. 45 C.F.R. § 1304.1(a)(2) (Government Printing Office 2002b).

Hilton/Early Head Start Training Program. (2000). *Case example of family in EHS* [Videotape]. Rohnert Park, CA: Sonoma State University, California Institute on Human Services.

Hilton/Early Head Start Training Program. (2001). *Continuous improvement report, December 2001.* Rohnert Park, CA: Sonoma State University, California Institute on Human Services.

Hilton/Early Head Start Training Program. (2002). *Continuous improvement report, December 2002.* Rohnert Park, CA: Sonoma State University, California Institute on Human Services.

Individuals With Disabilities Education Act (IDEA). Pub. L. No. 105-17, 20 U.S.C. § 1400 *et seq.* (1997).

Irish, K., Schumacher, R., & Lombardi, J. (2003). *Serving America's youngest: A snapshot of Early Head Start children, families, teachers, and programs in 2002.* Washington, DC: Center for Law and Social Policy.

Knapp-Philo, J., Corso, R., Brekken, L., Bair-Heal, H. (2004). Training to make and sustain change: The Hilton/Early Head Start Training Program. *Infants and Young Children, 17* (2), 171–183.

Kunc, N. (1992). The need to belong: Restructuring Maslow's hierarchy of needs. In R. A. Villa, J. S. Thousnad, S. Stainbeck, & W. Stainbeck (Eds.), *Restructuring for caring and effective education: Administrative guide to creating heterogeneous schools* (pp. 25–39). Baltimore: Brookes Publishing.

McWilliam, R. A. (1996). A program of research on integrated versus isolated treatment in Early Intervention. In R. A. McWilliam (Ed.), *Rethinking Pull-Out Services in Early Intervention* (pp. 49–69). Baltimore: Brookes Publishing.

Nelson, C. A. (1999). Neural plasticity and human development. *Current Directions in Psychological Science, 8,* 42–45.

Odom, S. L., & Bailey, D. B. (2001). Inclusive preschool programs. In M. J. Guralnick (Ed.), *Early childhood inclusion* (pp. 253–276). Baltimore: Brookes Publishing.

Odom, S. L., & Diamond, K. E. (1998). Inclusion of young children with special needs in early childhood education: The research base. *Early Childhood Research Quarterly, 13,* 3–25.

Rainforth, B., York, J., & MacDonald, C. (1992). *Collaborative teams for students with severe disabilities: Integrating therapy and educational services.* Baltimore: Brookes Publishing.

Shonkoff, J. P., & Hauser-Cram, P. (1987). Early intervention for disabled infants and their families: A quantitative analysis. *Pediatrics, 80,* 650–658.

Office of Special Education Programs. (2001). *Twenty-third annual report to Congress on the implementation of the Individuals With Disabilities Education Act.* Washington, DC: U.S. Department of Education.

ABOUT THE AUTHOR

Linda Brekken has more than 25 years of experience with state, regional, and national training and technical assistance programs to improve services to infants and preschoolers with disabilities and their families. She is currently director of the Hilton/Early Head Start Training Program, a public–private partnership between the Conrad N. Hilton Foundation and the Head Start Bureau at the California Institute on Human Services at Sonoma State University. She is also principal investigator for StoryQuest: Celebrating Beginning Language and Literacy.

EARLY HEAD START AND STATE PARTNERSHIPS

Mary M. Bogle

F
or more than 35 years, Head Start has delivered comprehensive services and forged important collaborations on behalf of families through a federal-to-local structure. More recently, states have joined with Head Start to expand and enhance services for low-income preschool children and their families. "State action" on Early Head Start (EHS) varies broadly—from the use of state revenues for program expansion to the creative allocation of existing federal resources.

This chapter documents the progress of state action on EHS, describes one of the most extensive EHS–state partnerships (the Kansas Early Head Start program), and concludes with recommendations for the future.

SETTING THE STAGE FOR STATE ACTION

Prior to the birth of EHS, three changes in the federal–state policy environment set the stage for state action with respect to the new program. These changes were

- the growth of state investments in preschool Head Start and in prekindergarten programs in general;

- the establishment of Head Start–State Collaboration offices; and

- welfare reform.

First, in a little more than a decade, from 1991 to 2002, state annual investments in preschool education expanded from $700 million to more than $1.9 billion (Head Start Bureau, 2002; "In early-childhood education and care," 2002; Schulman, Blank, & Ewen, 1999). Federal investments in Head Start grew from $818 million in 1981 to $6.5 billion in 2002. By 2000, 39 states and the District of Columbia were providing state-financed prekindergarten for at least some of their 3- to 5-year-olds—up from about 10 states in 1980—and by 2000, 21 states and the District of Columbia were investing in preschool Head Start ("In early-childhood education and care," 2002). State and federal investment in early education was driven by a series of studies - confirming the positive outcomes of preschool and the 1990 adoption of "school readiness" as the first of six national education goals (National Education Goals Panel, 2002).

Second, greater investments in early education sparked closer collaboration between Head Start and the states. Promising partnerships between Head Start and other state and local initiatives were not new—they had existed throughout the program's history. However, until the early 1990s, there was no systematic mechanism for collaboration between Head Start and the states around mutual policy goals in areas such as health care, welfare, child care, education, national service activities, family literacy services, services to homeless families, and activities relating to children with disabilities. In 1990, the Head Start Bureau funded Head Start–State Collaboration Projects in 12 states to fill this gap; the offices were charged with developing links between Head Start and relevant state initiatives and service systems, and all 50 states and the District of Columbia had established collaboration projects with Head Start by 1997 (Administration on Children, Youth, and Families, 2000). Thus, by the time EHS began, preschool Head Start had already had several years of experience with formal state collaboration.

Finally, the passage of welfare reform in 1996 meant that more low-income mothers with young children were required to join the workforce and that more Head Start families needed full-time child care. Many Head Start and EHS programs—especially those that provided part-day or home-visiting services—looked to state resources for assistance in meeting this need. Thus, Head Start and state officials were more eager than ever to work together, particularly around policies concerning child care, work programs, and child support enforcement.

STATE ACTION ON EARLY HEAD START

When EHS began in the mid-1990s, some states quickly recognized the opportunity the program presented. For example, Oklahoma's First Start program, a reduced-in-scope EHS model (see Table 10-1, p. 180) was launched only 2 years after the federal program began in 1995 (Oklahoma Department of Commerce, 2001). As a result of the Head Start–State Collaboration Projects, many state policymakers were already familiar with strategies for leveraging Head Start resources. Therefore, the launching of EHS provided state officials with yet another mechanism for responding to the family support and child-care challenges that low-income families with infants and toddlers would face under welfare reform.

State action on EHS can be initiated either by state legislators or by state executives. Strategies that depend on state general funds are generally approved by the state's legislature. When federal-to-state funding streams such as the Child Care Development Fund (CCDF) and Temporary Assistance for Needy Families (TANF) are used, state action on EHS typically is generated by the top child-care or TANF administrators in the state's social services agency, often at the urging of Head Start–State Collaboration office executives. For example, Kansas and Missouri run almost identical state-sponsored EHS programs. However, because Kansas transfers federal TANF dollars to support its EHS initiative, the impetus for the program arose from the vision of the governor and the efforts of executive branch officials, such as those of the Kansas Head Start–State Collaboration office. In Missouri, state action on EHS is partially supported by state levies on its riverboat gambling industry and tobacco settlement funds; therefore, legislative approval is required to maintain the program's momentum.

In 2002, at least 14 states (Georgia, Indiana, Kansas, Minnesota, Missouri, Nebraska, Nevada, New Mexico, North Carolina, North Dakota, Oklahoma, South Carolina, Vermont, and Wisconsin) and the District of Columbia were targeting funds to EHS.[1] State investment in EHS promotes three policy goals:

1. expanding the number of low-income infants and toddlers participating in high-quality, comprehensive programs;

2. supporting low-income working families; and

3. improving the quality of community child care for infants and toddlers.

State action to achieve the three goals takes one or more of the following forms:

• expanding the capacity of Head Start and EHS in the state, thereby increasing the number of children and their families who receive high-quality infant–toddler services;

• extending EHS services to meet the complete child-care needs of already enrolled families, thereby accommodating the schedules and needs of working families; and

• encouraging partnerships between community-based infant–toddler child-care providers and EHS, thereby improving the quality of care for children enrolled in EHS and in the partner child-care program.

Some states expand the capacity of Head Start programs to serve infants and toddlers in their state or jurisdiction. For example, in Washington, D.C., early childhood administrators worked with the federal Head Start Bureau so that preschool Head Start resources could be reallocated to enroll infants and toddlers in EHS, where unmet demand was greater. Although most states use expansion dollars to enroll families with infants and toddlers who are already eligible for EHS, Kansas, Missouri, and South Carolina direct expansion funds specifically to working-poor families. The now-discontinued Indiana initiative funded three EHS providers to seek diverse and hard-to-reach families, such as newly arriving immigrants.

Some states extend EHS services to cover the complete child-care needs of enrolled families. This is necessary because federal funding sometimes covers less than the amount needed by programs to provide high-quality child care to all enrolled working families. In addition, the employment status of families enrolled in programs often changes over time.

Kansas, Missouri, Nebraska, and the District of Columbia encourage partnerships between EHS and child-care providers so that EHS programs' extensive professional expertise and technical assistance resources can be used to improve community child care. For example, in Kansas and Missouri—where state-sponsored EHS grantees provide many of their comprehensive infant and toddler services through community child-care partners—state and federal resources support early childhood education training and additional planning time for infant–toddler teachers in community child-care settings. In Washington, D.C., policymakers enhance quality by offering child-care partners subsidies that approach the level of EHS rates per child.

In addition to the states that take direct action on EHS, many Head Start and EHS programs across the country benefit from investments that states make in community-based planning groups. For example, Iowa's goals for its Community Empowerment Initiative (CEI) are quite broad and reach beyond early childhood. The state delegates decision-making authority about the best ways to achieve CEI goals to local planning boards. Since 1999, local CEI boards have supplemented nine EHS agencies to provide additional home-visiting services to low-income families (Anita Varme, personal communication, August 2002).

THE KANSAS APPROACH

In 1998, Governor Bill Graves transferred $5 million in Kansas TANF dollars through the state's child-care fund to create 13 state-sponsored EHS programs (Kansas Social and Rehabilitation Services [KSRS], 2002b). The Kansas Early Head Start (KEHS) initiative achieves all three of the state policy goals discussed above: expansion of comprehensive services to more children, support for working families, and improvement of community child-care resources. From July 1998 to July 2003, Kansas invested $35.2 million in the KEHS initiative. Federal EHS competitive grants representing

31% of the overall funding were given to support professional development of EHS child-care partners as well as for federal technical assistance.

The KEHS programs applied to KSRS for their grants. Only existing federal Head Start programs were eligible to apply, and the KEHS application was identical in almost every way to the federal application for EHS funding. There were, however, some important differences designed to ensure achievement of Kansas policy goals: (a) that applicants must provide their services through existing local child-care providers; and (b) families must meet the Head Start income guidelines and be employed, attending school, or in a job training program to enroll (Kansas Social and Rehabilitation Services, 1998).

The partnership requirement spreads the benefits of EHS beyond each KEHS program because KEHS grantees must share their training, financial, and other resources with child-care partners who, in turn, must meet the rigorous Head Start Program Performance Standards for the KEHS children under their care. According to KSRS, about 825 low-income children across 32 Kansas counties receive direct comprehensive KEHS services per year. An estimated 3,000 additional children per year benefit from KEHS because they are served by partner child-care providers. These children are not enrolled in KEHS and represent families from across the income strata (Kansas Social and Rehabilitation Services, 2002a). These numbers have increased since 2002 (see Table 10-1).

How Kansas Early Head Start Got Started

Similar to most innovative policy initiatives, the KEHS program grew out of a mix of lucky timing, political savvy, and bureaucratic finesse. For one thing, EHS began just as welfare reform had risen to the top of every governor's agenda. For another, EHS enjoyed the history, technical support, and resources of the seasoned preschool Head Start program while also being an exciting new entry into the resource-poor field of infant–toddler care.

In 1997, Kansas Governor Bill Graves convened an Early Childhood Advisory Committee composed of state, federal, and local officials responsible for overseeing programs such as special education, Head Start, and child care throughout the state. The committee's charge was to recommend a state strategy for supporting infants, toddlers, and their families. On the basis of the committee's findings and recommendation, Graves selected EHS as the model for Kansas efforts (Rae Anderson, personal communication, May 2001).

From there, child-care administrators with KSRS and the advisory committee worked out the details of the program with federal Head Start and child-care officials. The timing was serendipitous because regional and central office Head Start staff members had already noted Kansas' remarkable success in winning 3 of the original 68 EHS programs. In their view, the state was fertile territory for a new and innovative approach to linking EHS and child-care programs (Lynda Bitner, personal communication, July 2001).

Together, state and federal planners blended the best of what federal, state, and local resources have to offer. Federal Head Start staff offered $750,000 to KEHS programs in the first year. Since 1998, the federal contribution has risen to $2.5 million annually. KEHS programs use federal funds to cover professional development for teachers and other aspects of making the child-care partnerships viable. In addition, KEHS programs and their partners have full access to federal technical support such as the EHS Quality Improvement Centers, nationwide conferences, and training in WestEd's Program for Infant/Toddler Caregivers (Lynda Bitner, personal communication, July 2001 and November 2002).

Those who were involved in planning KEHS agree that the state–federal teamwork was extraordinary. Linda Lewis, regional administrator for Head Start and other federal children's programs in the Midwestern states, ascribes the cooperation to several factors: "We couldn't have done this except through an infant–toddler program because the terrain is so different from preschool with regard to provider shortages, cost of care, and other unique conditions of the marketplace. Crisis led to opportunity. The fact that Early Head Start was new and fresh helped, too . . . . Ultimately, the KEHS programs do not represent a new model, but a new way of doing business—we also could not have pulled this off without our network of strong relationships with the Kansas early childhood administrators" (personal communication, July 2001).

The View From the Ground

Martha Staker, director of the Project Eagle EHS program in Kansas City, says, "Through KEHS we are able to help so many other children indirectly. There are thousands of children who are eligible for Project Eagle and who we cannot enroll. With the state funds, [Project Eagle] has been able to serve an additional 370 children who are cared for by our child-care partners right alongside Early Head Start children" (personal communication, August 2002).

Korey Powell-Hensley, director of the Heartland Head Start and EHS programs that serve three rural counties in Salina, Kansas, agrees that KEHS has made a big difference: "Both locally and statewide, child care is feeling in less competition with Head Start than they have in the past. In our community, they feel it's a partnership. We are all interested in looking beyond what's good for each program and are now looking at just what's good for the children" (personal communication, August 2002).

The Heartland program received a KEHS grant of $751,000 in 2002. Heartland KEHS also receives nearly $100,000 in federal monies to provide training and other resources to their child-care partners. The KEHS child-care partners—three centers and four family child-care homes—provide full-day care to enrolled KEHS children. On a direct basis, Heartland provides all other EHS services, including

- recruitment and enrollment;
- home visits at least every other week to support family health and the parent–child relationship;
- breast-feeding and infant massage support groups for new parents;
- fathers' groups;
- English-as-a-second-language classes; and
- self-sufficiency services, immunizations, and other direct and facilitative health services for children.

Heartland families are transferred between the agency's federal and state EHS programs, depending on their employment status.

The Project Eagle KEHS is integrated with the agency's federal EHS program, which offers several program options, including home-based, center-based, and combination models. The 2002 KEHS grant is for $700,000—of which Project Eagle uses $350,000 to cover contracts with child-care partners. The rest is available to provide the required comprehensive services of EHS. The reach of the Project Eagle KEHS program is extensive because the 64 enrolled children are spread out over 25 centers and family day care homes.

KEHS staff members and other child-care providers receive 120 hours of intensive education and training so that they can meet the requirements for the Infant/Toddler, Family Child Care, or Home Visitor Child Development Associate (CDA) credentials. In addition to the training, the state requires that teachers have 480 hours of experience in working with children from 0 to 3 years of age (Kansas Social and Rehabilitation Services, 2002b). KSRS provides a training program for EHS staff members and child-care partners that combines the curricula of the highly regarded Parents As Teachers program, Healthy Families, and the CDA certificate programs (Kansas Social and Rehabilitation Services, 1998).

Teachers from Heartland's child-care partners attend monthly training sessions. In addition, the program finances bachelor's-level early childhood courses. Teachers who have an associate degree or higher receive an incentive of $1,000 per year from Heartland to encourage them to stay in a field with a notoriously high staff turnover rate. Teachers from Project Eagle's child-care partners receive tuition for early childhood courses from the Kansas City Kansas Community College (KCKCC); a meal allowance and a $7 per hour stipend to cover their expenses while in class, especially their own child-care needs; and the guidance of Project Eagle's academic facilitator at KCKCC.

Powell-Hensley and Staker say that the state's support is essential to creating strong partnerships with neighboring child-care providers. As federal EHS providers, both programs had already been in less formal partnerships with child-care partners prior to the advent of KEHS. With KEHS, however, came the funding, staff, and policy support for making these arrangements comprehensive and systems-changing. Says Staker, "If we didn't have these new dollars, none of this training would have happened. Through this program, we have supported 75 child-care providers to receive college degrees or Infant/Toddler Child Development Associate certificates. And they are not just for Early Head Start; they are resources to the entire community now."

Heartland and Project Eagle employ specialists with master's degrees in early childhood to regularly monitor and offer technical assistance to their child-care partners. Child care partners in Kansas City receive visits every 2 weeks. Heartland partners receive weekly calls from their consultants. Like all the KEHS programs, Heartland and Project Eagle monitors use the Infant/Toddler Environmental Rating Scale to assess the quality of partner-provided child care. Also, KEHS home visitors frequently observe each enrolled child in her child-care setting to assess the provider's success at meeting the child's specific learning needs. KEHS staff members convey a message of collegial partnership during visits to the child-care partners. As Hensley says, "They know we're not there to judge them; we're there to help them."

By aligning local, state, and federal efforts, the KEHS initiative has improved and brought greater coherence to the early childhood efforts of at least 13 Kansas communities. Says Rae Anderson, a former Head Start fellow and the first Kansas administrator for the program, "What this program did was enable us to serve families based on their need, not just based on what Early Head Start had to offer or what child care had to offer" (personal communication, May 2001).

Anderson's federal colleague Linda Lewis concurs: "We always have seen this as bigger than either child care or Head Start. It's modified the way federal, state, and local people look at our work together—we're all talking about quality first now" (personal communication, July 2001).

NEXT STEPS

State strategies for using EHS to advance policy goals on infant well-being, parent employment, and improved child-care resources show great promise. EHS's role as a laboratory for state action on very young children and their families should continue. We suggest a few recommendations on how to proceed.

First, states should consider investing their TANF, general revenue, and child funds to expand EHS programs or extend the length of the EHS day or year. States can maximize their spending on infants and leverage additional federal investment by sponsoring initiatives similar to those observed in Kansas and Missouri, which expand services and support quality. Today, fewer than a dozen states take action on EHS. Although these efforts are promising, most of them are funded on a very small scale and reach relatively few children. In a climate of tight state budgets, allocating resources wisely—for example, through state sponsorship of EHS programs—will deliver cost-effective results for children and families.

In considering this recommendation, state policymakers should be aware of emerging outcomes in states such as Kansas and Missouri and in the District of Columbia, where action on EHS is more extensive than in other places. Though limited, early data suggest that state-encouraged EHS–child care partnerships are reaping notable benefits. For example, according to data from the Midwest Child Care Research Consortium (2002), of a sample of programs that covered Kansas and three other Midwest states, 42% of EHS and Head Start child-care partners have met Head Start requirements for teacher receipt of CDA certificates—compared with only 17% of child-care providers in general across the four-state sample.

According to a Kansas state database, 70% of all KEHS programs fall in line with the CDA requirement (Kansas Social and Rehabilitation Services, 2002b). And according to a 2001 survey of teacher quality in Head Start's Midwest region, teachers from child-care partners in Kansas and Missouri are also pursuing higher education far more aggressively than their counterparts in neighboring states. Ninety-six partner teachers in Kansas and 128 partner teachers in Missouri reported taking college-level early childhood classes, compared with only 19 total across two nearby states. In addition, all 13 KEHS programs have been jointly monitored and are in compliance with Head Start Program Performance Standards (Kansas Social and Rehabilitation Services, 2002b).

Second, there should be an annual survey and comprehensive report about how states are addressing the needs of their youngest citizens to help inform policy-makers, practitioners, and the general public. Much of the information in this chapter is based on review of secondary sources and informal interviews with state officials. Thus, this chapter does not necessarily identify every state that has an EHS initiative, nor does it capture all of the important details about state action on EHS. Information about state initiatives for infants and toddlers, in general, is also limited. An annual 50-state survey of state-sponsored infant–toddler initiatives would help the field track progress and share promising practices across the states.

Third, federal officials should provide states with additional technical assistance for action on EHS (in general), and on ways to support partnerships between EHS programs and neighboring child-care providers (in particular). During the past few years, federal resources have begun to support technical assistance to states and communities for promising ways to promote partnerships and leverage federal dollars. For example, the Quality in Linking Together (QUILT) Project documented scores of promising collaborative efforts across the country and continues to serve as a critical resource for the dissemination of information about these efforts. In addition, the Child Care Bureau and the Head Start Bureau held an important partnership seminar in 2002 that convened teams of EHS staff members, child-care partners, and parents from 12 communities. Each team included a federal and a state official. Today, these teams continue to work together to initiate or expand EHS–child-care partnerships in their communities (Administration for Children and Families, 2002; Adrienne Sparger, personal communication, October 2002). Such efforts should be expanded further so that programs, communities, and states develop a deeper understanding of the potential of such partnerships.

In summary, creative state leaders, in concert with local program managers and federal officials, have set an important example of how good leadership can meet worthwhile policy goals regarding infant and family development. The time is ripe for others to take note and follow suit. State action on EHS—coupled with strong, sustained federal support—provides a coherent means of supporting healthy babies and families across the 50 states.

TABLE 1O.1 **State Action on Early Head Start**

State	Action on EHS	Financing
District of Columbia	*Expand* EHS by converting existing preschool HS slots to high-demand EHS infant–toddler slots. *Extend* the length of day for high-quality child care for working EHS families by enhancing child-care reimbursement rates to HS and EHS providers and their child-care partners. *Improve* the quality of community child care by encouraging formal partnerships with EHS programs.	The district reprogrammed federal HS preschool funds in February 2002. In FY 2002, a line item for EHS was created in the regular HS expansion budget. The district also has used CCDF and TANF child-care reimbursement funds since 2000.
Georgia	*Extend* the day of service and length of service year by supplementing EHS programs.	Georgia provided $2 million in state lottery funds in FY 2002, and $523,000 in FY 2003, from the Office of School Readiness (OSR) for contracts with HS and EHS. An estimated $1.6 million from CCDF funds was awarded in FY2002 to 10 EHS programs. In FY2003 an estimated $2.4 million from CCDF funds was awarded to 12 EHS programs. State funds in the amount of $500,000 were awarded to EHS/HS program. These funds were granted to programs interested in providing extended day/year services.
Indiana*	*Expand* three EHS programs in 2001 for 2 years to reach out to, enroll, and provide high-quality infant–toddler care and comprehensive services to culturally diverse or hard-to-reach working families with infants and toddlers.	Indiana provided $604,320 of CCDF funds to HS and EHS for 2 years; an average of $100,720 was made available to each program for 2001 and 2002.
Kansas	*Expand* high-quality infant–toddler care and comprehensive services for low-income working families through 13 state-funded EHS programs that have been in operation since 1998. *Improve* the quality of community child care by requiring formal partnerships between EHS and child-care providers. Only HS and EHS agencies were eligible to apply in competitive process, which stipulated that they must serve only low-income working families and provide all high-quality child care through pre-existing community child-care partners. Programs are treated as part of the national EHS system and must follow federal standards and they have access to federal technical assistance and monitoring resources. State funds have made it possible to serve more than 800 children annually, and an estimated 3,000 non–EHS children have been affected	Kansas used $35.2 million from July 1998 to July 2003. In the first year, the funds were from TANF transfer dollars to CCDF, and after the first year the funding was allocated from CCDF "quality" dollars. In FY 2002 Kansas invested an estimated $7.5 million; 31% of overall funding is through federal competitive grants to support state–federal–community partnerships and give priority to professional development of EHS and child-care partners.

Continues

TABLE 10.1 State Action on Early Head Start (Continued)

State	Action on EHS	Financing
Kansas cont'd	because of higher quality child care. FY 2003 began the first year of statewide outcomes for all 13 Kansas EHS programs. Outcomes in most areas were met or exceeded. A new assessment tool to measure expressive language in children 3 months to 40 months was implemented in collaboration with Juniper Gardens Children's Project from the University of Kansas and a Language Intervention Toolkit from Kansas State University.	
Minnesota*	*Extend* EHS services to full-year for enrolled EHS families through annual supplements to seven EHS programs since 1997.	Minnesota allocated $1 million in state funds for FY 2002 and 2003 to the seven EHS programs funded in 1997. The original selection process was competitive. In 2003, the Minnesota State Legislature cut all of the State Head Start Birth to Three funding for FY 2004 and 2005. However, Minnesota HS grantees now have flexibility through their State Head Start allocation to serve birth to 3 based on community need.
Missouri	*Expand* high-quality infant–toddler care and comprehensive services for low-income working families through 11 state-funded EHS programs that have been in operation since 1999. *Improve* the quality of community child care by requiring formal partnerships between EHS and child-care providers. Only HS and EHS agencies are eligible to apply, and they must improve the quality of community child care through formal partnerships with EHS programs. Programs are treated as part of the EHS federal system with access to technical assistance, standards, and monitoring resources. State funds for this year have increased the number to be served to 652, cumulatively over 4 years, by 2008. The impact on increasing quality child care for infants and toddlers in the state is 3,000 per year because of higher quality child care statewide (better qualified providers and higher quality environments).	In FY 2002, $20 million in TANF and Missouri gambling and tobacco settlement funds were used; 44% of overall funding is through federal competitive grants to support state–federal–community partnerships and give priority to professional development of EHS and child-care partners.

TABLE 1O.1 State Action on Early Head Start (Continued)

State	Action on EHS	Financing
Nebraska	*Improve* the quality of community child care by funding EHS programs to provide professional development and technical assistance on quality infant–toddler care to neighboring child-care providers. Provider liaisons from EHS programs visit providers regularly to provide onsite consultation, materials, supplies, invitations to trainings, and information about an infant–toddler curriculum that can be used in home-based and center-based child-care settings.	In FY 2002, $146,831 from the CCDF infant–toddler quality enhancement set-aside was used to award noncompetitive grants to all eight EHS programs.
Nevada	*Extend* high-quality infant–toddler care to full-day for enrolled EHS families by allowing all EHS programs to negotiate with the state for the funds they need to do so.	In FY 2002, Nevada used $324,000 in CCDF funds to grant awards to all EHS programs through contract negotiation.
New Mexico	*Expand* high-quality infant–toddler care and comprehensive services for low-income families by allowing previously existing HS supplements to apply to EHS programs as well. One HS/EHS provider in Albuquerque received a supplement in 2003 to serve teen mothers and homeless families, including those with infants and toddlers.	New Mexico used $6 million in state general allocation funds in FY 2002 and $2 million in state funds for FY 2003 to supplement four HS/EHS programs, one of which is an EHS. A total of $700,000 was allocated to the HS/EHS program in Albuquerque.
North Carolina*	*Expand* high-quality infant–toddler care and comprehensive services to additional families. *Extend* services to full-day care for enrolled EHS families by offering supplemental funding to EHS programs.	North Carolina used $605,000 in direct state funding in FY 2000 and 2001; in FY 2002, state funds were discontinued when additional federal EHS funds became available.
North Dakota*	*Extend* care to full-day/full-year services for enrolled EHS families in their original setting by offering supplemental funding to Head Start and EHS programs. Only one EHS program was funded in Minot, North Dakota.	North Dakota allocated a total of $500,000 in TANF funds to be available to all EHS/HS programs through an RFP process. A total of $12,000 was also awarded in FY 2000 to the one EHS program. However, for the 2001–2003 biennium and the 2003–2005 biennium (July 1, 2003–June 30, 2005) the North Dakota Head Start State Collaboration Office no longer has access to supplemental TANF funds (nor general funds) to be used for full day/full year services as a result of budget cuts.

TABLE 10.1 State Action on Early Head Start (Continued)

State	Action on EHS	Financing
Oklahoma*	*Expand* high-quality infant–toddler care and some services to additional families by adapting a portion of the EHS design as a model for new programs. "First Start" was created as an EHS hybrid program funded by the state since1998, making Oklahoma the first state to take action on EHS. The 26 programs funded during FY 2002 followed the Head Start Program Performance Standards except for those covering home visits, policy councils, and prenatal services. Any early childhood provider could apply. Oklahoma also layered a stipend on top of child-care payments to cover enhanced services.	In FY 2002 Oklahoma used $3.123 million in CCDF funds to award competitive grants to applying early childhood agencies to participate in First Start. This program is no longer being funded.
South Carolina	*Extend* high-quality infant–toddler services to full-day and through summer for enrolled working EHS families through supplemental funding available to all Head Start grantees in the state (Head Start, EHS, and Native American). Migrant Head Start programs already provide full-day services.	In FY 2002, $1.5 million in CCDF funds was awarded to all HS grantees using a funding formula. They each had a choice of participating.
Vermont	*Expand* EHS services to additional at risk children and families by contracting with one EHS program to support four infant–toddler classrooms with enhanced EHS services and to include infants and toddlers not eligible for HS. *Extend* high-quality infant–toddler services through one EHS program to full-day, full-year care for enrolled EHS and subsidy-eligible families.	Vermont used $117,130 in CCDF funds toward expanded and extended EHS services.
Wisconsin	*Expand* high-quality infant–toddler care and comprehensive services to additional EHS families.	In FY 2003, $3.7 million in TANF funds and $3.7 million in state funds were allocated for HS. With some HS programs not taking their full allocation, additional funds remained, so some programs applied to use these funds to increase their EHS slots.

*Funding no longer available

Sources:
District of Columbia: Beverly Jackson, personal communication, August and October 2002 and July 2003.
Georgia: Robert Lawrence, Bonnie Murry, Gail Ormsby, and Delores White, personal communication, May and October 2002; Lisa Harden, personal communication, July 2003.
Indiana: Donna Hogle, personal communication, May, July, August, and September 2002 and July 2003.
Kansas: Lynda Bitner, personal communication, August and October 2002; Mary Weathers, personal communication, July 2002 and July 2003.
Minnesota: Sandy Simar, personal communication, April, August, and October 2002 and July 2003.

Missouri: Lynda Bitner, personal communication, August and October 2002 and July 2003.

Nebraska: Diane Bishop, personal communication, August and October 2002 and July 2003; Paulsell et al., 2002, p. 66.

Nevada: Kathy Biagi, personal communication, July, August, and October 2002, and July 2003.

New Mexico: Donna Dossey, personal communication, July and September 2002.

North Carolina: Janice Fain, personal communication, April, July, August, and October 2002, and July 2003.

North Dakota: Corinne Bennett, personal communication, May 2002; Linda Rorman, personal communication, October 2002 and July 2003; Cheryl Ekblad, personal communication, October 2002.

Oklahoma: Luann Faulkner and Nancy VonBargen, personal communication, August and October 2002 and July 2003; Oklahoma Department of Commerce (2002).

South Carolina: Mary Lynn Diggs, personal communication, August, September, and October 2002, and July 2003.

Vermont: Kim Kaiser, personal communication, June and October 2002, and July 2003.

Wisconsin: Julia Herwig, personal communication, April, May, August, and October 2002, and July 2003.

ACKNOWLEDGMENTS

Rachel Abbey, project manager for the Better Baby Care Campaign at ZERO TO THREE, contributed to this chapter by researching state EHS initiatives.

NOTE

1. Although 14 states were identified in 2001–02 as investing in EHS, at least 5 states had reduced or eliminated funding by 2003 as a result of budget constraints (see Table 10-1).

REFERENCES

Administration for Children and Families. (2002). *Application for the Early Head Start and Child Care Partnership summer seminar.* Washington, DC: U.S. Department of Health and Human Services.

Administration on Children, Youth, and Families. (2000). *Head Start–State Collaboration offices: Annual state profiles, 2000.* Washington, DC: U.S. Department of Health and Human Services.

Head Start Bureau. (2002). *Head Start statistical fact sheet.* Retrieved from www2.acf.dhhs.gov/programs/hsb/research/02_hsfs.htm in September 2002.

In early-childhood education and care: Quality counts [Executive summary]. (2002). In *Quality counts 2002: Building blocks for success.* Retrieved from www.edweek.org on October 8, 2002.

Kansas Social and Rehabilitation Services. (1998). *Kansas Early Head Start 1999 request for proposal.* Topeka, KS: Author.

Kansas Social and Rehabilitation Services. (2002a). *2002 business plan.* Topeka, KS: Author.

Kansas Social and Rehabilitation Services. (2002b). *Kansas Early Head Start and Head Start programs (KEHS/KHS).* Retrieved from www.srskansas.org/kidsnet/kehskhs.htm on October 17, 2002.

Midwest Child Care Research Consortium. (2002, October). *Child care quality and workforce characteristics in four Midwestern states.* Lincoln: University of Nebraska Center on Children, Family, and the Law.

National Education Goals Panel. (2002). *History 1989 to present.* Retrieved from www.negp.gov on November 13, 2002.

Oklahoma Department of Commerce. (2001). *Invitation to Bid: 2002 Oklahoma First Start program*. Oklahoma City, OK: Author.

Paulsell, D., Cohen, J., Stieglitz, A., Lurie-Hurvitz, E., Fenichel, E., & Kisker, E. (2002). *Partnerships for quality: Improving infant–toddler child care for low-income families*. Washington, DC: U.S. Department of Health and Human Services.

Schulman, K., Blank, H., & Ewen, D. (1999). *Seeds of success: State prekindergarten initiatives 1998–1999*. Washington, DC: Children's Defense Fund.

U.S. Department of Health and Human Services. (1994). *The statement of the Advisory Committee on Services for Families With Infants and Toddlers*. Washington, DC: Author.

ABOUT THE AUTHOR

Mary M. Bogle is the former executive director of Grantmakers for Children, Youth, and Families. Previous to that position, she was a program specialist for the Head Start Bureau. She served on the Early Head Start design team and is a staff coauthor of *The Statement of the Advisory Committee on Services for Families with Infants and Toddlers* (U.S. Department of Health and Human Services, 1994) and the initial Federal Register announcement that launched Early Head Start. Currently, she is a private consultant on early childhood, youth development, and nonprofit management.

CHAPTER 11

EARLY HEAD START
LOOKING FORWARD: TOWARD A
NATIONAL COMMITMENT

Joan Lombardi

A nation committed to having all children enter school ready to learn must do more than offer them a preschool program. For at-risk children to have a genuine head start toward school success, intervention must begin prenatally and continue throughout the early years of life.—Edward Zigler (1993, pp. 3–4)

Ten years after the launching of Early Head Start (EHS), the promise of the program is clear and the case for program expansion strong. Research continues to document that the first few years of life are critical to healthy child development. Research also provides compelling evidence that effective interventions can change the balance of risk and protection in children's lives, shifting the odds for poor children in favor of more positive outcomes and altering the course of development in early childhood (National Research Council and Institute of Medicine, 2000).

Yet public policies have not kept up with what is known about the importance of early development or what can be done to ensure its success. EHS remains out of the reach of the vast majority of eligible young children. In 2001, Head Start served about 60% of all eligible preschool children (National Head Start Association, 2002), but EHS serves only about 3% of the eligible infants and toddlers.

This chapter addresses two emerging policy issues: Why should the United States increase investments in EHS, and what are the logical next steps to expand the program and ensure continuous improvement?

WHY INCREASE INVESTMENTS IN EHS?

There are three central reasons to increase investments in EHS. First, as the nation continues to face high rates of poverty among its youngest children, threatening their healthy development, EHS provides a promising strategy to address early inequities. Second, as more and more low-income mothers with very young children are required to enter the workforce, their children need good-quality out-of-home care. EHS has the potential to address the child-care needs of working families as well as the developmental needs of vulnerable children. Finally, as the nation continues to focus on improving educational outcomes for children, EHS serves as a national laboratory for developing new strategies to reach vulnerable infants, toddlers, and their families and to improve education right from the start.

EHS raises the chances that poor children will have equal access to education by promoting healthy child development. In the United States, babies who are born into poor families and who live in poor communities begin life at a higher risk of compromised development than their more affluent peers. According to Song & Lu (2002), although the poverty rate for very young children has dropped in recent years, it still remains high, particularly for Black and Hispanic children. Song & Lu also report that from 1993 to 2000, the number of children under age 3 living in poverty dropped from 3.3 million to 2.1 million, or from 27% to 18% of all children in this age group; still, the poverty rate for children under age 3 is about 80% higher than the rate for adults or the elderly (2002). Moreover, Song & Lu also report that the poverty rate for Black and Hispanic infants and toddlers is three times higher than that of White children. Thus inequality in education begins well before young children enter the preschool door.

Infants and toddlers who live below the official federal poverty line are by no means the only young children who experience economic hardship. More than 2.6 million infants and toddlers live in families on the edge of poverty. In total, nearly 40% of children under age 3 lived in poor or near-poor families in 2000 (Song & Lu, 2002).

A growing body of evidence documents the consequences of growing up in poverty. Infants and toddlers living in low-income families are at risk for inadequate nutrition, lack of access to health services, exposure to environmental toxins, the effects of maternal depression, trauma, neglect, abuse, and parental substance abuse. These conditions are of particular concern during the prenatal period and the first years of life, which are critical stages of brain development.

The relationship between economic hardship and compromised child development is one of the most consistent associations in developmental science (National Research Council and Institute of Medicine, 2000, p. 275). Although the exact pathways that affect child development are still being discovered, evidence indicates that income has an effect on the developing child (Duncan & Brooks-Gunn, 1997). Although researchers have brought forth many theories about how low income affects development, a combination of several factors is probably at play. They include limited family resources to provide stimulating experiences for children and economic pressures that can lead to tension in the family, maternal depression, and a harsh parenting style. Moreover, many low-income families experience instability in their work schedules and limited benefits, which also affect family life. These factors, combined with lack of access to quality early education services, contribute to an intergenerational cycle of poverty that affects development from a very young age.

The effects of poverty on development are evident as poor children enter preschool. The third progress report of the *Head Start FACES: Longitudinal Findings on Program Performance* (U.S. Department of Health and Human Services, 2001, p. 15) provides some indication of what children look like when they enter the Head Start program. The FACES report includes a national random sample of children as they enter Head Start and follows their progress as they leave the program. The study reports that 75% of Head Start children start the program with vocabulary skills that are below the "low-average" to "average" range; similarly, 82% of Head Start children start out with early writing skills below the "low-average" to "average" range. For very young children in poverty, this lag in early development can take years to overcome. Without support, far too many children simply never catch up.

EHS provides an opportunity to change this pattern of development. The findings of the national evaluation illustrate the program's potential to affect early education (see Chapter 2). EHS has positive effects on very young children's cognitive, language, and social–emotional development—all important to success in preschool and beyond. At the same time, the program has favorable effects on a wide range of parenting outcomes, including progress toward self-sufficiency (Administration for Children and Families, 2002). As noted by U.S. Department of Health and Human Services Secretary Tommy Thompson upon the release of the findings, "The [Early Head Start] program improves the chances for our youngest and most disadvantaged children to grow up healthy, to learn, and to prepare for school while providing support to mothers and fathers to improve their parenting and other skills" (U.S. Department of Health and Human Services, 2002a).

EHS supports families and promotes economic self-sufficiency by ensuring access to quality child care. As the nation continues to encourage low-income families with infants and toddlers to move toward greater self-sufficiency, it has not taken full advantage of this opportunity to promote healthy child development by providing the best child care and family supports possible. Although public investment in early childhood education has increased over the past 2 decades, investments in services for families with infants and toddlers still lag far behind. In their review of state investments in early education, Cauthen, Knitzer, and Ripple (2002, pp. 6–7) found significant—but uneven—growth in state efforts to promote child development and support. Even though 80% of states are investing in programs for preschoolers, only about 60% are investing in programs for infants and toddlers. Cauthen and colleagues also found that even in states that invest in early childhood development services, per capita spending remains extremely low—on average, about $157.

The scarcity of federal and state support for families is most evident in the area of ensuring high-quality child care to families with infants and toddlers. Today, more than half the infants and toddlers in the United States regularly spend time in child care (National Research Council and Institute of Medicine, 2000). The need for care among infants and toddlers has escalated since the beginning of welfare reform. Previously, women on welfare with children under the age of 3 were exempt from work requirements; however, since 1996, women with children as young as 1 year old have been required to work or participate in a work activity. Furthermore, even though states can exempt women with children under age 1, almost one half of the states have chosen to require women with children under age 1 to participate (Kirby, Ross, & Puffer, 2001).

These policy changes have resulted in an increased demand for infant and toddler child care. Yet even though financial assistance for child care has increased during the past decade, it reaches only one out of seven eligible children (Mezey, Greenberg, & Schumacher, 2002). Child-care expenses continue to drain the resources of low-income working families and push far too many children into poor-quality care. In their review of infant and toddler care, Phillips and Adams (2001) note that "in virtually all large-scale studies of child care in the Untied States, approximately 20% of the settings that participate in the research have been found to fall below minimal thresholds of adequate care." The licensing requirements of most states do not insist that caregivers for infants have preservice training. Moreover, many infants and toddlers are in unregulated, informal care. In sum, the scarcity of good infant and toddler care and the high cost of the good care that exists mean that the families who need high-quality care most are often the least likely to get it.

EHS has begun to address this critical shortage. Recognizing the importance of high-quality child care for low-income families, program planners required that care for participating infants and toddlers—whether provided within the EHS program or in a community-based setting—meet Head Start Program Performance Standards. This innovative approach has led to a wide variety of partnerships and strategies to improve the quality of community-based child care. The Early Head Start National Research and Evaluation Project found that these creative partnerships have the potential to raise the quality of care provided to low-income children across the country (Administration for Children and Families, 2002; see also Chapter 3).

EHS serves as a national laboratory for promising practices in the delivery of services to expectant parents, infants and toddlers, and families with very young children. Just as Head Start has served as a national laboratory for the delivery of high-quality, comprehensive preschool services, EHS has made a similar contribution to the field of infant–family policies and programs. Although Head Start has been serving infants and toddlers in Parent and Child Centers and in migrant programs for decades, only with the launching of EHS has Head Start issued performance standards that define high-quality, comprehensive services to expectant parents, children from 0–5 years old, and the families of these children. As states begin to invest in services for infants and toddlers, these standards can serve as a benchmark for high-quality programs.

Along with performance standards, EHS has developed a wide variety of new strategies and materials to help staff serve pregnant women, reach out to young fathers, identify very young children with special needs, address the mental health needs of low-income infants and their families, and foster young children's cognitive development, language, and literacy skills. Furthermore, EHS has defined new job categories (such as infant–toddler specialists), stimulating innovations in higher education and vocational training.

Finally, the Early Head Start National Research and Evaluation Project has highlighted the importance of program implementation to the achievement of desired outcomes and the potential for new partnerships to deliver comprehensive services. Indeed, the dissemination effort launched by the Early Head Start National Research and Evaluation Team has served as a model for how to translate research findings into program improvements, particularly as researchers, program staff, and federal officials work together to learn from the evaluation. Through printed summaries and conference presentations, the research findings are providing guidance to new and existing services within EHS and beyond.

THE NEW EARLY HEAD START AGENDA

The future of EHS must be shaped to fit the changing needs of families and the increasing interest in state-funded prekindergarten. Although Head Start should continue to serve as an important provider of comprehensive services to preschool children, an expansion of preschool services alone will not guarantee success for low-income children. As evidence has shown, inequality begins before children enter preschool. Thus, in the 21st century, as state resources for prekindergarten grow, more and more Head Start resources should be focused on serving very young children. The following five principles should guide the new EHS agenda:

1. all expectant parents and families with infants and toddlers living in poverty should have access to EHS;

2. implementation of EHS Program Performance Standards must not be compromised as the program expands to serve more children;

3. EHS programs must fit into the constellation of services in their communities through innovative partnerships and collaboration;

4. training and technical assistance should help build the capacity of programs to successfully serve expectant parents and families with infants and toddlers; and

5. research must inform policy, practice, and continuous improvement.

Taking into account these principles, investments in EHS should be increased to

- expand the program to serve all eligible expectant parents and children from birth to age 3,

- build the capacity of EHS programs to ensure quality services, and

- continue to experiment to improve services and to disseminate promising practices.

These three goals are discussed below.

Expand EHS to serve all eligible children and to meet the diverse needs of families. Today, only about 10% of the overall Head Start budget is used to serve pregnant women, infants, and toddlers. Even though more than 950,000 children were served by Head Start in fiscal year (FY) 2002, only 62,000 of these children were served in EHS. Given that 2.1 million income-eligible infants and toddlers are living in poverty, expansion of services to families with children under age 3 should be a top priority. Serving at least 1 million poor infants and toddlers a year by the end of the decade would allow us to reach one half of the poor children under age 3 in the United States. Reaching this goal would be an important step forward in efforts to serve all eligible children. Given existing data about the effectiveness of EHS, the most vulnerable children in the nation should not have to wait another 3 decades to receive the services that they need.

Expansion of Head Start services to very young children should proceed through a combination of approaches. First, existing Head Start programs in good standing should be able to serve children from birth to age 5 based on a community needs assessment. For years, Migrant Head Start programs have been allowed to serve children under age 3 in recognition of the needs of families of migrant workers. Now that so many other Head Start families are working, this important precedent should be extended to all children in the program.

Based on the needs of their families and communities, Head Start programs should be able to convert existing preschool spaces, use expansion dollars, or both to serve children from birth to age 5. Each Head Start grantee interested in providing services to infants and toddlers should go through a three-part planning and approval process that focuses on

- assessing the capacities and resource needs of the program and community,

- developing a plan to meet the program performance standards, and

- ensuring the staffing levels and training capacity to serve younger children.

Second, along with increased flexibility for Head Start grantees to serve younger children, the specific set-aside for EHS should continue to grow, either as a percentage of the overall Head Start budget or as a percentage of any increase. This set-aside will allow some new agencies to join the Head Start community.

The EHS evaluation provides important insight into the ways that expansion should proceed to ensure the most effective services and to meet the wide range of family needs. For example, the study found that the earlier children enroll in EHS, the better the outcomes; therefore, new efforts should be made to enroll more pregnant women and very young children. Furthermore, the study indicates that a mixed model—that is, one that combines center-based services with home-based services—may provide the strongest effects. Even though this finding needs further exploration and discussion to understand what combination of services is appropriate for an individual family, it does appear to underscore the importance of focusing on both the child and the parent.

Given the demands of welfare reform, more and more infants and toddlers will be served in community-based child care, particularly family child-care homes and kith-and-kin providers (neighbors, friends, and relatives). Special efforts are needed to develop partnerships between EHS and these community-based providers.

The U.S. Department of Health and Human Services (2002b) reports that in FY 2000, more than 600,000 infants and toddlers were served though the federal child-care assistance programs, including the Child Care and Development Fund. The majority of these children live in families below the federal poverty level and therefore are eligible for EHS. Although the number of poor and near-poor children served by federal and state child-care funds represents about 10 times the number of children served in EHS, very few resources are available to improve the quality of care, link providers to comprehensive services, or monitor and ensure that the poorest children in child care receive the types of services that can help them attain the language and cognitive skills that they will need to be prepared for preschool or the elementary grades. Partnerships between child-care providers and EHS can help low-income working families access the opportunities that their very young children need to be ready for school.

Head Start expansion cannot occur without significant new investments, including assurance that programs will be able to meet the performance standards and that the cost per child will reflect adequately the special needs of programs serving very young children. Although the majority of funding to expand EHS should come from the federal level, states should also be encouraged to use funds from the Child Care and Development Block Grant; Temporary Assistance to Needy Families; Title I; and state family support, child care, or other early childhood funds to serve more children or expand the EHS day. In recent years, 11 states and the District of Columbia have launched innovative partnerships with EHS (see Chapter 10), but such efforts are still relatively small. Technical assistance, collaboration initiatives, and other incentives should be used to encourage states to invest in the EHS model.

Build the capacity of programs and communities to provide high-quality services to infants and toddlers and their families. Even though the results of the EHS evaluation are promising, new efforts must be made to ensure that programs and communities have the capacity to expand in order to serve more children. Only through such a continuous-improvement system can the program reach its full potential and strengthen its effects. Ron Lally, a pioneer in providing services to infants and toddlers, put it this way: "We need to take seriously the need to continuously upgrade local initiatives so that each child is given a high-quality experience. The first evaluation is an indication of a strong start for EHS, but only the first step of implementation has been realized. Now we need to move the program from a good start-up effort to a mature model that enhances strong intellectual, language, social, emotional, and physical development in all the children it serves" (personal communication, July 2002).

Because the heart of any good program is the relationship between its staff and the children and families it serves, capacity-building and continuous-improvement efforts must focus on ensuring that the programs are able to recruit and retain the most qualified staff possible. Such an initiative should focus on expanding the training and technical assistance system, improving the staffing requirements and increasing compensation, and building the capacity of local colleges and universities to deliver high-quality professional preparation for those interested in working with expectant parents, infants, toddlers, and the families of very young children.

Even though the training and technical assistance network that has been put in place for EHS has provided critical support during the initial period of program growth, as EHS expands, so should the ability to deliver high-quality training and supports directly to programs. Although this national focus should continue and should be expanded as the program grows, consideration should be given to developing an infant and toddler resource and technical assistance center in every state. Along with a national focal point of support, such a network could focus and expand professional preparation and programming based on the EHS model and could help develop the capacity of all infant–toddler programs that serve low-income families.

At the same time, it is important to improve the higher education system to ensure that colleges and universities have the capacity to train staff for infant and toddler programs. Special incentives, perhaps through the Higher Education Act are needed to help states develop the capacity to deliver high-quality training on infant and toddler issues. Furthermore, although about one half the Head Start programs now have teachers with at least a 2-year college degree, EHS programs still fall short of meeting such a standard. As programs expand, efforts should be made to hire staff with higher degrees in early education and with a specialization in or experience with infants and toddlers. At the same time, 4-year undergraduate- and graduate-level training, with specialization in infant development and parent–child relationships, will be needed for supervisors and others working with classroom staff and home visitors.

Continue to experiment with new ways to improve services to very young children and their families and to disseminate promising practices. The role of EHS as a national laboratory of innovation has only just begun. During the next 5 years, new initiatives should be launched to

- develop, implement, and evaluate improved curriculum for infant–toddler programs, particularly in the area of language development;

- experiment with ways to expand the intensity of family services for families at very high risk, particularly through partnerships with mental health and child welfare agencies;

- improve outreach to and support for fathers and continue to disseminate the findings about father involvement;

- continue to define, implement, and evaluate quality services to very young children with special needs;

- explore the best practices for serving families with infants and toddlers whose first language is not English;

- experiment with various strategies to strengthen services to teen parents; and

- explore best practices for supporting kith-and-kin as well as family child-care providers.

During the next few years, a key role of innovation will be the development of an outcomes framework that can guide the programs' progress. Although measuring outcomes has become an integral part of Head Start since 1994, efforts to develop an outcomes framework for programs serving expectant parents, infants and toddlers, and the families of very young children have been launched only recently. Although such efforts must proceed with caution and must be guided by sound developmental principles, delineating clear program expectations and creating mechanisms for tracking service delivery can become important instruments for continuous improvement.

Finally, it is not enough to develop innovative practices and to disseminate findings. The lessons of EHS should be translated into improved child-care policies that ensure health outreach, encourage parent involvement and family services, and provide high-quality early childhood development experiences to all infants and toddlers and their families.

EARLY HEAD START: THE BEACON OF HOPE

This year alone, an estimated 700,000 babies will be born into poverty in the United States. Although EHS cannot be seen as a panacea for addressing all the issues that poor families face, it does provide one of the most promising strategies ever identified for helping to promote healthy child development while supporting the parental role and encouraging families as they move toward economic self-sufficiency. During the next decade, the nation should build on this foundation, working to improve and strengthen the EHS model, helping communities build their capacity to provide services to expectant parents and families with infants and toddlers, and expanding the program to serve all eligible children.

By taking these important steps forward, the United States can provide a beacon of hope to its most vulnerable children—helping to ensure equal opportunity, supporting families, and meeting the great potential of the nation.

DISCLAIMER

The opinions presented in this chapter are solely those of the author and do not necessarily represent the views of ZERO TO THREE.

REFERENCES

1998 Amendments to the Higher Education Act of 1965. Pub. L. 105-244. (Government Printing Office 1998).

Administration for Children and Families. (2002). *Making a difference in the lives of infants and toddlers and their families: The impacts of Early Head Start.* Washington, DC: U.S. Department of Health and Human Services.

Cauthen, N. K., Knitzer, J., & Ripple, C. H. (2002). *Highlights from findings: Map and track: State initiatives for young children and families.* New York: National Center for Children in Poverty.

Duncan, G. J., & Brooks-Gunn, H. J. (1997). Income effects across the life span: Integration and interpretation. In G. J. Duncan & H. J. Brooks-Gunn (Eds.), *Consequences of growing up poor* (pp. 596–642). New York: Russell Sage Foundation.

Higher Education Act of 1965. Pub. L. 89-329. (Government Printing Office 1965).

Kirby, G., Ross, C., & Puffer, L. (2001, July 27). *Welfare-to-work transitions for parents of infants: In-depth study of eight communities.* Princeton, NJ: Mathematica Policy Research.

Mezey, J., Greenberg, M., & Shumacher, R. (2002, October 2). *The vast majority of federally-eligible children did not receive child care assistance in FY 2000: Increased child care funding needed to help more families.* Washington, DC: Center for Law and Social Policy.

National Head Start Association. (2002, July). *Full funding: A modest proposal target 2003.* [Presentation]. Alexandria, VA: Author.

National Research Council and Institute of Medicine (2000). *From neurons to neighborhoods: The science of early childhood development.* Committee on Integrating the Science of Early Childhood Development. J. P. Shonkoff & D. A. Phillips (Eds.). Board on Children, Youth, and Families, Commission on Behavioral and Social Sciences and Education. Washington, DC: National Academy Press.

Phillips, D., & Adams, G. (2001). Child care and our youngest children. *The Future of Children, 11*(1), 44.

Reauthorization of the Higher Education Act of 1965. Pub. L. 107-139. (Government Printing Office 2002).

Song, Y., & Lu, H. (2002, March). *Early childhood poverty: A statistical profile.* New York: National Center for Children in Poverty.

U.S. Department of Health and Human Services. (1993, December). *Creating a 21st Century Head Start.* Final report of the Advisory Committee on Head Start Quality and Expansion. Washington, DC: Author.

U.S. Department of Health and Human Services. (2001, January). *Head Start FACES: Longitudinal findings on program performance.* Third progress report. Washington, DC: Author.

U.S. Department of Health and Human Services. (2002a, June 3). Study shows positive results from Early Head Start program. *HHS News.* Washington, DC: Author.

U.S. Department of Health and Human Services. (2002b, August 29). *ASPE child care eligibility and enrollment estimates for fiscal year 2000.* Washington, DC: Author.

Zigler, E. (1993, January). *An Early Head Start planning and intervention program for economically disadvantaged families and children ages zero to three.* A paper prepared for the Clinton Administration. New Haven, CT: Yale University.

ABOUT THE AUTHOR

Joan Lombardi served as staff director for the Secretary's Advisory Committee for Head Start Quality and Expansion in 1993 and was primary author of *Creating a 21st Century Head Start* (U.S. Department of Health and Human Services, 1993). While serving as the first associate commissioner for the Child Care Bureau within the U.S. Department of Health and Human Services, she served on the Advisory Committee on Services for Families With Infants and Toddlers and was part of the original planning team that launched the Early Head Start program.

MEMBERS OF THE ADVISORY COMMITTEE ON SERVICES FOR FAMILIES WITH INFANTS AND TODDLERS

Susan Aronson	Joan Lombardi
Kathryn E. Barnard	Harriet Meyer
Mary Jane Bevins	Evelyn K. Moore
Helen Blank	Genoveva P. Morales
Sue Bredekamp	Dolores Norton
Urie Bronfenbrenner	Maria Elena Orrego
Bettye Caldwell	Carol Brunson Phillips
Jane Campbell	Deborah Phillips
Gayle Cunningham	Ed Pitt
Sharon Darling	Gloria Johnson Powell
Amy L. Dombro	Linda Randolph
Anne Cohn Donnelly	Julius B. Richmond
Robert Emde	Ann Rosewater
Lily Wong Fillmore	Shirley Senegal
Susan Fowler	Lisbeth B. Schorr
Olivia Golden	Helen H. Taylor
Sarah Greene	Sally Vogler
Judith Jerald	Bernice Weissbourd
Linda Kills Crow	Edward Zigler
J. Ronald Lally	Barry Zuckerman

Source: U.S. Department of Health and Human Services. (1994). *The statement of the Advisory Committee on Services for Families With Infants and Toddlers*. Washington, DC: Author.

ABOUT THE EDITORS

Joan Lombardi

Joan Lombardi is one of the nation's leading experts on early childhood education. She is the director of The Children's Project, a nonpartisan effort to improve public, private, and civic investments in children and families. Through The Children's Project, she serves as an advisor to a number of national organizations and foundations across the country and helps creates partnerships that support children and families.

Lombardi served as the deputy assistant secretary for External Affairs in the Administration for Children and Families, U.S. Department of Health and Human Services. Prior to this appointment, she served as the first associate commissioner of the Child Care Bureau. In that role, she managed the nation's largest child care program—the Child Care and Development Fund—and was instrumental in planning the 1997 White House Conference on Child Care and the President's 1998 Child Care Initiative.

Lombardi also served as the staff director of the Secretary's Advisory Committee on Head Start Quality and Expansion and was the primary author of the committee's landmark report, *Creating a 21st Century Head Start*. Prior to joining the administration, she served as a senior advisor to a number of national organizations. She is the co-author of *Right From the Start: The Report of the National Early Childhood Task Force* and *Caring Communities: The Report of the National School Readiness Task Force*, both publications of the National Association of State Boards of Education.

In 2001, working with several national and state organizations, Lombardi launched the Better Baby Care Campaign to help improve the quality of infant care in the United States. More recently, she completed the book, *Time to Care: Redesigning Child Care to Promote Education, Support Families, and Build Communities* (Temple University Press, 2003).

MARY M. BOGLE

Mary M. Bogle is president of Bogle Consulting, which provides community-based organizations and foundations with expertise and assistance in the areas of organizational development, nonprofit sustainability, community building, and the healthy development of children from infancy through adolescence. She is also the strategic coordinator for the Annie E. Casey Foundation's initiative to improve the economic well-being of families and nonprofit capacity in several high-poverty neighborhoods in the District of Columbia.

Bogle is the former executive director of Grantmakers for Children, Youth, and Families (GCYF), a foundation affinity group of more than 400 funders with an interest in strengthening children, youth, and families. In that capacity, she developed and sustained GCYF as a forum to discuss grantmaking strategies, exchange information about effective programs, examine public policy developments, and maintain dialogues with national leaders.

In the early- to-mid-1990s, Bogle was a program specialist for the Head Start Bureau. As such, she served as the federal project officer for the Comprehensive Child Development Program, a unique initiative funded by Congress in 1989 to demonstrate the effectiveness of comprehensive, integrated, and continuous family support and child development services. In addition, she was a member of the federal design team for the Early Head Start program, a Head Start initiative to serve families with infants and toddlers. In that capacity, she coauthored the program's founding document, *The Statement of the Advisory Committee on Services for Families With Infants and Toddlers*. Before joining Head Start, Bogle worked in the Office of the Secretary for Health and Human Services as a budget and program analyst on a wide range of programs serving low-income children and families. She has also worked as an advocate and counselor for runaway and homeless youth and victims of domestic violence. Bogle earned a master's degree in Social Services Administration from the University of Chicago.